About this book

This book explores how the events of September 11 2001 and the subsequent 'war on terror' have impacted on the lived experiences of British Muslims. The 2001 attacks on the World Trade Centre and the Pentagon were an act of extreme actual and symbolic violence and the 1.6 million Muslims who live in Britain as minorities were just as astonished as majority society. Since then, however, British Muslims have experienced a range of threatening responses – from increasing racist attacks and Islamophobic hostility to direct and indirect questions being raised about 'loyalty' to the state and the nature and direction of British Muslim 'citizenship'.

The 2001 attacks have far-reaching implications that go beyond the current 'war on terror' and are inextricably linked to wider economic, political, religious, and cultural difference issues. This important collection is a cogent exploration of how these events have influenced Muslims living in Britain today, covering areas such as aspects of community life, perceptions of Islamophobia, education, media, politics, identity, and gender. It situates the analysis within the particularity and the diversity of the South Asian experience in post-war Britain, taking into consideration implications for both policy and practice.

The contributors to this volume are leading authorities in the fields of sociology, social geography, anthropology, theology, and political science. A number of the chapters contain previously unpublished primary empirical material, making this one of the most pertinent and timely compilations in the field.

Critical praise for this book

'Plunged into a post-Rushdie and now post-September 11 world, British Muslims have had to face urgent issues of Islamophobia, gender, identity and media representation. Dr Tahir Abbas' excellent collection has brought together some of the leading authorities to help make sense of these issues in a rapidly changing and even threatening world'. – Professor Akbar Ahmed, Ibn Khaldum Chair of Islamic Studies and Professor of International Relations, American University, Washington DC, USA.

'A wide-ranging and invaluable guide to the highly complex and diverse nature of British Muslims from South Asia. Those wishing to get to the heart of Muslim communities should read this book.'
– Professor Ziauddin Sardar, author of *Desperately Seeking Paradise: Journeys of a Sceptical Muslim*.

'We are at an important moment in the process of integration between British society and its Muslim communities. The events of 11 September 2001 focused attention on questions which had been simmering but only very carefully placed into the public debate. With increasing vitality, this process has come into the open, often in surprising and usually in surprisingly constructive ways. This collection of papers is a major contribution to that debate and will help move it forward.' – Jorgen S. Nielsen, Professor of Islamic Studies, University of Birmingham

'No question in British public debate, for Muslims and non-Muslims alike, is of more pressing contemporary importance than that of relations between the Islamic world and western society. The volume in question is a rich and stimulating contribution to debate on these questions. It should be read by all, within Islamic communities and without, who are concerned with understanding and developing policy on such issues.' – Fred Halliday, Professor of International Relations, LSE, author of *100 Myths about the Middle East*, *Islam and the Myth of Confrontation* and *Arabs in Exile: Yemeni Migrants in Urban Britain*.

'This essential collection brings a variety of important new data, informed insights and innovative perspectives on key issues affecting British Muslims today. It is a highly welcome and important contribution to the subject.' – Steven Vertovec, Professor of Transnational Anthropology, University of Oxford and Director of the ESRC Centre on Migration, Policy and Society.

Muslim Britain
Communities under Pressure

edited by
Tahir Abbas

Foreword by
Tariq Modood

ZED BOOKS
LONDON & NEW YORK

500278361

Muslim Britain: Communities Under Pressure
was first published in 2005 by
Zed Books Ltd, 7 Cynthia Street, London N1 9JF, UK and
Room 400, 175 Fifth Avenue, New York, NY 10010, USA.

www.zedbooks.co.uk

Editorial Copyright © Dr Tahir Abbas, 2005
Individual chapters © Individual authors, 2005

The right of the contributors to this volume to be identified as the authors of
this work has been asserted by them in accordance with
the Copyright, Designs and Patents Act, 1988

Cover designed by Andrew Corbett
Set in 10/12 pt Georgia by Long House, Cumbria, UK
Printed and bound in Malta by Gutenberg Press Ltd

Distributed exclusively in the USA by Palgrave Macmillan, a division of
St Martin's Press, LLC, 175 Fifth Avenue, New York, NY 10010.

A catalogue record for this book
is available from the British Library

US Cataloging-in-Publication Data
is available from the Library of Congress

ISBN   Hb 1 84277 448 4
Pb 1 84277 449 2

Contents

List of figures

List of tables

Foreword
TARIQ MODOOD

The situation of British Muslims has been thrown into sharp relief by September 11 and its aftermath. There are many reports of harassment and attacks against Muslims; and Muslims, who have expressed both vulnerability and defiance, have become a focus of national concern and debate. They have found themselves bearing the brunt of a new wave of suspicion and hostility, and strongly voiced if imprecise doubts are being cast on their loyalty as British citizens.

There has been widespread questioning of whether Muslims can be and are willing to be integrated into European society and its political values – in particular, whether Muslims are committed to what are taken to be the core European values of freedom, tolerance, democracy, sexual equality and secularism. Across Europe, multiculturalism – a policy suitable where groups want to maintain some level of distinction among communities – is in retreat and integration is once again the watchword. These questions and doubts have been raised across the political spectrum, voiced by individuals ranging from Berlusconi in Italy and the late Dutch politician Pim Fortuyn to prominent *Guardian* intellectuals such as the late Hugo Young and Polly Toynbee. At the time of writing (February 2004) the French Parliament has passed, with an overwhelming majority, a bill the main purpose of which is to ban the wearing of the *hijab* in state schools. It thus aims at a forcible integration of Muslims and it is expected that this example will be followed by some German states and by Belgium and the Netherlands. In the UK, many politicians and commentators, as well as letter-writers and phone-callers to the media from across the political spectrum, have blamed Muslims for cultural separatism and self-imposed segregation, and attack a 'politically correct' multiculturalism that has fostered fragmentation rather than integration and 'Britishness'.

Certainly, the relation between Muslims and the wider British society and British state has to be seen in terms of the developing agendas of racial equality and multiculturalism. Muslims have become central to these agendas even while they have contested important aspects, especially the primacy of racial identities, narrow definitions of racism and equality, and the secular bias of the discourse and policies of multiculturalism. While there are now emergent Muslim discourses of equality, they have to be understood as appropriations and modulations of contemporary discourses and initiatives whose provenance lies in anti-racism and feminism.

The initial development of anti-racism in Britain followed the American pattern, and indeed was directly influenced by American personalities and events. Just as in the United States the colour-blind humanism of Martin Luther King Jr came to be mixed with an emphasis on black pride, black autonomy and black nationalism as typified by Malcolm X, so too the same process occurred in the UK. Indeed, it is best to see this development of racial explicitness and positive blackness as part of a wider socio-political climate that is not confined to race and culture or non-white minorities. Feminism, gay pride, Québecois nationalism and the revival of a Scottish identity are some prominent examples of these new identity movements, which have become an important feature in many countries.

What is often claimed today in the name of racial equality, especially in the English-speaking world, thus goes beyond the claims that were made in the 1960s. Just as the ideas of equality as colour-blindness were spreading across the world, a new idea was born – a new ideal of equality that was not satisfied with allowing excluded groups to assimilate and live by the norms of dominant groups, but encouraged groups to assert and, if necessary, to redis-cover, their heritages and identities. This significant shift takes us from an understanding of equality in terms of individualism and cultural assimilation to a politics of recognition; to equality as encompassing public ethnicity – and, by extrapolation, to minority religious identities.

Muslim assertiveness in Britain, though sometimes triggered or intensified by what are seen as attacks on Muslims in places such as Palestine, Kashmir, Bosnia, Kosovo, Chechnya, Afghanistan, Iraq and so on, is primarily derived not from Islam or Islamism but from contemporary Western ideas about equality and multiculturalism.

While simultaneously reacting to the latter in its failure to distinguish Muslims from the rest of the 'black' population and its uncritical secular bias, Muslims positively use, adapt and extend these contemporary Western ideas in order to join other equality-seeking movements. Of course political Muslims do, therefore, have an ambivalence in relation to multicultural discourses. On the one hand, as a result of previous misrecognition of their identity, and existing biases, there is distrust of 'the race relations industry' and of 'liberals'; on the other hand, the assertiveness is clearly a product of the positive climate created by liberals and egalitarians.

Even before September 11 and its aftermath, it was generally becoming acknowledged that, of all groups, Asians face the greatest hostility, and many Asians themselves feel this is because of hostility directed specifically at Muslims. In the summer of 2001 the racist British National Party began explicitly to distinguish between good, law-abiding Asians and Asian Muslims. Much low-level harassment (abuse, spitting, name calling, pulling off a headscarf and so on) goes unreported, but the number of reported attacks since September 11 was four times higher than usual (in the United States it has increased thirteenfold, including two deaths).

Reaffirming multiculturalism

This book builds a detailed and composite picture of the circumstances of British Muslims today. It is clear that there are real causes of concern. Nevertheless, it is not difficult to see that some positive developments are taking place, too. We must not, therefore, give up on the moderate, egalitarian multiculturalism that has been evolving in Britain, and has proved susceptible to gradually accommodating Muslim demands.

Other than Muslims themselves, a leading actor in bringing Muslim concerns and racial equality thinking into contact has been the Runnymede Trust, recognising Islamophobia as one of the chief forms of racism today when it set up its Commission on Islamophobia. The demand for Muslim schools within the state sector was rejected by the Swann Report on multiculturalism in the 1980s and by the Commission for Racial Equality even in the 1990s, but it is now government policy. Adapting the census to measure the extent of socio-economic disadvantage by religious groups has been achieved, religious discrimination, albeit in a weak form, has been outlawed and some support for incitement to religious hatred legislation has been built. Talk of Muslim identity used to be rejected by racial egalitarians as an irrelevance ('religious not political') and as divisive, but in the last few years Muslim organisations have co-organised events and demonstrations with anti-racist groups.

Certainly, there must be an emphasis not just on 'difference' but on commonality too. British anti-racists and multiculturalists have indeed been too prone to ignore this; but to do so is in fact less characteristic of Muslims than of the political left (see, for instance, the various statements of the Muslim Council of Britain from its inception in 1998, and its choice of 'The Common Ground' as its motto). To take up some recent issues, of course wanting to be part of British society means having a facility in the English language, and the state must be protective of the rights of those oppressed within their communities, as in the case of forced marriages. But blaming Muslims alone for segregation ignores how the phenomenon in the northern cities and elsewhere has been shaped by white people's preferences as individuals, and the decisions of local councillors, not least in relation to public housing.

We need to recognise, however, that there is an incompatibility between radical secularism and any kind of moderate multiculturalism in which Muslims are an important constituent. Integration cannot be left to a laissez-faire approach; we must be willing to redefine Britain in a more plural way. The French approach of ignoring racial, ethnic and religious identities does not mean that they, or the related problems of exclusion, alienation and fragmentation, vanish. They are likely, on the contrary, to become more radical; and so the French may actually be creating the unravelling of the republic that they fear.

The Future of Multi-Ethnic Britain, the commendable report of the Commission on Multi-Ethnic Britain, published in 2000, tried to answer the question: how is it possible to have a positive attitude to difference and yet have a sense of unity? Its answer was that a liberal notion of citizenship as an unemotional, cool membership was not sufficient; better was a sense of belonging to one's country or polity. The report insisted that this 'belonging' required two important conditions:

- The idea that one's polity should be recognised as a community of communities as well as a community of individuals;
- The challenging of all racisms, including anti-Muslim racism, and related structural inequalities.

Here we have a much more adequate concept of social cohesion than that which has emerged as a panicky reaction to the current Muslim assertiveness and which runs the risk of making many Muslims feel that they do not belong to Britain. Integration and assertiveness are far from incompatible. Rather, the political mobilisation and participation of minority groups, especially protest and contestation, has been one of the principal means of integration in Britain. As activists, spokespersons and a plethora of community organisations come to interact with and modify existing institutions, there is a two-way process of mutual education and incorporation: public discourse and political arrangements are challenged but adjust to accommodate and integrate the challengers. Political contestation seems to have been an almost necessary stage in the integration process at a time when identities and the solidarities and divisions that they create or constrain are increasingly shaped by public sphere discourses. One of the most profound contemporary developments has been how increasingly 'blackness' or 'ethnicity' is less experienced as an oppositional identity than as a way of being British, and something similar is probably happening to 'Muslim' at the moment.

This process can be facilitated by extending to Muslims existing levels of protection from discrimination and incitement to hatred, and the duties on organisations to ensure equality of opportunity, not the watered-down versions of legislation proposed by the European Commission and the UK government. Moreover, we should target more effectively, in consultation with religious and other representatives, the severe poverty and social exclusion of Asian Muslims. And we should recognise Muslims as a legitimate social partner and include them in the institutional compromises of church and state, religion and politics, that characterise the evolving, moderate secularism of mainstream Western Europe.

Ultimately, we must rethink 'Europe' and its changing nations so that Muslims are not a 'Them' but part of a plural 'Us', not mere sojourners but part of its future. A hundred years ago, the African American theorist W. E. B. Du Bois predicted that the twentieth century would be the century of the colour line; today, we seem to be set for a century of the Islam–West line. The political integration or incorporation of Muslims – remembering that there are more Muslims in the European Union than the combined populations of Finland, Ireland and Denmark – has not only become the most important goal of egalitarian multiculturalism but is now pivotal in shaping the security, indeed the destiny, of many peoples across the globe.

Preface

There are approximately one million South Asian Muslims in Britain, representing nearly two-thirds of all Muslims in the UK. The study of British South Asian Muslims after September 11 is important in the current climate, not only because of their numerical importance as distinct religious, ethnic and cultural groups but also because of the ways in which their lives have been affected by local, national and international developments. With a focus on international security and the 'War on Terror' at one level, and the redefining of what it means to be a citizen or English or British at another, the following collection of research papers and polemical essays eloquently expresses some of the important debates and issues in relation to this group.

Written by British scholars engaging with various issues in this area, this book presents discussions and analyses in relation to economic and social history, social geography, race equality policy and practice, religious discrimination, Islamic identity, the role of the state, media representations, education, Islamic political radicalism, local governance, and multicultural citizenship. A number of chapters are based on primary research carried out specifically for this book, and the authors include some of the established figures in this field.

Tariq Modood's Foreword sets our scene in relation to the post-September 11 debates currently impacting on British South Asian Muslims, highlighting local area tensions, international radicalism and the development of British multiculturalism.

Part I of the book gives a broad picture of the state of South Asian Muslims in Britain. I have written a historical (pre-1945) account of relations between Islam and the West (Britain), and what it has meant over time, why matters are problematised and how relations have been exacerbated in the current period. The focus is historical but there is also an emphasis on the state of British multiculturalism and citizenship in the current period. Ceri Peach provides the latest breakdown of South Asian Muslim numbers from the 2001 census, generating a detailed picture of the changing social demography of Muslims in Britain. The analysis shows the extent to which they are an important part of the population but also emphasises their social exclusion and economic marginalisation. Examples in relation to housing, education and employment are given. Muhammad Anwar explores the policy and practice in place to ameliorate the plight of disadvantaged and discriminated-against Muslims in Britain. Instances of discrimination and underperformance in education, high rates of unemployment, poor housing, limited political partici-pation, protection or otherwise under the law, and policy in relation to practice, as perceived by Muslim interviewees, are discussed in this chapter. Anwar shows the extent of racism's impact on the lives of Muslims in Britain and how it is important to remain especially sensitive to both structural and cultural racisms experienced by Muslims in general.

Part II of the book is an articulation of the role of Islamophobia and its impact on British multiculturalism. Chris Allen, studying Islamophobia in Britain today, explores the case in Britain after September 11. He discusses the shift from the marker of 'race' to markers of religion as important. He provides an eloquent discussion of how anti-Muslim feelings have intensified in the post-September 11 period. Anomalies in the legislation, the roles of far-right groups and the media, and the negative voices of parliamentarians are all elaborated upon in an essay that analyses the nature of pre- and post-September 11 anti-Muslim sentiment. Ron Geaves elaborates on the nature and orientation of British multiculturalism after September 11. He questions what it means to be a citizen and Muslim, and how it has been affected by recent episodes, including the Salman Rushdie affair of 1989. Internationally, the first Gulf War (1990–1) and subse-quent events concerning Muslims impacted on the development of a transnational Muslim solidarity. Changes in identity politics and the ways in which British Muslims are involved in wider political campaigns such as the Stop the War Coalition to help in their struggle are some of the examples of changes that have occurred. Stephen Lyon provides a fascinating case study of two very different

South Asian Muslims – one who has become more 'radical' in the light of reactions to September 11 and the other who seeks his refuge in a more integrated approach to life in Britain. Lyon thus offers a detailed picture of the different multicultural citizenship options open to British South Asian Muslims. This chapter provides an experiential and perceptual analysis of two British South Asian Muslim men who are dealing with identity conflicts during the post-September 11 period in quite different ways. Despite their differences, both case studies highlight how greatly state reactions to September 11 have influenced British South Asian Muslims – encouraging some to adopt the norms and values advocated by the state, compared with others who regard state moves after September 11 as further calls to assert their religion and to interpret their rights and responsibilities in its light. Jonathon Birt writes on how British Muslims united around the Stop the War campaign and what this means for multicultural citizenship. In particular, there is a focus on how the Muslim lobby was managed by the state, and the implications for Downing Street–British Muslim relations. The chapter suggests that Muslim community leaders and parliamentarians were caught in a quagmire when New Labour sought their voices in support of the war on Afghanistan (2001). For New Labour, these Muslim leaders were not the moderate forces that New Labour needed at the time. These problems and concerns are explored to show how they have led to the tensions and issues of the current period. A particular focus of attention is the Muslim Council of Britain (MCB) and the coming together of different Muslim bodies to form part of the Stop the War coalition.

Part III of the book explores the role of the media in representing Islam and British Muslims. Tahira Ahmed offers a valuable account of the reporting of Muslims in the press at the time of and after September 11. Using discourse analysis, this chapter provides a detailed study of the different reporting of the events of September 11 in mainstream and Muslim media. It explores the growing significance of Muslim media sources as an important influence on people's knowledge. It also analyses the ways in which young British Muslims are using different media to articulate their views and concerns. Audrey Osler and Zahida Hussain discuss the experiences of young South Asian Muslim women in education. While there is a commitment towards state-funded schooling, this policy is at odds with other government initiatives. This chapter focuses on the views of mothers in relation to their daughters' education on the development of Islamic values; educational qualifications and future economic independence; identity, self-esteem and confidence as Muslims; and preparation for life in a multicultural society. Humayan Ansari explores the issue of radical Islam through surveys and interviews with young Muslims. He identifies the extent of the radicalism in this body of people and suggests reasons for its articulation. Specifically, the controversy over the idea of Jihad is explored, analysing the theological differences between those who see the ideal delivered through violence and those who look to peaceful methods (as something that is carried out in the inner self as opposed to an outer expression of faith: an extension of the latter is the idea of martyrdom). Ansari provides a useful analysis, based on a descriptive analysis of his interview sample of young British Muslims, of how this concept is understood, internalised and actualised. Parveen Akhtar provides an exhaustive discussion of the movement towards radicalism among British South Asian Muslims. Focusing on recognised British Muslim organisations, namely Hizb al-Tahrir and al-Muhajiroun, Akhtar argues that radicalism is found in both the East and the West, because it is the only remaining way in which Muslims can challenge their subordination. In the West, Muslims suffer from economic, political and social marginalisation. In the East, corrupt and inept regimes are the perpetrators of their oppression.

In Part IV, the issue of identity is further considered, but from the point of view of specific spatial dimensions. London's East End, the North-east of England and Northern Ireland are the settings of discussions of the impact of September 11 on British Muslim communities. Halima Begum and John Eade discuss the impact of the 'War on Terror' on British Muslims in the East End in terms of how an anti-war movement was maintained. A helpful history of the immigration and settlement of Bangladeshis in the East End is provided. In that economic, social, political and cultural space, Bangladeshis are asserting their ethnic identities and mobilising political action in a number of ways. In the past, disadvantaged socio-economic positions prevented any considerable involvement with the Salman Rushdie affair or the creation of the Muslim Parliament (later fused with the Muslim Council of Britain). The response of Bangladeshi Muslims has therefore rested on broad-based organising principles, emphasising not only anti-poverty and social exclusion issues but also their frustration with US–British foreign policy in relation to Muslim nations. Nilufar Ahmed provides an informative account of the experiences of first-generation Bangladeshi

women and the development of their ethno-religious identities, pre-
and post-September 11. Processes of migration, religious identity,
racism and the post-September 11 environment are contextualised.
In a period when the Bangladeshis are establishing themselves as
communities in the East End, the often alienated and marginalised
experiences of Bangladeshi women have been exacerbated by
September 11 and its aftermath. It has required these women to
revaluate (and in many cases sharpened) their religious, ethnic and
cultural identities. It has also led to further insecurities, however,
with many first-generation Muslim women of Bangladeshi origin
now more isolated than ever. Issues of belonging and identity are
right at the fore for this body of people.

Paul Bagguley and Yasmin Hussain discuss citizenship and
identity in the post-September 11 period in the context of the disturbances in northern England of the same year. This chapter
offers a unique insight into the multifarious nature of post-2001
identity formation among young British Pakistanis. It explores in
detail the nature of the disturbances and contextualises state and
civil society responses – suggesting that, in effect, state reaction
merely added to the essentialising of British Muslims as well as
binging their specific group loyalties into question. A social path-
ology was developed and emphasis was laid on inter-generational
differences and cultural deficits within communities. Using first-
hand interview accounts from young Pakistani respondents in the
North, the perceptual data in relation to changing ethnic, religious
and cultural identities in the post-2001 climate are enriched.
Gabriele Marranci discusses the experiences of Pakistanis in
Northern Ireland after the events of September 11. There are less
that two thousand Pakistanis in Northern Ireland according to the
2001 census but they nevertheless underwent the same kind of
social, cultural, political and religious questioning experienced by
British Muslims on the mainland. Again on the basis of first-hand
interview accounts, this chapter explores the ways in which British
Muslims in the context of Northern Ireland face challenges to their
ethno-religious identities. An historical analysis reveals the extent
to which there is inter-generational change in relation to religious
identity. In particular, the chapter reveals how attention became
more focused on the group within the sectarian politics of the
region. It is a fascinating discussion of how issues impacting on
British Muslims in wider urban settings are specifically revealed in
micro-community settings.

The indefatigable John Rex offers his insightful thoughts on the situation of British South Asian Muslims in the post-September 11 world in which we live. His is a fitting last word to this collection.

I would like to thank the many different authors who contributed to this collection. Without their efforts, this book would not have come about. I am especially indebted to Nadia Hashmi, particularly for her assistance in the early stages of conceptual and editorial development of this book. Finally, I thank Robert Molteno and Anna Hardman of Zed Books, for whose advice, support and encouragement I am extremely grateful.

T. A.
Centre for the Study of Ethnicity and Culture
University of Birmingham

PART I
From Islam to British Muslims…

Chapter 1
British South Asian Muslims:
before and after September 11

TAHIR ABBAS

Introduction

At 08:46 and 09:03 the morning of Tuesday, 11 September 2001, as staff of varying ethnicities, religions and cultures, working in various investment and finance firms, switched on their computers to begin the day's work, two planes, brimming full of high-octane fuel and frightened passengers, were flown directly into the Twin Towers in New York. At 09:45 a third plane crashed into the Pentagon.

Over 3,000 people died in the burning, crumbling aftermath of the impact on the World Trade Centre. The shocking scenes reverberated around the world in seconds, and as more news came in of the attack on the Pentagon, for some it signalled the end of the world. For a very tiny minority, it was perceived as a victory against an oppressive US regime. Muslims all over the globe, some not always confident of their positions in society, especially in recent periods, condemned the attacks as inhumane un-Islamic acts of extreme violence.

Amid high levels of anger and frustration, the Bush administration, which had gained power in January 2001 in a tainted election, launched its 'War on Terror' – first against Osama bin Laden in Afghanistan and then against Saddam Hussain and his infamous but altogether missing 'weapons of mass distraction' (Rampton and Stauber 2003). This 'war' could be read as one against terrorist organisations, and ever since the Iranian Revolution of 1979 and the fall of the Berlin Wall in 1989 nearly all these new terrorists have been Islamic by name (although certainly not by deed). There are a billion Muslims on this earth and every one of them would have been affected by both September 11 and the subsequent attempts to fight this new 'evil' discovered within their own religion. The target was, and still remains, that of 'radical political Islam' – but the problem for Muslims is how far they see this as an attack on everyday Islam, which tends to be marginalised or politicised in both the East and the West. For many, what has followed after September 11 is an acceleration of an already developed process. Without doubt, for many Muslims, both in the East and the West, the 'War on Terror' is perceived as a war on Islam.

It is because of the wider impact of this event that this book has come about. It is about the impact of that attack on the US on the lives of British South Asian Muslims, who make up about a million of Britain's 1.6 million Muslims (ONS 2004).[1] These South Asian Muslims are predominantly Pakistani and Bangladeshi, but also include a small percentage of Indians (see Ceri Peach in Chapter 2 on more recent calculations). The repercussions of September 11 have had far-reaching consequences for South Asian Muslims in Britain. In the US the Patriot Act was legislated in a matter of weeks. In Britain the International Terrorism Act resulted in the outlawing of certain Muslim organisations, detailed scrutiny of the financial dealings of those that remain and increased powers to the security forces and the police.

The everyday norms and values of British South Asian Muslims have been questioned in more ways than were necessary, perhaps never more insensitively than in the remarks of Home Secretary David Blunkett MP. He accused impoverished, marginalised, disempowered and racialised British South Asian Muslims in the northern towns, where severe disturbances took place between young Muslims and the police (instigated by far-right groups who helped to orchestrate the events), of indulging in 'self-styled' segregation, of not speaking English within the home and of not marrying partners from this country. He also conflated the practice of female genital mutilation with the cultures of these South Asian Muslim groups, and all this within a few short months of September 11. It is a poignant example of how Muslims – rather than the hostile and racist structures of post-war British society and the institutions that form the very fabric of it – are considered perpetrators of their own misfortunes. These sentiments are writ large in a number of right-of-centre speeches by parliamentarians, while tabloid newspaper editors and the burgeoning right-of-centre presence in British politics and the media all seek to target Muslims as the new 'enemy other' and 'enemy within'.

This chapter introduces the case of British South Asian Muslims and their experiences of post-September 11 multicultural citizenship. It charts the historical relations between Britain (the West) and Islam (the East) and discusses the impact of September 11 on British ethnic relations and public policy thinking. How September 11 changed a benign multiculturalism to a malevolent one is explored, and the state of British multiculturalism in the wake of September 11 is discussed to draw out the implications for British Muslims.

In the beginning…

It is important to ask how it all started – how Islam and the West came into contact with each other and how the tensions and ambiguities that exist today originated.

For Muslims throughout the world, the life of Prophet Mohammed, who died in 632, symbolises the origins of Islam. For thirty years after the death of the prophet, the Caliphs spread Islam to the four corners of the world.[2] The speed of this advance was breathtaking. By the death of the fourth Caliph, Hazrat Ali, in 661, half the known world was under Islamic rule (Robinson 1996), a fact that helps to explain the tension among the ruling élite. After Ali, Mauwiyah (governor of Syria for the previous twenty years) took the Caliphate. He was the originator of the Umayyed dynasty, and was succeeded by his son, Yazid. Secessionists gathered around Ali's son, Hussain, and rebelled against Yazid. Hussain, his entire family and a small group of loyal followers were tragically slaughtered by Yazid's army in 680. The Umayyed dynasty established Muslim power through conquest and industry.

It was five centuries of the Abbasids, succeeding the Umayyeds from 750 onwards, that provided the Golden Age of Islam. Muslims mass-produced books after learning the art of paper making from the Chinese. This fuelled the generation of knowledge and the dissemination of ideas. Muslims translated all they could find into Arabic – this included what were considered lost Greek texts – the works of Aristotle are known to the Western world because of Muslim endeavour. As a result of these translations, Islamic, and through it much of Greek thought became known to the West, and Western schools of learning began to flourish. The oldest university in the world, still functioning today after eleven hundred years, is the Islamic University of Fez, Morocco, known as the Qarawiyyin (although Alizhar University in Cairo, slightly younger, is a much more robust survivor). The Islamic educational system was emulated in Europe, and to this day a university 'chair' reflects the lineage of the Arabic *kursi* (literally seat) upon which a teacher would sit to teach his students in the *madrassa* (school of higher learning). Advances in astronomy, mathematics, chemistry, zoology, psychology, botany and veterinary science, to name but a few, were originated by the Muslims. Five hundred years before Galileo discovered the rotation of the earth around its axis, Al-Baruni measured the circumference of the globe. In 1121, Al-Khazini published his *Book of the Balance of Wisdom*. He identified a universal force directed to the centre of the earth. Newton's apple (allegedly) fell on his head 566 years later. Muslims developed hospitals too; there were 60 in Baghdad at one time. These were remarkably advanced and, again, laid the foundations for modern-day practice. They contained pharmacies, libraries, lecture theatres for medical students, separate wards for men and women and out-patient facilities. Muslims excelled in surgery, medicine, optics and the human blood system. They travelled extensively; indeed, to every part of the known world. They developed charts and maps, even a postal system. Town planning and natural and wildlife reserves were formalised. What remains of the architecture of the time speaks for itself (Sardar and Malik 1999).

As European civilisation grew and reached the high Middle Ages, there was hardly a field of learning or form of art, whether it was literature or architecture, where there was not some influence of Islam. Islamic learning became in this way part and parcel of Western civilisation. With the advent of the Renaissance, the West not only turned against its own medieval past but also sought to forget the long relation it had had with the Islamic world, one which was based on intellectual respect despite religious opposition. A defining event for the changing relation between Islam and the Western world was the series of Crusades declared by the Pope and supported by various European kings. The purpose, although political, was outwardly to recapture the 'holy land' and especially Jerusalem for Christianity. Pope Urban II launched the First Crusade on 27 November 1095. Although at the beginning there was some success and local European rule was set up in parts of Syria and Palestine, Muslims finally gained the upper hand and in 1187 Saladin, the celebrated Muslim leader, recaptured Jerusalem and defeated the Crusaders. The eighth and last of the great Crusades was in 1270, headed by St. Louis IX, King of France, son of Louis VIII and Blanche of Castile. There were no further attempts to recapture the holy lands after

1291. English participation in the Crusades was minimal and Richard I was the only King of England to participate personally (Edward I participated when he was heir to the throne).

At the same time, within the Islamic world there were divisions, fed by feuds and the corrupt and luxurious lifestyles of rulers. This was compounded by the sacking of Baghdad by the Mongols in 1258. Coupled with the loss of Spain to Ferdinand and Isabella, this period marked the end of the ascendancy of the Islamic world. On 2 January 1492, Broadbil, Moorish Prince of Granada, knelt before Ferdinand, ending eight hundred years of Muslim rule in Spain. These events fuelled a gradual decline. At the end of the fifteenth century, the *Ulama* (religious scholars) reduced the concept of *Ilm* from 'all knowledge' to 'religious knowledge', reduced *Ilma* from meaning the 'consensus of the community' to that of the *Ulama* itself. The interpretation of the Qur'an was frozen in history. It lost its dynamism; this transformed society from an open to a closed one. The printing presses were closed, depriving Islam and Muslims of the oxygen on which they once thrived.

The British, the colonials and Islam

The era marking the expansion of both Islam and Islamic culture reached a zenith with the conquest of much of India in 1526 by Babur, one of the Timurid princes. He established the powerful Moghul Empire, which produced such legendary rulers as Akbar (1556–1605), Jahangir (1605–1627), Shah Jahan (1627–1653) and Aurangzeb (1658–1707). After 1707, the Moghul Empire gradually lost its substance to its various vassals – princes, maharajahs, sultans and other dependants – whilst the British colonial presence took over. Despite the gradual rise of British power in India, the Moghul Empire lasted over three hundred years until 1857, when it was officially abolished. The British blinded and exiled Bahadur Shah II. His three sons were publicly executed, thus ensuring that a thousand years of Muslim rule came to an end.

India was the 'Jewel in the Crown' for the British. The Raj managed to hold on to power with very little effort, but the British standpoint is to regard the events of 1857 as a mutiny. This view is correct in so far as there was a mutiny by sections of the military, yet fails to account for the sections of the civilian population who also engaged in civil unrest. Most British writers and observers of the events were and are agreed in calling it a mutiny because of the failings of the army, in terms of discipline and command. Although not accepted by all South Asian historians, traditional Indian nationalist views of the events of 1857 depart from the British scenario of a series of isolated and uncoordinated mutinies. Instead, nationalists see a war of independence, the first act by Indians to gain self-rule. For half a century after 1857, writing on the uprising was basically confined to British observers and scholars. Racist ideologies were very much in place at this time, with differences in preconceptions concerning Hindus and Muslims becoming reified – the latter were thought not to be open to Western education, for example. Indian nationalist tradition defines the post-1857 period as leading to a return to Indian rule.

At the height of European colonial expansion in the nineteenth century, most of the Islamic world was under colonial rule, with the exception of a few regions such as the heart of the Ottoman Empire, Persia, Afghanistan, Yemen and certain parts of Arabia. But even these areas were under foreign influence or, in the case of the Ottomans, under constant threat. After the First World War and the break-up of the Ottoman Empire, a number of Arab states such as Iraq became independent. Others, like Jordan for example, were created as new entities and yet others like Palestine, Syria and Lebanon were either mandated or turned into French colonies. As for Arabia, it was at this time that Saudi Arabia was finally consolidated, too. In other parts of the Islamic world, Egypt, which had been ruled by the descendants of Muhammad Ali since the nineteenth century, became more independent as a result of the fall of the Ottomans. Turkey was turned into a secular republic by Ataturk and the Pahlavi dynasty began a new chapter in Persia, which now reverted to its traditional Eastern name as Iran. Most of the rest of the Islamic world, however, remained under colonial rule.

Decolonisation and British South Asian Muslims in the post-war period

At the end of the Second World War, Britain was no longer able to hold onto its colonies. As a parting gesture, the Raj gave Pakistan the independence it wanted in 1947. The region was in turmoil, with the displacement of ten million people and as many as a million dead. There was now a Pakistan in two segments (East and West) with India in between. It was widely held that Kashmir should have been part of the newly formed Pakistan, and that the alliance between Lord Mountbatten and Kashmir-born Pandit Jawaharlal Nehru had tilted the decision India's way (Ali 1989; Choudhury 1968). The two countries have gone to war three times over this issue, although in the current period real attempts at a solution seem to be emerging, despite election-driven gesturing and politicking. International pressures will probably determine the outcome.

In Britain, meanwhile, manpower was needed to work in certain industrial sectors that were in decline partly because employment conditions were no longer attractive to the existing workforce. In response, people from the former New Commonwealth nations, having fought alongside British troops, now elected to make a life in Britain (Anwar 1979; Khan 1979). The economic recession of the late 1950s, however, eliminated the demand for labour – whether domestic or immigrant. By then local communities and national institutions had already developed overt hostilities towards ethnic minorities. It was increasingly the case that South Asian Muslims were concentrated in the inner areas of older industrial towns and cities, living close to those working-class white indigenous inhabitants who were unable or unwilling to make their way out of the locality through 'white flight'.

The somewhat limited acceptance of immigrants by the white indigenous working class was based on the belief that ethnic minority and Muslim workers would eventually return to their regions of origin when their employment terminated. Rarely was it imagined or, for that matter, wished that ethnic minorities would remain, forming communities and putting down roots over time. The pattern was one in which immigrant labour in Britain, as in a number of other advanced Western European economies, originated in once-colonised lands and filled lower-echelon gaps in the society. South Asian Muslim immigrants were placed at bottom of the labour market, disdained by the host society, and systematically ethnicised and racialised in the sphere of capitalist accumulation. These workers were recruited into those industrial sectors most in decline and accordingly their positions in society were located below the white working class. The latter was able to attain social mobility, progressing from lumpenproletariat to proletariat and from petty bourgeoisie to bourgeoisie (Castles and Kosack 1973).

At the beginning of the 1960s, the number of immigrants entering Britain from South Asia was at its peak. Towards the end of the 1960s, however, immigration from South Asia had all but ended. Both the high point in 1961–2 and the decline in 1968 were the result of the Commonwealth Immigrants Act (1962) and the Commonwealth

Immigration Act (1968). The 1962 Act changed the pattern of South Asian immigration – rather than 'pioneer' men, it was their wives, fiancées and children that arrived, with many South Asians from India and Pakistan seemingly rushing to 'beat the ban' created by the Act (Deakin 1970). Subsequent amendments to the original 1962 Act in 1968 led to wider restriction of immigration from New Commonwealth countries. On each occasion the move was affected by the politicisation of ethnic minorities in Britain. As a consequence of changes to the legislation, the South Asian settlement became more permanent and family-orientated. At the turn of the 1970s, Britain had a large number of distinct South Asian Muslim communities living and working in different parts of the country – although these were largely restricted to inner city areas in de-industrialised zones.

The South Asian Muslim groups in Britain are more likely to be living in the most inferior housing stock, possess the poorest health, underachieve in education, and are 'underemployed' or more likely to be unemployed in the labour market. Many of the South Asian Muslims, specifically those from the rural areas of Azad Kashmir in Pakistan and Sylhet in North-west Bangladesh, are working in declining or ultra-competitive manufacturing, textile and catering sectors, living in inner-city housing built at the beginning of the twentieth century (and often in need of substantial repair and maintenance), and as joint and extended families in restricted zones of ethnic and cultural maintenance. They remain close to kith and kin and the religious and cultural manifestations of their lives directly shape their presence in Britain. In the current period younger generations of these families have begun to question their religious and cultural values, as well as the increasing links between local and global capitalism. De-industrialisation, technological innovation and the internationalisation of capital and labour have helped to ensure that British South Asian Muslims remain at the bottom of society. This was the pattern early in the immigration and settlement experience of South Asian Muslims, but these social divisions are no less pronounced today – largely as a function of pernicious structural and cultural racism as well as increasingly competitive labour, education, housing and health markets (Brown 2000; Modood *et al.* 1997; Strategy Unit 2003).

In Britain, notions of cultural and social identification of the 'other' stem from an understanding and experience of imperialism and colonialism. As a result of British laissez-faire mercantilism and later capitalism, Muslims from South Asia have come to represent a minimal contributory role within the socio-economic and socio-political milieu of society. As New Labour passes the midway mark of its second term, Back *et al.* (2002) argue that although there have been genuine shifts in New Labour's approach to multiculturalism, citizenship and social justice, during the second term it is the policy of assimilation that has been rejuvenated. Blair's Britain is defining a new ethnicity – Englishness as opposed to Britishness in an era of globalisation and devolution. Eager to embrace the capitalist project, Blair is also at pains to offer answers to the economic, political and social anxieties and tensions faced by Britain's poor, a significant proportion of whom are members of ethnic minorities (Kundnani 2000). The young South Asian Muslim men of Oldham, Bradford and Burnley, who battled with the police in such dramatic scenes during the summer of 2001, do not suffer from 'under-assimilation'. Indeed, their predicament is that of a society divided by racism and discrimination.

The nature, origin and significance of Islamophobia

The fear or dread of Islam or Muslim is described as Islamophobia. Although the term is of relatively recent coinage, the idea is a well-established tradition in history. Since the genesis of Islam, awareness of Muslims in Europe has been negatively tinged. Throughout the history of Western European contact with Muslims, it has been convenient for the established powers to portray Islam and Muslims in the worst possible light, so as to prevent conversions to Islam and to drive the inhabitants of Europe to resist Muslim forces at their borders. Although there have been periods of learning and understanding on the part of the British, ignorance and demonisation have also led to conflict (Bennett 1992). Muslims have been characterised as barbaric, ignorant, blinkered semi-citizens, as maddened terrorists or intolerant religious zealots (Esposito 1999). This characteristic behaviour is still present today in the negative representation and treatment of the Muslim other, in an effort to aggrandise the established powers, legitimising existing systems of domination and subordination.

As much as present-day Islamophobia relies on history to provide the substance of its stereotypes, the fear of Muslims today has it own idiosyncratic features, connecting it to more recent experiences of colonialism, decolonisation, immigration and racism. The Runnymede Trust (1997) stated that Islamophobia is created analogously to xenophobia, the disdain or dislike of all things 'foreign'. Seven features of Islamophobia were identified: Muslim cultures are seen as monolithic; Islamic cultures are substantially different from other cultures; Islam is perceived as implacably threatening; Islam's adherents use their faith to political or military advantage; Muslim criticism of Western cultures and societies is rejected out of hand; the fear of Islam is mixed with racist hostility to immigration; and Islamophobia is assumed to be natural and unproblematic. This taxonomy of the features of Islamophobia is very relevant today.

Muslims in Britain feel that part of the reason for their continued existence as an unaccepted and often despised minority is based on the presence of the 'evil demon' – the media (Ahmed and Donnan 2004). The charge of media bias needs to be taken seriously. In recent periods the extent of coverage of 'extremist groups' and 'Islamic terrorism' has dramatically increased. The language used to describe Muslims often connotes violence, thereby inferring that the movements the individuals represent are violent too. Arabic words have been appropriated into universal journalistic vocabulary and have been invested with new meaning, which is generally extremist and aggressive. *Jihad*, for example, has been used to signify a military war waged by Islamists against the West. The true Islamic meaning of the term is, in fact, far broader. Words such as 'fundamentalist', 'extremist' and 'radical' are regularly used in apocalyptic headlines across all sectors of the British press (Abbas 2000).

Islamophobia is also present in British politics. A recent illustration of this is New Labour's idea of community cohesion (Cantle Report 2001). This notion, in keeping with New Labour rhetoric of inclusion, masks what is a case of blaming the victim. Home Secretary David Blunkett MP, whilst promoting the notion of cohesive communities, proclaimed the need for a test of allegiance. He referred to the problems of the 'excess of cultural diversity and moral relativism' that prevents positive change. He also made reference to English language issues and female circumcision – conflating many different behaviours and cultures with those of the South Asian Muslim community in the North-west of England. Although Britain cannot tolerate female circumcision and forced marriages, these were *not* the factors that caused the Bradford riots. Segregation of Muslims was seen to be self-imposed and the cause of racism rather than a result of it. British South Asian Muslims may be economically disadvantaged and socially marginalised but they are willing to participate in society. Segregation is the result of racism and discrimination, yet, at the same time, identification with Islam is the reason given for segregation. It is easy to blame people and their values and to ignore processes and institutions. Muslims everywhere have been soft targets since the end of the Cold War, and they remain so here in Britain.

British state policy towards Muslims has been at best inconsistent, at worst patchy. Muslims experience some of the worst unemployment, housing and health of all South Asian groups – locally, regionally and nationally. They are also becoming increasingly over-represented in prisons. Nonetheless, in terms of wider race equality policy and practice, there are a number of positives that have materialised and it is important to build upon them. For example, there is provision of *halal* foods and more sensitive dress codes in the army, and the wearing of the *hijab* (headscarf) for women is now possible in the Metropolitan Police Service (Anwar and Bakhsh 2003).

Lessons from history and the impact of September 11

Now that British South Asian Muslims (Bangladeshis, Indians and Pakistanis) have reached the third generation, issues of concern have shifted from cultural assimilation and social integration to religious identity and discrimination. The first generation of South Asian Muslims maintained religious and cultural norms hidden within the private realm or community spheres. Subsequent generations have grappled with issues of integration and racism in the climate of the early 1960s; cultural pluralism in the 1970s; free-market economic determinism and the rolling back of the frontiers of the state in Thatcher's and Major's Britain; and, the 'third way' centre-left politics of assimilationist New Labour. At the same time, identification with Islam is strengthening amongst some of the current generations of South Asian Muslims, both as a reaction to racist hostility and as a deeper understanding of Islam.

Ever since the Iranian Revolution of 1979, Muslims across the globe have become a focus of attention (Asad 1990; Parekh 1990). Pictures on television screens shown all over the world of three million men and women on the streets of Tehran on the day of Ayatollah Khomeini's return from exile shocked many in Western Europe. The Salman Rushdie affair in 1989 highlighted the extent to which the media and the British Muslims who demonstrated against the book's publication become 'emotionally unhinged' (Parekh 1992) over the issue, and how the South Asian Muslims of Britain were shown to be weak and intolerant, when, in fact, they were merely expressing their opinions in relation to the publication of *The Satanic Verses* (Goddard 1990; Modood 1990; Parekh 1990). It is a work of fiction that gravely offended Muslims and gave rise to discussions on freedom of speech, blasphemy laws and the protection of non-Christian religions in Britain. The first Gulf War (1990–1), the genocide in Bosnia-Herzegovina (1993–6), the Oklahoma bombing (1995), the Taliban in Afghanistan (1997–2002), Grozny and Kosovo (1999), the recent Palestinian Intifada (since September 2000) and the War on Iraq (2003) have all played a part in creating a transnational Muslim solidarity; a genuine and conscious identification with others of the same religion. Huntington's 'clash of civilisations' thesis (1996) – positioning East and West, Islam and Christianity, as diametrically opposed and irreconcilable – has served only to escalate growing anti-American sentiment and increased Orientalism through oversimplification and generalisation.

Nothing, however, could have prepared the world for the September 11 attacks on the World Trade Centre and the Pentagon. Reactions were swift and associations between Islam and terrorism, and the antagonistic juxtaposition of Christianity and Islam, fuelled additional anti-Islamic sentiment. It gave rise to the efforts of far-right groups in Britain who could now paint Muslims as the epitome of unwanted difference, and almost excused anti-Islamic violence. In the days following the attack, an Afghan taxi driver was attacked and left paralysed in London. A Sikh petrol station owner was shot dead in Arizona, USA. To the murderers, the beard and attire resembled Osama Bin Laden – the man thought to be behind the September attacks. Since then, books and television programmes about Islam, Qu'ran, *jihad*, international terrorism, international security, political Islam, radical Islam and Islamic militancy have been published, and debates on Muslims and Islam have proliferated. The study of Islam and Muslims has become more vigorous too, with a greater emphasis on trying to understand the nature and orientation of British Muslims in anthropological, sociological, theological, and political science perspectives. There appears to be genuine desire to learn more and debate the issues in relation to a religion that for many has remained relatively unfamiliar.

In the aftermath of the September 11 attacks, Blair was keen to present the imminent action against al-Qa'ida as *not* a war on Islam (although Bush's comment that the 'War on Terror' would be a 'crusade' left little doubt in the minds of British Muslims that political Islam was his main target). Sahgal (2002: 2) writes that Blair's dilemma was how 'to balance the bombing of Muslims abroad with wooing them at home'. On Friday, 28 September 2001, just hours after the attack on Afghanistan, a delegation from the Muslim Council of Britain (MCB) was invited to Downing Street and paraded to the media (cue smiles and handshakes). On 9 October 2001, the MCB issued a press release strongly denouncing the war. New Labour was furious about this. Although the MCB did not support the demonstrations against the war, it was clear that they did not want to further alienate the government – an important trade-off took place, with the politicians winning. This was the beginning of the end for MCB's cosy relationship with No 10. Furthermore, pressure was applied to several British Muslim parliamentarians at the time – apparently leading to their signing a letter denouncing the events of September 11 and in part justifying Downing Street's position on Afghanistan (*Guardian*, 13 November 2001). However, Khalid Mahmood MP denied that he had signed any such letter (*Guardian*, 16 November 2001). Regardless of the accuracy of these claims, it is clear is that there are difficult struggles taking place over issues of consultation, dialogue and the maintenance of the Muslim presence within New Labour.

The exact impact of the events on September 11 on Muslims in their everyday lives in Britain remains to be fully documented. It appears, nevertheless, that the attacks, and the reactions that have followed, seem to have permeated many areas of everyday life for Muslims around the world. As an event, it has far-reaching implications that go beyond 'international terrorism' merely, and are linked to politics, religion and issues of cultural difference in the context of maintaining harmony in Western societies and democracies containing significant Muslim minorities. In the East, as revealed in the aftermath of the war on Iraq, further unrest, political turmoil and violent action and reaction are the main features of the current climate. In the near future, as Western sites are increasingly targeted – the mid-March 2004 bombings in Madrid are presumed to be a case in point – relations between Muslims and their Western hosts will remain somewhat vulnerable.

The state of British multiculturalism

Indeed, there were both external and internal forces at work affecting the positions of British Muslims before September 11. After

September 11, we have a scenario in which these have been exacerbated. Externally, after September 11 the international agenda dominates domestic politics. There is a tightening of security and anti-terrorist measures and there are citizenship tests for new immigrants, for example – although, with a General Election in 2005, every effort is being made to ensure a smooth victory. Important to consider, too, are the disturbances in the North in 2001, as government reaction to them has had direct implications for British South Asian Muslims. Internally, young British Muslims are increasingly found to be in the precarious position of having to choose one set of loyalties in relation to the other (Islamic vs British), being impacted by radical Islamic politics on the one hand and developments in British multicultural citizenship on the other. This creates tensions and issues: it encourages some to take up the 'struggle' more vigorously, while others seek to adopt more Western values.

The recent case of British Muslims returning from Guantanamo Bay, and the ways in which their experiences are now being told, re-told and discussed, further illustrates the extent to which the study of British Muslims is topical and pertinent for a number of reasons, including issues around post-September 11 multicultural citizenship. In the post- September 11 climate, British Muslims are at the fore-front of questions that turn on what it means to be British or English: issues on the global agenda as well as local area concerns in relation to 'community cohesion', citizenship and multicultural and integration philosophy. The social construction of Islam in Britain, therefore, is a function of the historical, the local and the global.

It is true that British multiculturalism is a distinctive philosophy that legitimises the demands on unity and diversity, of achieving political unity without cultural uniformity, and cultivating among its citizens both a common sense of belonging and a willingness to respect and cherish deep cultural differences. This is an amiable ambition and not one that is easy to achieve. In fact, there are few examples one can use to verify its success, save for attempts in Canada and Australia. The New Labour experiment has had both high successes and low failures – the Race Relations (Amendment) Act (2000), the Human Rights Act (1998), the Stephen Lawrence Report – but then, as a result of September 11 and the Northern 'riots', public policy focus has been on domestic security and the war against international terrorism. Both of these fronts significantly impact on British Muslims in the current period. The important point to emphasise here is that there is a complicated story of integration and exclusion that cannot be understood in the terms set around 'assimilation' and 'integration'. Multiculturalism has strong limitations because it rejects 'cultures' that do not correspond to nation states. Cultural nationalism is about present politics, not ancient memory, although that memory is used as an instrument (Parekh 2000).

To move multiculturalism forward, there is a need for different ethnic groups, majority and minority, to appreciate its inherent value and the importance it carries for society, but it is also true that this cannot be achieved unless there is a significant elimination of ethnic social inequalities. In the present climate, it is the experiences of British Muslims that are important to consider, as they are at the sharp end of multiculturalist rhetoric, ideology and philosophy.

Notes

1   The vast majority of Britain's 1.6 million Muslim population originate from South Asia (around 1 million; two-thirds of whom are from Pakistan, under a third from Bangladesh and the remainder from India). The other 0.6 million are from North Africa, East Europe and South East Asia. More than half of all British Muslims are under the age of seventeen. The Muslims of Britain are also concentrated in older post-industrial cities and conurbations in the South-east, the Midlands and the North.

2   The first four Caliphs were (1) Abu Bakr Siddiq (close companion of the Prophet, who died two years after gaining power at his death in 632); (2) Umar al-Kattab, who was Caliph during the years 634–44; (3) Othman bin Affan, who was murdered 12 years after taking power, in 656; and (4) Hazrat Ali, who was assassinated in 661.

Chapter 2
Britain's Muslim Population: an Overview

CERI PEACH

Introduction

September 11 magnified the focus already trained on the Muslim population of Britain. Although there is no necessary relationship between ethnicity and religion, over the last fifty years British discourse on racialised minorities has mutated from 'colour' in the 1950s and 1960s (Banton 1955; Rose *et al.* 1969) to 'race' in the 1960s–1980s (Rex and Moore 1967; Smith 1989), 'ethnicity' in the 1990s (Modood *et al.* 1997) and 'religion' in the present period (Runnymede Trust 1997). Within religion, Islam has had the highest profile.

British popular discourse has shifted from seeing minorities as an undifferentiated mass to discerning differences within and between Afro and Asian origins; and, within Asians, to differences between Indians, Pakistanis and Bangladeshis, and thence between Muslims, Hindus and Sikhs. Religion has emerged as a major social signifier. In Britain the strong resurgence in interest in religion has come both from the awareness within the minority ethnic population of Islam and from the raised international profile of the faith. However, until the inclusion of a question on religion in the 2001 census of the United Kingdom, comprehensive data on British Muslims were not available. The 2001 census showed that the British Muslim population numbered 1.6 million. It has probably grown to that number from about 21,000 in 1951.

There has been a Muslim presence in Britain since the beginning of the nineteenth century when a small number of Muslim seamen and traders from the Middle East began settling around the major British ports. For example, Yemeni Muslims settled in South Shields and established a Muslim community there. Similar Yemeni communities grew up around the ports of Liverpool and Cardiff (Halliday 1992; Weller 1993). However, the major growth of the Muslim population dates from the post-war immigration of Pakistanis, Bangladeshis and Indians to fill the labour shortage in the industrial cities of London, the Midlands and the former textile towns of Yorkshire and Lancashire. In the 1990s there has been an influx of refugees: European Muslims fleeing from Bosnia and Kosovo as well as other streams from Afghanistan and Somalia. Two-thirds of the British Muslim population originate in South Asia.

The size of the Muslim population of the UK was the subject of controversy during the 1980s and 1990s. The rise in political importance of Islam, internationally and domestically, after Ayatollah Khomeini's Iranian revolution in 1979 led to an inflation of local estimates of numbers. Estimates in the early 1990s varied from a low of 900,000 (Peach 1997) to a high of 3,000,000 as given by the Muslim Parliament (Siddiqui 1992: 3) (Table 2.1).

Table 2.1 Estimates of the Muslim population of Great Britain, 1980–93

Year	Author	Estimate of GB Muslims
1980	Nielsen (1981: 25)	800,000
1981	Nielsen, (1992: 41)	750,000
1985	Brierley (1990: 250-3)	800,000
1986	Nielsen (1992: 41)	936,000
1986	Kettani (1986)	1,250,000
1987	Peach (1990: 417)	673,000 to 717,000
1989	Wahhab (1989: 8)	939,500
1990	*Independent* (9.1.90)	1,000,000 to 2,000,000
1990	Brierley and Longley (1992: 239)	990,000
1991	Peach (1997)	900,000 to 1,000, 000
1992	Siddiqui (1992: 3)	2,000,000 to 3,000,000
1993	Anwar (1994)	1,500,000

The census of 2001 showed that 71.6 per cent of the population of the United Kingdom considered themselves Christian. Muslims were the second-largest religion with 2.7 per cent. Hindus accounted for

1 per cent, Sikhs for 0.6 per cent, Jews for 0.5 per cent and other religions for 0.3 per cent; just under a quarter of the population had no religion or did not state one (Table 2.2).

Table 2.2 Religion of the UK population, 2001

	Thousands	%
Christian	42079	71.6
Buddhist	152	0.3
Hindu	559	1.0
Jewish	267	0.5
Muslim	1591	2.7
Sikh	336	0.6
Other religion	179	0.3
All religions	*45163*	*76.8*
No religion	9104	15.5
Not stated	4289	7.3
All no religion/not stated	*13626*	*23.2*
Base	*58789*	*100*

Source: Census 2001 (ONS 2004)

The 2001 census showed that 68 per cent of the Muslim population was of South Asian origin (Table 2.3). Pakistanis alone account for 43 per cent of the Muslim population and are the largest and dominant individual group. The number of white Muslims in England and Wales (179,000) is higher than expected. About a third of these are defined in the census as white British. The other two-thirds are described as 'other white'. These include the Turks, Bosnians, Kosovans and Albanians, but also those originating from North Africa and the Middle East. The religion by birthplace tables (Table S150 of the 2001 census) shows that 60,000 Muslims were born in Eastern Europe. These are assumed to be largely Bosnian and Kosovan refugees.

The same census table shows that 36,000 Muslims were born in North Africa and 93,000 Muslims were born in the Middle East. It is thought that many of these would have been counted among the

Table 2.3 Religion by ethnic group, England and Wales,
April 2001 (%)

Ethnic group	Hindu	Muslim	Sikh	Ethnic population	Ethnic Muslim population
	(%)	(%)	(%)	(No.)	(No.)
White	**1.3**	**11.6**	**2.1**	**47,520,866**	**179,409**
British	1.1	4.1	1.9	45,533,741	63,412
Irish	0.00	0.1	0	641,804	1,547
Other white	0.2	7.5	0.2	1,345,321	115,997
Mixed	**1.0**	**4.2**	**0.8**	**661,034**	**64,958**
White and black Caribbean	0.0	0.1	0	237,420	1,547
White and black African	0.0	0.7	0	78,911	10,826
White and Asian	0.6	2.0	0.6	189,015	30,933
Other mixed	0.3	1.4	0.2	155,688	21,653
South Asian or Asian British	**84.9**	**67.8**	**91.6**	**2,032,463**	**1,048,612**
Indian	84.5	8.5	91.5	1,036,807	131,463
Pakistani	0.1	42.5	0.1	714,826	657,316
Bangladeshi	0.3	16.8	0	280,830	259,833
Other Asian	**11.7**	**5.8**	**4.6**	**241,274**	**89,704**
Black or black British	**0.5**	**6.9**	**0.2**	**1,139,577**	**106,717**
Black Caribbean	0.3	0.3	0	563,843	4,640
Black African	0.2	6.2	0.1	479,665	95,891
Other black	0.1	0.4	0	96,069	6,187
Chinese or other ethnic groups	**0.6**	**3.7**	**0.7**	**446,702**	**57,225**
Chinese	0.0	0.0	0.0	226,948	
Other ethnic groups	0.5	3.6	0.7	219,754	55,679
All people	**100**	**100**	**100**	**52,041,916**	**1,546,626**
Base	552,421	1,546,626	3293,58		

Source: Census 2001 (ONS 2004), Table S101 (Ethnic Populations)

Table 2.4 Ethnic group by religion, April 2001, England & Wales

	Hindu	Muslim	Sikh	Christian	Buddhist	Jewish	Any other religion	No religion	Religion not stated	All people
Indian	45.0	12.7	29.1	4.9	0.2	0.1	1.7	1.7	4.6	100
Pakistani	0.1	92.0	0.0	1.1	0.0	0.0	0.0	0.5	6.2	100
Bangladeshi	0.6	92.5	0.0	0.5	0.1	0.0	0.0	0.4	5.8	100
Other Asian	26.8	37.3	6.2	13.4	4.8	0.3	0.9	3.4	6.8	100
Sub-total of Asian or British Asian	23.5	50.1	13.9	4.1	0.6	0.1	0.9	1.4	5.5	100

Source: Census 2001 (ONS 2004)

white population and account for many of the 116,000 'other white' Muslims in Table 2.3. There were 96,000 Black African Muslims in England and Wales, but the census tables so far published do not allow us to establish their precise provenance. There were, however, only 7,500 Nigerian-born Muslims and a further 11,000 for 'other Central and Western African countries'. It is thought that a substantial part of the remaining Black African Muslim population is of Somali origin.

While Pakistanis accounted for 42 per cent of British Muslims, Muslims accounted for 92 per cent of British Pakistanis and a similar percentage of Bangladeshis. Only 13 per cent of the Indian population were Muslim (Table 2.4). Table 2.4 also confirms that half of the South Asian population, taken as a whole, were Muslim.

The ethnic composition of the Muslim population, as revealed by the 2001 census, allows us to back-project the Muslim population to the immediate post-war years when large-scale immigration to Britain started. This is achieved by applying the 2001 percentages of the different ethnic groups to the estimated ethnic composition of the population in the census years 1951 to 1991. This is a very approximate method since the ethnic diversity of the Muslim population of Great Britain has grown in the last decade through the arrival of refugees and asylum seekers from former Yugoslavia, Somalia, Afghanistan, Iraq and Iran. Nevertheless, the proportions originating from non-Asian or African sources should not produce too great a distortion, given the small size of the minority ethnic population between 1951 and 1981. The results are given in Table 2.5. The table shows that the probable Muslim population of the UK rose from about 21, 000 in 1951 to 55,000 in 1961, a quarter of a million in 1971, nearly 600,000 in 1981, a million in 1991 and 1.6 million in 2001. The rate of growth is rapid and the population is young, so that strong continued growth is expected.

The characteristics of the British Muslim population are predominantly those of the Pakistani, Bangladeshi and Indian Muslim population living in Britain. This population is largely young and rural in origin. It is poor, badly housed and poorly educated, suffers high levels of male unemployment and has a very low female participation rate in the labour market. Survey accounts (Modood *et al.* 1997) show it is a very religious population and holds strong family values. Marriage is almost universal and is a within-ethnic-group affair: 99 per cent of Bangladeshi women in 1991 were married to Bangladeshi men, 95 per cent of Pakistani women to Pakistani men (Peach 1999).

Table 2.5 Estimates of the Indian, Pakistani, Bangladeshi, Muslim, Hindu and Sikh Populations in the UK, 1951–2001

Year	Indian	Pakistani	Bangladeshi	South Asian Muslim = Pak+B'desh + 13.1 % Ind	Estimated Muslims = S Asian N x 1.32	Estimated Hindu is Indian x 0.45	Estimated Sikh is Indian x 0.32
1951	31,000	10,000	2,000	16,000	21,000	16,120	10,000
1961	81,000	25,000	6,000	42,000	55,000	42,000	26,000
1971	375,000	119,000	22,000	190,000	251,000	195,000	120,000
1981	676,000	296,000	65,000	450,000	593,000	352,000	216,020
1991	840,000	477,000	163,000	750,000	990,000	436,800	269,000
Actual 2001	1,053,000	747,000	283,000	1,168,000	1,591,000	545,000	336,000

Source: Pakistani figures 1951 -1966 based on Peach and Winchester, 1974) adjusted for separation of Bangladeshi component. Figures for 1971 based on Peach 1990a.
Indian figures based on Vaughan Robinson's table 1, chapter 4 in Peach, 1996b
For calculations of the estimated religion figures, see text.
2001 ethnic figures from http://www.statistics.gov.uk/statbase/Expodata/Spreadsheets/D6588.xls

However, although South Asian groups represent Islam in Britain, there is a danger in essentialising Islam and arguing that South Asian characteristics are fully representative of Islam itself. Pakistanis and Bangladeshis may be almost entirely Muslim, but Islam is pan-ethnic and there are Muslims in Britain of Arab, Albanian, Bosnian, Iranian, Nigerian, Somali, Turkish and many other groups of origin whose characteristics and socio-economic profiles are very different from those of the South Asian groups. There are huge differences between Sunni Barelwi Pakistanis and East African Ismailis. What is true of the Pakistani and Bangladeshi populations as a whole is not necessarily true of individuals drawn from those populations.

We can illustrate the comparative position of Muslims in Britain with a series of diagrams showing the age distribution, educational level, occupational structure and housing tenure of the main religious groups. For convenience, the data relate to England and Wales, which contain 97 per cent of the United Kingdom total (data for Scotland and Northern Ireland are located in different censuses).

Figure 2.1 shows that the Muslim population has the youngest age structure of all the religious groups in England and Wales. One-third of the Muslim population is aged 0–15 compared to the average for

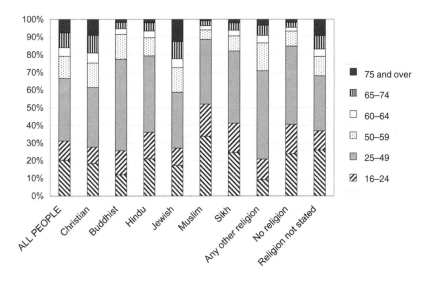

Figure 2.1 Religious groups by age, England and Wales, 2001

the whole population of 20 per cent. Less than 10 per cent are aged 60 or over compared to 18 per cent for the population as a whole. Educationally, the Muslim population is relatively poorly qualified. Figure 2.2 shows that over 40 per cent had no educational qualifications in the 2001 census. However, the profile is not too dissimilar to that of the population as a whole.

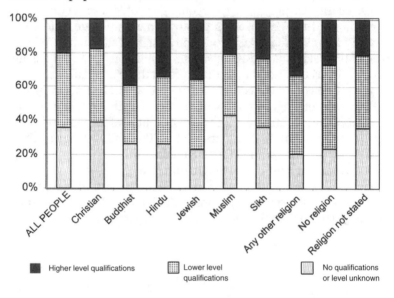

Figure 2.2 Religious groups by educational qualifications, England and Wales, 2001

In terms of occupation, however, the combination of a young age structure, poor educational qualifications and the small proportion of the female population engaged in formal economic activity results in a high age dependency ratio (25 per cent); correspondingly, Muslims have the lowest proportion (25 per cent) of population engaged in economic activity compared to other religious groups (Figure 2.3). Figure 2.3 also shows that Muslims have the smallest percentage of their population in the top three professional occupations.

In turn, the combination of young age, poor qualifications and poor jobs leads to an unfavourable tenure pattern in housing compared to other religious groups. Figure 2.4 shows that Muslims

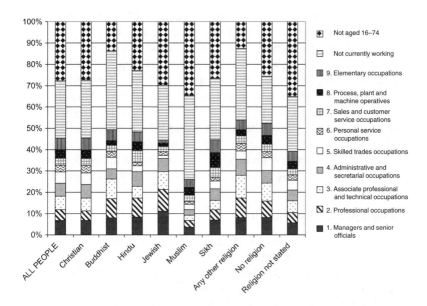

Figure 2.3 Religion by occupation, England and Wales, 2001

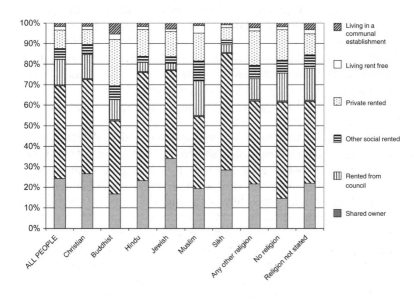

Figure 2.4 Housing tenure by religion, England and Wales, 2001

have the lowest proportion of owner-occupied homes of all of the religious groups (apart from the very small Buddhist population). They also have the highest dependence on social housing.

The overwhelming majority of Muslims in Britain are from the Sunni tradition. We have survey data from half of the mosques in our Oxford Leverhulme survey. If we take the proportion of mosque affiliations as the best available guide to the proportional strengths of the main traditions, Sunni mosques account for 87 per cent of the total. Shi'as account for 7 per cent. Multi-traditional mosques form a further 3 per cent and Ahmadiyyas, a group that is not recognised by many Muslims as truly Islamic, represent a further 2 per cent.

Geographical distribution

The Muslim population of Britain is highly concentrated into a small number of large urban areas: London (607,000), the West Midlands Metropolitan County (Birmingham) (192,000), Greater Manchester (125,219) and West Yorkshire Metropolitan County (the Bradford–Leeds urban area) (150,000) (ONS 2004, Table S103).

Ten of the twenty local authorities with the largest totals and highest proportions of Muslims in England and Wales are London boroughs. Tower Hamlets in the East End of London has the highest percentage of Muslim population of all the local authorities in the UK (36 per cent) and is also the third largest in size. It is the centre of the Bangladeshi population in Britain and the borough contains nearly a quarter of the total Bangladeshi population of the UK. Although this total has grown by 66 per cent between 1991 and 2001, the percentage of the national Bangladeshi population living in Tower Hamlets has remained constant.

Within the urban areas in which they have settled, Pakistanis and (particularly) Bangladeshis have shown high rates of segregation. On a scale from 0 (no segregation) to 100 (complete segregation), Pakistanis segregated from whites averaged 54 while Bangladeshis averaged 65. Bangladeshis showed the highest degree of segregation of any ethnic population in Britain in the 1991 census (Peach 1996a). They showed a moderately high degree of segregation from the Pakistanis (46), while the Pakistani/Indian segregation level was lower than the Pakistani/Bangladeshi level (39 versus 46). Thus, even though Pakistanis and Bangladeshis share a religion and once shared a nationality, ethnicity appears to be a stronger bond than religion among these Muslims.

Socio-economic status

Pakistanis and Bangladeshis represent some of the poorest minority ethnic populations in Britain, with Bangladeshis being worse off than Pakistanis. The majority of both groups originate from peasant backgrounds: Pakistanis from the Punjab and Azad Kashmir; Bangladeshis from Sylhet in the north-east of the country.

The 2001 census still shows Bangladeshis and Pakistanis to be the most economically marginal of the minority ethnic groups in Britain. They have the lowest percentages of all ethnic groups in higher managerial professions (2.1 and 3.6 respectively, compared to 6.1 for the population as a whole). They have the highest percentages of 'never worked or long-term unemployed' of all ethnic groups (17.1 and 16.2 respectively, compared to 2.7 per cent for all people); the highest percentages of persons looking after the home (13.1 and 12.2 per cent, compared to the average of 4.7 per cent); and the highest percentages with no educational qualifications (31.1 and 28.8 per cent, compared to the average of 26 per cent).

Bangladeshi and Pakistani women had the lowest economic participation rates of any ethnic minority group in Britain. Only 22 per cent of Bangladeshi women aged 16 and over – and only 27 per cent of Pakistani women in the same category – were economically active. These percentages were half those of Indian women (55 per cent). Although Pakistanis and Bangladeshis were both poorly off, in terms of home ownership Pakistanis were dramatically advanced. In 2001, 70 per cent of Pakistanis owned or were buying their homes with a mortgage, compared to 38 per cent of Bangladeshis.

The British 2001 census allows us to examine the situation of Muslims as such rather than to use Pakistanis and Bangladeshis as surrogates. Data published so far combine male and female and refer to England and Wales, rather than to the United Kingdom (however, the overwhelming majority of the Muslim population live in England and Wales). The broad picture confirms that Muslims as a whole occupy an underprivileged position.

Whereas the proportion of the total working population of England and Wales in the three white collar classes (higher managerial and professional occupations, lower managerial and professional occupations, and intermediate occupations) was 26 per cent, the Muslim proportion was 13 per cent, only half of the national total. The Hindu percentage, by comparison, was 30 per cent and the Sikh percentage was 21 per cent. While unemployment is much lower in

England and Wales than in the rest of Europe at 2.4 per cent, for Muslims it was nearly double at 4.6 per cent (Hindus 2.6 per cent and Sikhs 3.3 per cent). The Muslim figure for 'never worked or long-term unemployed' was five times higher than that for the population as a whole (16 per cent compared to the average of 3 per cent). The reason seems to be the non-participation of Muslim women in the official labour force. The Muslim percentage of those with higher educational qualifications was just below the England and Wales average (13.5 per cent versus 14.3 per cent). On the other hand, the Hindu percentage with higher educational qualifications was 27 per cent and for Sikhs it was 17 per cent. Home ownership showed Muslims as below the England and Wales average: 54 per cent compared to 69 per cent (Hindus 76 per cent and Sikhs 85 per cent.).

The low participation rate of Muslims, and of Pakistanis and Bangladeshis compared to Indian women, reflects traditional Islamic values of *purdah* (protecting Muslim women from contact with men outside their immediate family) and *izzet* (family honour) (Ballard 1990). It is also reflected in the low proportion of Pakistani and Bangladeshi women with higher educational qualifications. There are severe economic consequences arising from these traditional values. Unlike the Hindus and Sikhs, where both husbands and wives often work and there are dual incomes in the household, Pakistani and Bangladeshi households often have only one breadwinner. The younger age of marriage for Pakistani and Bangladeshi girls also results in family formation starting sooner and progressing later, so that average family sizes are larger than for Indian, Hindu or Sikh families. From this it follows that housing conditions are poorer and the degree of crowding greater than for Indians.

Chapter 3
Issues, Policy and Practice

MUHAMMAD ANWAR

It is a fact that 1.6 million Muslims now reside in Britain, where they are the largest religious minority group and an integral part of the society. However, all the socio-economic indicators show that Muslims, particularly of Pakistani and Bangladeshi origin, are one of the most deprived groups in Britain. In particular since the 9/11 catastrophe there has been an intensification of anti-Muslim attitudes in Britain that has sometimes resulted in attacks on individuals and property, and also more marked direct religious discrimination. In December 2002 the European Monitoring Centre on Racism and Xenophobia (EUMC) reported that Islamophobia and anti-Semitism, fuelled by the September 11 attacks and the Middle East conflict, are in danger of becoming acceptable in Europe. It is a fact that religious minorities cannot keep their ethnicity and identity confined to their homes. In addition, society needs to reflect the diverse nature of communities in terms of adapting various services and provisions to meet the specific needs of all communities (Bakhsh and Sullivan 1985). Therefore, the presence of Muslims and other non-Christian religious groups in Britain poses a challenge to the policies and practices of the institutions of society as well as to the faith communities themselves.

This chapter examines the current policy and practice towards Muslims of central and local government and other organisations. The empirical work reported here was undertaken as part of a research project on 'State Policies towards Muslim Minorities in the European Union', funded by the European Commission.[1] The project was undertaken in Britain (with results that provide the basis of this chapter), Germany and Sweden. The study was mainly qualitative and over eighty persons participated in it. The fieldwork included one-to-one interviews, focus group meetings and two round-table discussions – one in London and one in Birmingham.

Interviewees were asked to comment on various services and public policy areas relevant to Muslims. Eleven areas of concern in relation to British Muslims were mentioned by the respondents. Five of these are discussed in this chapter: education, employment, housing, political participation, and religious and racial hostility leading to discrimination or violence.

Education

Research shows that educational achievement levels of Muslim children in Britain are generally lower than white and some other ethnic groups. In 2002, the proportion of Muslim children achieving five or more A*–C grades in subjects taken for the General Certificate in Secondary Education (GCSE) in maintained schools was lower than for white, Chinese and Indian groups. For example, Pakistani (40 per cent) and Bangladeshi (45 per cent) pupils achieved lower grades in the GCSE than Indian (64 per cent), Chinese (72 per cent) and white (50 per cent) pupils (Department of Education and Skills 2003). These figures clearly show a significant gap between Muslim and non-Muslim children. It is worth pointing out that across all ethnic groups, girls were achieving higher grades than boys. However, Muslim children in Glasgow and some areas of London were performing better than Muslim children in Birmingham and Bradford (Anwar 1998). Detailed analysis shows that these differences are linked to their social class backgrounds and the length of stay in Britain. In higher education, despite the differential acceptance rates between Muslims and whites with the same qualifications by the British universities (40 per cent to 54 per cent), the proportion of Muslim children in higher education is slowly increasing. Other education issues which relate to Muslims include mother-tongue teaching, religious education, provision of *halal* meals, prayer facilities, uniforms for girls, single-sex education and state funding of Muslim schools. It is worth mentioning that there are at present over eighty Muslim independent schools in Britain, and after a long campaign only five have recently received state funding while several thousand (almost 7,000) Church of England and Catholic schools have been receiving state funding, which has also been extended to Jewish schools.

One professional man in the study said that 'Muslims have fallen behind'. This illustrates the urgent need to redress this situation and the perception of all respondents that education is an area of serious concern. It further appears from the tenor of the responses that this is something all respondents accepted. Apart from a reference to the high academic standards in the few Muslim schools that exist, there were no positive comments from any of the respondents in relation to the wider education system, which is seen as failing Muslim pupils. Half of the respondents referred to the failure of the British education system to meet the specific needs of Muslim pupils. Some of them referred to the lack of Muslim schools as a problem, and to the lack of funds available for existing schools. A significant number felt that mainstream schools lacked facilities for Muslims, such as prayer facilities, *halal* food and understanding the needs of fasting pupils.

A number of respondents said that there were too few Muslim teachers and governors. One spoke of the problem as one of 'very few role models for Muslim pupils in society/ schools'. Another referred to the lack of understanding of Muslim culture within educational psychology services and said this 'tends to stereotype parents' views'. A further comment illustrates the consequence of the

> low level of educational attainment in particular for Bangladeshi and Pakistani communities in Britain. Links with high levels of unemployment and living in deprived areas with poor housing and little support. Many young people may feel disillusioned with educational institutes, some may not be meeting specific needs of Muslim communities.

Half of the respondents mentioned some aspects of the education system that go beyond a failure to meet the needs of Muslims, being more actively hostile to Islam, Muslim pupils and their parents. For example, a few referred to the stereotyping of Muslim pupils, particularly girls – including an expectation of underachievement. Some others quoted bullying of Muslim pupils as a problem that schools are failing to tackle adequately and one of them explained that 'bullying and attacks on Muslims in state schools ... are common. Some respondents mentioned the Christian bias in religious education, and the misrepresentation and denigration of Islam ('Islamophobic religious education lessons'). A number of responses related to the high rate of exclusion of Muslim pupils. Others felt that Muslim parents are discouraged from involvement with the schools

and one felt that parents were, 'often subtly excluded by being intimi-
dated, made to feel unwelcome or uncomfortable within the school
context'. They also said that there was, 'no communication by schools
with parents'.

A small number of respondents referred to factors within Muslim
communities that have a detrimental impact on the education of
Muslim pupils, such as high levels of illiteracy amongst the adult
Muslim immigrant population and the fact that some Muslim
parents tended not to encourage their children to study.

Employment

First-generation migrant Muslims were granted access only to a
limited range of occupations upon arrival, and as a consequence they
are most numerous in certain industrial sectors: this has also led to
their concentrations in certain towns, cities and regions (Anwar
1979). There is now a growing number of Muslims working in the
service sector as well as an increasing number who are starting their
own businesses. Muslims working in the manufacturing industry are
mainly manual workers in the textile and metal industries. However,
the percentage of employed Muslims working in the textile industry
has been halved in the last 20 years from over 20 per cent to 10 per
cent because of the virtual demise of this industrial sector. Overall, it
appears that as second-generation British-educated Muslims join
the labour market, the occupational pattern is slowly changing. It is
relevant to mention here that very few Muslim women work as
compared to white women and other ethnic groups. For example,
according to the 2001 census the economic activity rate for Pakistani
and Bangladeshi women was very low, 29 and 25 respectively,
compared with 60 per cent for white, 62 per cent for black and 57 per
cent for Indian women. Generally, Muslims hold menial jobs, are
employed in older industries, have lower incomes and are vulnerable
to unemployment.

Evidence from the 2001 Census and Labour Force Surveys clearly
shows that the unemployment rate for Muslim groups was almost
three times as high as the rate for whites, although in the 1990s
unemployment rates fell for all groups. However, the overall employment position of Muslim groups at the end of the decade remained
considerably worse than that of the white population (LFS, Spring-
Winter 2000). A difference of 10–15 percentage points remained
between Muslim groups and whites. The 2001 census has confirmed

this trend. It shows that 14 per cent of Pakistanis and 16 per cent of Bangladeshis were unemployed compared with only 5 per cent of whites.

Almost half of the respondents felt that Muslims were disadvantaged in the field of employment. This is clearly a serious issue. If Muslims are disadvantaged in the workplace, they are disadvantaged both economically and socially in a society that defines status largely by reference to employment. It is therefore important to consider the factors that are causing the disadvantage. Fourteen respondents specifically referred to discrimination against Muslim workers, both at the point of recruitment and within the workplace. One said, 'young Muslims ... tend to need more qualifications than their white counterparts to secure a job'. Some said that there was discrimination within public sector employment: they mentioned local authorities, government and the BBC. One referred to the practice of appointing from within without advertising posts as a way to exclude Muslims from promotion. Another felt that discrimination was greatest against Muslims from Bangladesh. Others felt that since Muslims do not participate in social events at work and that this affects their promotion prospects:

> Muslims don't fit into the social life of the British, therefore making it harder to make 'contact' with peers. Social attitudes of *hijab* and non-drinking of alcohol being interpreted as disinterest in social activities at place of employment. Hence, being discriminated against for promotion.

One respondent offered a comment that ranged across various aspects of the problem:

> Level of unemployment for Muslim communities is significantly higher than other groups; young Muslims who do not do well in education tend to need more qualifications than their white counterparts in order to secure a job. Others who do not do as well will go into manual employment with little scope. Those who have the means would probably become self-employed. There is now a growing awareness of young Muslims to do well at school, college and university in order for them to better their chances of securing employment. There is probably a correlation between those Muslim families and parents who are educated and the likelihood their children will follow suit.

Some respondents felt that a problem for Muslims in employment was the lack of understanding of Islam, and the failure of employers to provide 'accommodation for religious needs, holidays, etc.' Some other comments referred to the fact that Muslims are not protected by existing anti-discrimination legislation ('unlike Jews and Sikhs') because they are identified by religion rather than race. Three comments might be mentioned in this context:

Muslims are being disproportionately discriminated [against].

Unlike Jews and Sikhs, Muslims are not protected by law. This should be changed because a huge number of young UK-born Muslims are preferring to identify themselves on grounds of religion rather than race.

The young Asian Muslims seem to be more assertive in relation to their religion.

A minority of respondents said that Muslims often received poor education and training, which adversely affected their employment opportunities. A number of respondents referred to factors within their own communities which limited employment opportunities. One felt that 'Muslims themselves do not exert adequately to obtain jobs in right professions or trades'. Another said that 'girls are often dissuaded from careers out of the house, though this varies'.

Housing

There is a strong correlation between the employment status of Muslims and the type and quality of housing in which they live. Housing segregation for some groups has clear implications for the quality of education, and bad housing certainly affects health. Some Muslim groups like Pakistanis have a high owner-occupation rate (69 per cent) compared with Bangladeshis (34 per cent). Overall, 70 per cent of whites are living in owner-occupied homes (Survey of English Housing 2001). One of the reasons why the owner-occupation rate for Bangladeshis is so low is because they are concentrated in inner London, particularly in Tower Hamlets, where it is difficulty to buy houses. Even when they do own their own homes, the condition of their houses is often poor. More Muslims live in terraced houses (64 per cent of Pakistanis) compared to whites (27 per cent) (Modood *et al.* 1997) As far as physical housing problems are concerned, the 2001 census has provided very detailed information regarding overcrowding, the lack of or need to share bathroom or WC facilities, lack of central heating, and whether the accommodation is self-contained. It appears that a significant number of houses occupied by Muslim groups are overcrowded (43 per cent Pakistani and Bangladeshi) compared to white households (2 per cent). Also, almost 60 per cent of Pakistani and Bangladeshi households are without central heating compared to 37 per cent of white households in this situation. Another relevant factor worth mentioning here is that an over-whelming majority of Muslims live in inner-city run-down areas where housing problems are endemic. Unless conditions in these areas are improved, housing disparities between Muslims and the general population are likely to continue in the near future.

An overwhelming majority of the respondents (68 per cent) felt that housing was an area of serious concern for Muslims. Only one respondent expressed a positive view: 'I have seen Asian Muslims benefit from council houses.' It was pointed out by one respondent that Muslims prefer to own their houses, and it is not owner occupiers but those living in council housing who suffer the problems. Another felt that the problems were experienced more severely by Bangladeshi Muslims than by those from India and Pakistan. One respondent explained the situation in the following way:

> Most Muslim communities tend to live in concentrated areas where there is a large proportion of black and ethnic minority communities. This is probably due to feeling more comfortable and confident living within their own community. Muslim Bangladeshi communities (most) live in deprived areas within council estates. Other factors around housing include preference given to areas where mosques are nearby. Most Muslim families (even if they have the means to live in a more affluent area) will prefer to stay where their own family and community are near.

However, it is important to note that several respondents felt that Muslims were allocated housing on poor estates. One said that 'Muslims have been living in inner-city ghettos and slums.' Some felt this specifically reflected discrimination on the housing lists. A signifi-cant minority of respondents spoke of racist attacks on Muslims on council estates and of the 'failure [on the part of the authorities] to tackle racist attacks and harassment directed at Muslims'. Some recommended better training of housing officers, the recruitment of more Muslims in this area and the need for better policing.

More than a third of respondents said that overcrowding was often a problem for Muslim families. This was attributed partly to economic factors but principally to the fact that 'Muslim families are larger'. The lack of four-bedroom council houses was seen as threatening the Muslim way of life. One said the 'extended family was at risk of being destroyed'. As one interviewee explained,

> Modern houses are too small for Muslim families. They [Muslims] need larger flats and houses, e.g., four-bed houses or flats. Often on the local authority housing list they [Muslims] are discriminated [against]. Muslims are offered poor houses or dumped in poor housing estates.

Several respondents said that Muslims tended to live in areas and on estates with a high concentration of other Muslims. One respondent felt this was by choice, 'probably due to feeling more comfortable and confident living within their own community'. Others, however, saw it as 'ghettoisation'. A few respondents raised the issue of sheltered or supported housing for elderly people, students and people with disabilities: they felt that there should be such housing specifically for Muslims. The number of elderly Muslims is likely to increase in the future and therefore appropriate sheltered housing for Muslims should be seen as a priority.

Political participation

Political participation is a good measure of the integration of Muslims in Britain. Most British Muslims have the right to vote and stand for elections. The concentration of Muslims in certain areas means that in statistical terms they are in a position to influence the political and electoral process in the areas of their settlement (Anwar 1994). Their participation in the electoral process has increased in the last twenty years but their representation has made slow progress. There are only two out of 659 Members of Parliament of Muslim origin in the House of Commons. There are five members of Muslim origin in the House of Lords. At local level, there are just over two hundred local government councillors. There is one Muslim Member of the European Parliament from Britain. However, there is no Muslim representation in the Scottish Parliament, the Welsh Assembly or the Greater London Assembly.

Two-thirds of respondents felt that Muslims lacked a sufficient voice in the political process. Such a situation has important repercussions for the welfare of British Muslims generally, in terms of both the impact of Muslims on the policies driving the nation and the relationship between the Muslim communities and the country in which they are living: a people without a political voice are a people forced out of the mainstream of national life. If this is the case for British Muslims, it is so despite the fact that they have contributed significantly in terms of economic growth. However, one respondent disagreed that Muslims lacked political representation, saying that 'representation seems okay, at local and now national level; although limited to Labour Party and lack of visible Muslim women'. However, of those who expressed concern about this situation, many did feel that at local levels Muslims were at least making their presence felt. Several respondents commented on the shortage of Muslim MPs and thought that there were too few Muslims in the House of Lords. It appeared that the problem was that parties did not put forward Muslims for safe seats and that this should be tackled. For example, one respondent suggested that 'all political parties should offer more safe seats in council and national elections to Muslim candidates'. Some felt that there was a need specifically for younger Muslims to become involved in the politics of central government: 'we need more sensible councillors and MPs from the new generation'. Local government was perceived by the respondents as an area in which Muslims are better represented. One respondent said that, although there were Muslim councillors, there was still a shortage of Muslims 'chairing key committees at local authority level'.

Generally it was felt that Muslims have contributed substantially in business and the economic growth of the country yet nonetheless lack power and a proper share of resources in British society. Some respondents expressed disillusionment with the attitude of the political parties towards Muslim issues. Some typical responses in this context included, 'tokenistic', 'little support by politicians for Muslims', 'Muslims feel badly let down by both the political parties', 'there is a lot of talk but very little action'. However, there was also the feeling that Muslims should make a greater effort to become involved in politics, because currently 'the burden of effectively representing the Muslim interests falls on an extremely small number of individuals who participate in politics'. On the whole, the political parties have a long way to go to provide the scale of representation for Muslims in the political institutions commensurate with their numbers in the population.

Religious and racial discrimination and violence

The first Race Relations Act in Britain was passed 39 years ago in 1965, the second in 1968 and the third in 1976 (current Race

Relations Act). The Race Relations Act deals with both direct and indirect racial discrimination. However, it was felt by academics and practitioners in the field of race relations that the 1976 Act was weak and that it needed strengthening. The Race Relations (Amendment) Act 2000, which came into force in April 2001, has strengthened the 1976 Act and extended it to include some public bodies and government functions that were not included in the scope of the 1976 Act. The new Act strengthens the 1976 Act in two major ways: it extends protection against racial discrimination by public authorities and it places a new, enforceable positive duty on public authorities. Under the 1976 Act, the Commission for Racial Equality (CRE) was set up and now there is a network of over one hundred local Racial Equality Councils, largely funded by the CRE. Many local authorities also have their own equalities and/or race relations units. These units are expected to work more effectively under the Race Relations (Amendment) Act because of the new duties of public authorities. The same applies to hospitals, police and government ministers. It is also expected that the standards for dealing with racial discrimination adopted by public bodies will influence practice in the private sector.

Religious discrimination can take different forms. For example, it may simply be attitudinal religious prejudice and/or there may be a deliberate act of direct discrimination based on religion. It is also possible that Muslims may be discriminated against as a result of institutional practices or procedures that are seen as indirect discrimination. For many Muslims, religious and racial discrimination and violence is a fact of life. Despite the existence of legislation in Britain against racial discrimination for the last 39 years, ethnic minorities including Muslims are still victims of racial discrimination. The Race Relations Act 1976 does not fully protect Muslims because religious discrimination is not unlawful in Britain. It is worth mentioning that, following on from case law, two religious groups, Sikhs and Jews, are protected by the Race Relations Act. Meanwhile, in Northern Ireland, religious discrimination is unlawful under the Fair Employment (Northern Ireland) Act (1989). A close examination of this Act shows that there is nothing in it that could not be implemented in Britain for Muslims and other religious groups: this anomaly could be removed if the political will were there (Anwar 2000). Some Muslim workers have been sacked because they wanted to offer prayers at their workplace, some Muslim women have been refused jobs because of their dress, and sometimes Muslim girls have been excluded from schools because they wanted to wear headscarves (Anwar and Shah 2000). Research funded by the Home Office showed that Muslims perceived and experienced religious as well as racial discrimination (Weller, Feldman and Purdam 2001). The Human Rights Act (1998), which came into force on 2 October 2000, also prohibits discrimination on the basis of religion. For example, under the Act, freedom from inhuman or degrading treatment may provide ground to challenge discriminatory treatment or harassment. Freedom of religion could help Muslims whose employers prohibit the observance of their religion in the workplace, and freedom of expression could apply to the wearing of clothing by Muslims for religious or cultural reasons at work or school.

Generally, it was felt that, although a tolerant community, the younger generation of Muslims do not feel they should put up with any sort of religious or racial discrimination or violence. Of all the questions put to respondents, this one drew the greatest response – reflecting the centrality of this issue to Muslims. Almost all respondents expressed a view and all felt that discrimination and/or violence were a major problem for Muslims. The importance of action around this issue can therefore hardly be overstated: it is clearly unacceptable for a community to be living in fear. An overwhelming majority of respondents said that Muslims experienced discrimination in their daily lives. Some of these specifically referred to 'Islamophobia' as the context for the discrimination and one referred to 'Islam as the most hated religion' – hated both by white people and by some other ethnic minorities.

Respondents also referred to different forms of discrimination in the workplace. Muslims may be passed over for promotion, as in the case of a Muslim doctor who had more experience but was not promoted to a consultant's post while a younger, less experienced white doctor *was* promoted. Discrimination may also take the form of employers who generally fail to be sensitive to the needs of Muslim employees:

> lack of facilities for prayers during the month of Ramadan, limited holiday allowance/entitlements if Muslims want to go away for Hajj, limited understanding of women wearing *hijab/burka* by fellow white people.

Some respondents referred to children facing discrimination in schools; one felt that there exists a 'conscious part in schools (in my opinion) to confuse students about their identity'. Misrepresentation of Islam by the media was also cited as one of the causes of the discrimination experienced by Muslims. In addition, several respondents spoke of racist violence directed towards Muslims, including 'violence against mosques and gangs of skinheads and National Front hooligans taunting Muslim women and children'. One said that hostility and violence had become worse since September 11. A couple of respondents mentioned domestic violence experienced by Muslim women and the lack of appropriate services to help.

Views on policy and practice

In the study a number of respondents from key agencies such as local councils, the health service, schools and central government departments were asked to point to examples of good practice from their own places of work. Twenty-six were able to give examples of good practice; only two said there were none. Examples included policies, provision for facilities, special initiatives and achievements. Several respondents referred to successful equal opportunities policies operating at their places of work. A typical answer was that 'any form of discrimination or harassment is not tolerated'. Others said that Muslim applicants were given equal access to jobs and that equal opportunities policies were followed. One respondent spoke of a racial equality plan being developed and implemented in a local authority, while another referred to the implementation of the *Religious and Cultural Guidelines in Schools* in his area.

A number of respondents said that their places of work had taken steps to enable prayer and to make *halal* food available, and had been extremely supportive during the month of Ramadan and flexible when it was time for staff to break the fast. Almost half of the respondents quoted initiatives they had adopted, including training in racial awareness; establishment of forums for consultation between community groups and service providers; positive action schemes for recruitment of Muslim staff; a process of sharing and cascading best practice in schools; and the formation of Black Workers' Groups. Several respondents spoke of good practice achieved in their work, including successful partnership between community groups/organisations and the local authority; a successful self-help group of Muslim women carers, now given Council funding; respect for clients; equality and democracy in the workplace; inter-faith dialogue and harmony; a new care centre that caters for the needs of Muslims and increased recruitment of Muslim staff.

The general view was that local councils are now prepared to take Muslim issues on board, following pressure from Muslim groups: 'under political and community's pressure, the local councils have often come forward to recognise the needs and demands of the Muslims'. Another typical answer was that the situation is improving because Muslims have taken initiatives and actively participated in local politics. Respondents also welcomed the anti-racist policies and initiatives being implemented in some councils. Several of them commented on initiatives relating to anti-racism and celebrating diversity as well as the appointment of specialist consultants on issues affecting local ethnic minority communities. It was pointed out that there has been an increase in literature in various languages and an improvement in the availability of interpreters. The Race Relations (Amendment) Act 2000, the Macpherson Report (1999) and the CRE Standard for Local Government initiatives were mentioned.

However, a significant number of respondents felt that some councils remain actively hostile to Muslims. Others felt that the policies adopted do not deal adequately with issues in practice. One respondent said that 'we have a long way to go yet'. Certain respondents noted that there are very few Muslim schools – only five having received government funding. Single-sex schools are discouraged although there is demand for such schools by a vast majority of parents. It was also felt that the practice of Islam in schools is 'looked down upon'. Some responses to the needs of Muslims were seen by one respondent as tokenistic: 'window dressing, e.g., appoint a few black faces on the staff'.

It was felt that there was insufficient representation in Parliament and that little attention is paid to Muslim needs. Concern is only raised when a situation occurs, such as the disturbances in 2001 in Oldham, Burnley and Bradford. Otherwise, Muslims' needs are not on the government's agenda. However, it was acknowledged by several respondents and those who participated in round-table discussions that some good government initiatives have been taken. In particular, 'initiatives for social inclusion are helpful and DfES [Department for Education and Skills] targeting [of] schools' exclusion [of pupils] and underachievement' were appreciated. It was also the view that there is an increased awareness of racial issues. However, there were others who were not satisfied and felt that there was a lack of interest in Muslim issues at central government level:

Muslims as a community have made no impact in affecting the national government policies.... As far as the CRE and RECs (Racial Equality Councils) are concerned a lot of work is being done to promote racial equality; however, in terms of very specific issues relating to the Muslim community there is not a single organisation which can be identified as being proactive. Other areas of the legal framework are very patchy.

Another respondent expressed it in this way:

Working in the equality field I am quite shocked to learn that not much is known about Islamophobia; worse still is that recommendations stated in the Runnymede Report are not known.

Two other concerns were also mentioned by several participants in the study. One was about the negative attitudes of the media towards Islam and Muslims. Typical comments were that 'the press and media are generally xenophobic' and that there is 'anti-Muslim hostility in the media'. The other concern was about the future of young Muslims in Britain. They were worried about the 'de-Muslimi-sation of the Muslim youth'. They were also worried about the 'future of the family unit, given high divorce rates in Britain'. Some also felt that there was a 'shortage of Muslim boys/girls when seeking a marriage partner for their children' and that this sometimes created practical problems in arranging marriages of Muslims in this country.

Conclusions

It appears from research evidence that hostility and discrimination against Muslims forces them to seek support from their own communities. Muslim school leavers as well as their parents face very high unemployment rates compared with whites and other local job seekers. This partly reflects racial and religious discrimination. In education, Muslim children are also facing disadvantage in terms of poor educational achievements and lack of facilities for the teaching of their religion and culture in schools. Muslim parents are generally concerned that their children are not able to learn about their religion in formal educational institutions. Although Muslim organisations provide such teaching facilities in mosques and community centres, these activities are not enough. The housing conditions of Muslims are also inferior to those of indigenous white people. Muslims are over-represented in the prison population (almost 10 per cent of the total). However, they are under-represented in the police, the judiciary, the civil service, the media, public appointments and also in the decision-making process. For example, there are only two MPs of Muslim origin in the House of Commons, out of 659: to reflect the Muslim population in Britain, however, there should be at least 20 MPs of Muslim origin.

Legislation in Britain against racial discrimination has been in operation since 1965, but there is still widespread racial and religious discrimination against Muslims and other ethnic minorities. The Race Relations Act 1976 does not fully protect Muslims because religious discrimination is still not unlawful in Britain. Article 13 of the Treaty of Amsterdam provides a legal basis for the European Union to take action against discrimination on grounds of religion or belief, in addition to racial or ethnic origin. The European Union Employment Directive, which came into force in December 2003, covers religious discrimination in employment, but religious discrimination in other areas is not covered. There is also recognition of this in the Human Rights Act 1998, the Scotland Act 1998 and the Greater London Authority Act 1999. However, very few participants were aware of these developments. Muslims feel that they need to be protected by law as Sikhs and Jews are protected from religious discrimination as a result of case law. In particular, since September 11 hostility and attacks against Muslims, both verbal and physical, have increased. Recently there have been numerous press reports of violent assaults and attacks on individuals and property such as mosques. Generally, there seem to be an increase in Islamophobia (EUMC 2001). Research has shown that general hostility towards Islam and Muslims in Britain can be found in services, the media and the general public (Weller, Feldman and Purdham 2001). Racism and religious discrimination against Muslims in the workplace (Hepple and Choudhry 2001), in schools and on council estates is widespread (Parekh 2000). The public services have in the main failed to meet the specific needs of Muslims in terms of prayer facilities, *halal* food, religious holidays and so on.

With the significant demographic change that has taken place within the Muslim communities in Britain – a shift from first-generation migrants towards second- and third-generation British-born citizens – the question of identity is now part of an ongoing discussion within Muslim communities in Britain. It is relevant, among other factors, to community facilities and the responses of relevant authorities to the needs of Muslims in the areas of their settlement. Muslim practice is often misunderstood by non-Muslims in Britain leading to integration problems. Young Muslims generally feel that while they are getting the same education and training as white indigenous young people, they are not being treated equally and are in practice second-class citizens. They also feel that, on the whole, their parents have tolerated prejudice, discrimination and harassment, perhaps as the price of settling in Britain. However, it appears that young Muslims are not prepared to accept racial and religious discrimination and harassment. Unless Muslim young people receive equal treatment the tensions between Muslim young people and non-Muslims are likely to grow, as was seen in street disturbances in Oldham, Burnley and Bradford in the summer of 2001. Therefore, positive policies and measures are needed by the state agencies and others to facilitate the integration of Muslims by bringing their rights and their working and living conditions into line with those of their fellow-citizens. However, as research reported in this chapter shows, Britain has a long way to go to achieve this goal.

Note

1   For full details of the EU-funded study see M. Anwar and Q. Bakhsh (2003). I am grateful to Qadir Bakhsh for his help with this study.

PART II
Islamophobia, Identity Politics
and Multiculturalism

Chapter 4

From Race to Religion:
the New Face of Discrimination

CHRIS ALLEN

When one speaks of 'racism' towards 'Asians' in Britain, the descriptor 'Asian' is clearly inappropriate. In Pnina Werbner's deconstruction (1997: 244),

> it is not, after all, primarily *Asian* collective sacred icons and cultures which are violently targeted by racists in Britain, but the discrete national and religious icons of subgroupings within the broader South Asian collectivity. As we have seen, the most violent racism at present is directed against British Muslims.

A report that considered this 'anti-Muslim racism', 'anti-Muslim-ism' or (as most writers term it) 'Islamophobia' was the Runnymede Trust's *Islamophobia: a Challenge for Us All* (1997), undertaken following the recognition that racist attacks were increasingly 'explicit, more extreme and more dangerous' (*ibid.*: 3). So, while racism on the basis of markers of race obviously continues, a shift is apparent in which some of the more traditional and obvious markers have been displaced by newer and more prevalent ones of a cultural, socio-religious nature. However, while traditional markers of race have been afforded legislative protection, the same is not true for religious markers, in relation to which protection is restricted to ethnically definable religious communities. Despite Muslims being increasingly targeted with newer forms of racist prejudice and hatred, as multi-ethnic communities they remain outside the writ of current legislation.

Recent events have also seen Muslims presented and represented through myriad forms of communicative dissemination that have both reinforced and potentially 'justified' such racist beliefs. The socio-religious icons of Islam, and more specifically Muslims, have attained such prominence recently that they are almost immediately recognisable – and almost entirely negative and detrimental. Since 9/11, however, the situation has simultaneously deteriorated and intensified, and the anti-Muslimist discourse prevails to the extent that society is becoming increasingly receptive to such ideas (Allen and Nielsen 2002). This chapter intends to consider how rising Islamophobia and the impact of 9/11 have combined to shape the ways in which South Asian Muslims in particular have been caught up in this malaise.

The chapter begins with an overview of the changing face of racism, from its more racialised markers in earlier manifestations to newer and more culture- or religion-based identifiers, to put into context the way in which 9/11 has given both resonance and credence to already existent anti-Muslim ideas and expressions, and how in Britain these same ideas and expressions have taken on an increasingly South Asian character. Providing a background to the anomalies in legislation that have allowed Islamophobia to become legitimised, the chapter explores the way in which far-right groups have exploited this and found unprecedented success at the ballot box after highly inflammatory and insidious anti-Muslim campaigns. Using examples from across the media, as well as from other voices in the public domain, including mainstream politics, the chapter concludes with a consideration of how post-9/11 Islamophobia has impacted upon South Asian communities, and how 9/11 may be used in the future to justify the perpetuation of racist attitudes and beliefs.

Terrorists or apologists: post-9/11 Muslims and the new racism

Post-9/11 reificatory processes have therefore both re-established and newly established Muslims as chimerical, monstrous others, drawing upon the legacy of anti-Muslimism endemic to the European mindset. Increasingly, Muslims have found themselves identified in definite and bi-polar ways. As Ziauddin Sardar (2002) writes, contemporary Muslims are identified as either terrorists warring against the West or apologists defending Islam as a peaceful religion. Yet both types lack clarity, being visually identical when *all* Muslims are indiscriminately assigned the negative and stereotypical attributes of the terrorist. Combining the hyperbolic threat that so-called 'anti-Western' Muslims pose in the climate of fear initiated by 9/11, all

Muslims without distinction are widely seen as the enemy within (others, 'sleepers', fifth columnists) as well as without ('axis of evil', 'green menace').

Indeed, following the naturalisation of Islamophobia first reported by the Runnymede Trust (1997), since 9/11 much greater acceptance of this widely held public hostility has been apparent. Consequently, there was minimal mainstream public response to a post-9/11 Islamophobia report by the European Monitoring Centre on Racism and Xenophobia (EUMC) when it noted that 'across the entire spectrum of the EU member states incidents were identified where a negative or discriminatory act was perpetrated against Muslims or an entity that was associated with Islam'. Even though the report concluded that such hostility 'may well continue to become more tolerated', no proactive responses were forthcoming (*ibid.*: 33–43). Consequently, the forms of 'new racism' (Ansell 1997; Barker 1981; Mac an Ghaill 1999) that emerged following the legislative protection rightly afforded to minority communities and groups in the early 1980s would appear to have taken on an overtly 'Muslim' face since 9/11, stratifying into negative actions and reactions. As racist groups sought to continue to propagate their views in a new legislatory environment in the late 1970s and early 1980s, so they were forced to shift the foci of their hatred. As a result, racist ideology began to focus upon issues of difference – more specifically, cultural and religious difference – in order to make hostile assertions about the same groups and communities as before but now in ways where their difference was presented as either unacceptable or incompatible with the norms of society. Contemporary Islamophobia clearly has similarities with this new racism, and as the new racist ideologies target the same communities that were targeted in the pre-legislative period, so those same South Asian communities in Britain, now because of their Muslim identity, remain in focus.

As Britain is an integral part of the EU spectrum, the EUMC report noted a number of incidents that were recorded in Britain. Because they are the largest and most visually prominent of all religious communities in Britain – where the Muslim population currently numbers approximately 1.6 million, more than half of whom are ethnically South Asian (ONS 2004) – it is unsurprising that South Asian Muslims became the primary recipients of Britain's backlash. Yet whilst other, non-South Asian Muslims were also targets of Islamophobia, unlike their South Asian counterparts the majority had not previously figured as racialised victims of racism, since markers of 'Asian-ness' were then in the ascendancy. South Asian Muslims found themselves not only being identified on the basis of religion rather than race, but also being identified as the prime representatives of what had come to be seen as Muslim. To their communities were attributed the markers of cultural and religious difference that the shifting focus of new racism had identified. Consequently, they also came to be seen as communities that were presenting – in new racist terms at least – the biggest threat to 'our way of life' (Barker 1981): a threat that found even greater credence in the light of 9/11.

The roots of this transformation can be traced back through the recent history of the media. From the work of critics and scholars in the 1970s through to Barker, from writing about the *Satanic Verses* affair to the Islamophobia report of the Runnymede Trust, the media are highlighted as the major disseminators of images and messages that have both established and codified the markers of difference that are now so accepted. One of the most unlikely references in this process can be located in the mid-1970s situation comedy, *Mind Your Language*. Set in an English language class for non-English pupils, the show grossly exaggerated xenophobic stereotypes of different nationalities, including German, French, Chinese, Greek and Turkish, to what purported to be 'comedy' effect; three other pupils were South Asian. Whilst society might have lumped these last pupils together as Pakistani, the exploitation of the subtleties of difference that render the homogeneous 'Asian' useless were covertly yet stereotypically exploited to pit a Sikh against a Muslim, alongside a passive and counterbalancing Hindu. Even if much of this was lost on its audience, it does offer a focal point for identifying the beginnings of a potential cultural shift to a greater awareness of difference based upon religious identities. At the time, however, the interplay and differentiation were largely overlooked, itself a possible precursor of what was to ensue. Indeed, so sluggish has societal recognition of difference been that 'Asian' remained the preferred descriptor for some time afterwards, even holding some of its ground in the race legislation that emerged at around this time.

Protecting race: unprotecting religion

Prior to the 1970s, only the Church of England, as a religious institution rather than a community, was offered any legislative protection (through the blasphemy laws). Then, through the Race Relations Act (1976), protection was provided against discrimination on the grounds of statutory definitions of a 'racial group', based primarily upon markers of race and common national or ethnic origin – making it illegal to discriminate against South Asians because of their colour or nationality, but offering them no such protection with regard to their religion or beliefs. The definition of 'racial group' was later extended in the 1980s to include mono-ethnic religious groups, like Sikhs and Jews, but still neither non-ethnic nor multi-ethnic religious communities like Muslims and Buddhists. Definitions of 'racial group', developed in civil anti-discrimination legislation, were also adopted wholesale in criminal law through the Public Order Act (1986), introducing the criminal offence of incitement to racial hatred. This definition was also adopted for aggravated offences of harassment, violence and criminal damage motivated by racial hatred, both through the Crime and Disorder Act (1998) and, later, the Race Relations (Amendment) Act (2000). Repeatedly, religious identity was sidelined.

So whilst racial groups were protected, including South Asians, an iniquitous anomaly in the law established a hierarchy of protected faith communities. Mono-ethnic faith communities benefited from protection against discrimination, aggravated offences of harassment, violence and criminal damage, and against incitement to hatred. They also benefited from the imposition of a positive duty on public authorities to promote equality. Multi-ethnic minority faith communities, like Muslims, benefited from neither protection nor the equality provision. Unless it could be shown that discrimination was racial (on grounds of colour, for example) or because they were 'Bangladeshi' rather than 'Muslim', some forms of racism began to seem legitimised if not entirely legal. Differentiating between 'South Asian' and 'Muslim' is ironically something that Islamophobia fails to do, within its inherently unidimensionalist outlook (Runnymede Trust 1997). Racists and detractors began to exploit this. Muslim-ness provided the focus and basis of difference that the new racists necessarily required.

More recently, two separate initiatives have sought to address this anomaly. In civil legislation, from December 2003 the EU Employment Directive has outlawed religious discrimination in the workplace, although it falls far short of the positive duty standard in the Race Relations (Amendment) Act. In criminal law, the Anti-Terrorism, Crime and Security Bill (2001), a direct response to the events of 9/11, sought to address the anomaly but was only successful in retaining provisions of protection against religiously motivated harassment, violence and criminal damage to property, failing to legislate against incitement. Incorporating 'Muslim' concerns into legislation that dealt with 'anti-terrorism, crime and security' was also indicative to some of the institutional view of Muslims in relation to 9/11. So whilst the anomalies have been narrowed, in neither civil nor criminal law have they been eliminated; the loophole that accentuates and differentiates Muslims from racialised markers remains obvious. Consequently, the exploitation of the offence of incitement to religious hatred has been critical in the recent shifting focus of bigotry, from race to religion. In this shifting, the target remains the same, though 'not because he is Pakistani but because he is Muslim' or 'not because she is Chinese but because she is Buddhist'.

For South Asian Muslims, the loophole makes a mockery of the offence of incitement to racial hatred. One motive for introducing race legislation was to afford protection to those suffering at the hands of the far right on the basis of their race affiliations. Initially, legislation somewhat marginalised racist behaviour and attitudes, and with the policy changes made in the wake of the riots in the early 1980s a situation emerged that offered racial groups much more protection within society. However, the impact of the *Satanic Verses* affair in 1989 and the emergence of a specifically Muslim identity (Ahsan and Kidwai 1991; Kepel 2000; Ruthven 2000) highlighted a new opportunity for racism to realign itself. In building upon the already existent historical context of the archetypal Muslim and Islam's inherent otherness, those same far-right groups that had been somewhat restricted by legislative protection, located a window of opportunity with a clear and definable yet unprotected marker: Muslim identity.

International events and developments that followed, including the Gulf War, various terrorist incidents and the publication of Samuel Huntington's 'clash of civilisations' thesis (Huntington 1997), amongst others, saw anti-Muslim expression find a greater resonance and gave encouragement to previously isolated Islamophobic voices. Within Britain, intensifying anti-Muslimism led to the Runnymede Trust report and its recognition that the far right was beginning to focus on religion rather than race. Marked by both race and religion, South Asian Muslims, once the minority communities most heavily targeted by racists, were again under siege by their old foes, who were now even able to claim some legitimacy. The failure of the authorities to recognise the new situation left communities feeling isolated and increasingly agitated, a mood that was to culminate in the 2001 summer disturbances in the north of England (Allen 2003). South Asian Muslims were under fire not only on the ground but also through the ballot box at local elections, where the more organised far-right elements were capitalising upon an unprecedented resonance within the wider public when it came to anti-Muslimism.

Following 9/11, the far right's Islamophobic rhetoric turned up the volume right across Europe at both the mainstream and grass-roots political levels. As the EUMC confirmed, there was substantial evidence to suggest that the gap between mainstream acceptability and the previously outlawed views of the far right was closing fast. Because of the increasingly consensual ear that these messages – primarily, and at times solely, about Muslims – were locating in the mainstream of European societies, the EUMC concluded that this was a very serious cause for concern and a very worrying development (Allen and Nielsen 2002). Exploiting this acceptability, the ever-increasing newsworthiness of Muslims, and, especially in the British context, the latitude afforded by the smug 'it couldn't happen here' mentality, Muslims became ever more demonised, and fear and mistrust grew rapidly within the general public. Whilst the shift from race to religion clearly has its roots prior to 9/11, it was Ground Zero that provided the catalytic impetus to its quasi-justification.

'Islam out of Britain': ballot box rhetoric and success

In line with this closing distance between acceptable and unaccep-table, the British National Party (BNP) sought justification of its views and societal legitimacy by producing a wide body of materials and resources that exploited the specifically post-9/11 fears and threats, however real or absurd. Much of this was highly inflamma-tory: it encouraged insult, provocation and abuse, and employed language and images calculated to initiate or encourage hatred. At the same time, the BNP stressed the legality of its actions. Through a 'ghost' web project, *Oldham Harmony,* the message became clear: *the problem is Muslim.* In a BNP publication circulated in Oldham, the party called for whites to boycott local businesses, but not those 'owned by Chinese or Hindus ... only Muslims as it's their community we need to pressure'. Muslims were clearly being singled out within the all encompassing 'Asian'. Since 94 per cent of the Muslim community in Oldham are ethnically South Asian (ONS 2004), the legislation in place to protect such communities was rendered useless through the shift of markers towards Islam and Muslimness, leaving a large and distinct 'racial group' vulnerable.

A BNP campaign leaflet entitled *Islam out of Britain* unapologetically sought to explain 'the threat Islam and Muslims pose to Britain and British society'. However, the explicit South Asian-ness of the BNP's vitriol became apparent in its leaflet entitled *The Truth about I.S.L.A.M.* This employed 'I.S.L.A.M.' as an acronym for 'Intolerance, Slaughter, Looting, Arson and Molestation of women'. Widely distributed, it used highly inflammatory reasons to justify hatred of Muslims, suggesting that 'to find out what Islam really stands for, all you have to do is look at a copy of the Koran, and see for yourself ... Islam really does stand for Intolerance, Slaughter, Looting, Arson and Molestation of women'. Selectively quoting the Qur'an, it painted the most despicable picture of South Asian Muslims in particular, claiming that 'no-one dares to tell the truth about Islam and the way that it threatens our democracy, traditional freedoms and identity'. The venom of the diatribe reaches full strength when it suggests that understanding the Qur'an provides a context for the 2001 Bradford disturbances and 9/11. Drawing a timeline of anti-Muslim sentiment, juxtaposed alongside a knight from the Crusades, the leaflet states:

> the *Koran* is packed with sadistic descriptions of how Unbelievers will burn forever in the fires of Hell ... fire has been used against non-Muslims and their property from the earliest times. When the conquering Muslim army arrived in Egypt, the general in charge did not know what to do with the huge library at Alexandria, the greatest in the ancient world. He sent a message to Caliph Umar, Muhammad's successor, who replied: 'If these writings of the Greeks agree with the book of Allah, they are useless and do not need to be preserved. If they disagree, they are pernicious and ought to be destroyed.' The great library was therefore burnt to the ground, settling for all time the way Muslims deal with centres of infidel learning and religion. During communal riots in India (in which around three million Hindus have been murdered by their 'peace-loving' Muslim neighbours since 1947) it is common practice for Muslim mobs to trap their victims inside buildings and then set them alight, hoping to burn them alive. The same was done during the Islamic revolution in Iran, where Muslim

mobs chanted 'purification by fire' as they burnt down cinemas and brothels. The 'justification' for trapping people in burning buildings is found in S.22.22: *'And every time they want to get out of it (the fire) they are brought back into it. And it is said to them: "Taste the agony of burning".'* Here we see the source of the vicious mentality which, during this summer's anti-*kafir* violence in Bradford, led rioting Muslims to block the fire doors of a local Labour Club with burning cars.

Offering a very particular and quite inaccurate interpretation of events, the leaflet fails to mention, for example, that it was Arab Muslim scholars who found numerous, previously lost Greek texts and translated them, thus introducing Europe to the works of Aristotle and others. Nor does it recognise that the Qur'an is written in a largely poetic style that is in complete opposition to the narrative style of other religious scriptures, including the more commonly known Christian Gospels. So when the leaflet mentions Qur'anic references to 'fire', it is engaging in textual and literalist misrepresentation: in the Qur'an such references are much more metaphorical and represent a number of other ideas and themes. As a result, the style of the Qur'an is much more difficult to understand than other commonly known scriptural sources in Europe and therefore can be easily misrepresented. What is worrying about this lack of understanding is that it has become the widespread and accepted norm: inaccurately quoted Qur'anic sources are neither questioned nor queried. Consequently, misrepresentations and inaccuracies continue to find acceptance and resonance.

It is therefore unsurprising that similar quasi-theological inter-pretations were offered in relation to the role of fire in 9/11, by the BNP in other campaign material, by other far-right groups and more widely in the media. By compressing the past and the present, these materials created unidimensional and non-differentiated 'Muslims', a monolithicism also to be found in the Runnymede Trust report (1997), and located relevance and justification in both historical and contemporary frameworks. This stereotyping also reinforced the ideological separation and segregation of 'whites' and 'non-whites' that continued so clearly to underpin the new racism of the BNP and others: the functional capability of new forms to cover and smoke-screen the hostilities and hatreds of old, reinventing 'Asians' as 'Muslims' of South Asian descent.

The BNP explored these issues further through its two regular publications: *Identity* and *Freedom*. In both, the incitement to hatred of Muslims was a recurrent feature, yet it clearly remained within what was (and subsequently is not) legal. Three months after 9/11, the December 2001 edition of *Identity* complained that a campaign poster used in densely populated Muslim locales, emblazoned 'Islam out of Britain', would be outlawed under new anti-terrorism legislation. At the same time, the magazine employed explicit language to repeatedly derogate Muslims, in particular South Asians, as 'fundamentalists', 'hotheads' and 'terrorists', exaggerating the danger of a further 9/11 in Britain. This example illustrates two points: first, that the BNP acted with sophistication and clarity of knowledge of the current legislative framework, and, second, that it accurately gauged the post-9/11 climate, the heightened fears and potential threats, and the shifting attitudes against Muslims across society. Later, in the April 2002 edition of *Identity*, a new 'Islam out of Britain' leaflet was showpieced that remained within the new legal boundaries while also exploiting the post-9/11 climate. Even more cynical was the gloating in *Freedom* (December 2001) over the legislative loophole that allowed them to continue to target Muslims. Headed 'Police Drop a Clanger', their story told of a supporter who repeatedly displayed an 'Islam out of Britain' poster in his window,

> was then arrested and questioned, and then charged with 'incitement to racial hatred'.... The snag for the police, however, is that Islam is not covered by the anti-free speech Race Law ... it's legal to say anything you want about Islam, even far more extreme things.

Freedom, however, was generally more direct. In November 2001, it deliberately sought to inflame post-disturbance tensions between 'whites' and South Asian Muslims in Bradford within a post-9/11 context. One headline, 'Police seize Bradford mosque guns', was situated adjacent to another that read 'Osama Bin Laden Thugs in Britain'. Not only were the BNP seeking to create further mischief in these already tense areas, but they were also indiscriminately projecting the attributes, perceived or otherwise, of the perpetrators of 9/11 onto ordinary Bradford Muslims, 92 per cent of whom are of South Asian descent (ONS 2004). In drawing further links between Muslim communities in the UK and South Asia, another article, 'Bangladesh: Election Bloodbath', repeatedly described Muslims as 'zealots' and 'fanatics' before a concluding diatribe against 'the anti-democratic doctrines of Islam'. On the same page, the BNP linked these reports to the 'injustices' that they felt underpinned the 2001 disturbances in Bradford, Burnley and Oldham:

of £50 million allocated for improvements over ten years, 25 per cent of the money went to the Pakistanis and Bangladeshis.... According to Oldham council's Housing Department, the average *white* family getting a Home Improvement Grant got £3,059, the average *Pakistani* family got £11,336 and the average *Bangladeshi* family got £14,863 – that's nearly *five times as much* as white people living in the same town [original emphases].

Whilst the BNP's campaign non-differentially referred to 'Islam' and 'Muslims', it is not difficult to identify the surviving strain of 'racially motivated' racism that had imbued the campaigns of similar far-right groups when they targeted South Asians some thirty years before.

As a direct consequence of the inroads made by the far right and the deepening receptivity of society, South Asian Muslims also found themselves targeted by other minority communities with whom previously they had been lumped together as 'Asian'. Following anecdotal evidence that Indians in Manchester were adopting an overtly Hindu identity in order to deflect any potential Islamophobic backlash, and the incidental targeting of Sikhs because of their visual similarity to media images of bin Laden and the Taliban, the BNP exploited intra-Asian tensions by issuing an audio resource piously entitled *Islam: a Threat to Us All*. The venture, undertaken in conjunction with fringe Sikh and Hindu organisations, was set up to provide 'insider' (that is, Asian) justification of both its own skewed view of Islam and the need to rid Britain of Muslims. The press release claimed to

give the lie to those who falsely claim that we are 'racists' or 'haters'. We sympathise and identify with every people in the world who want to secure or preserve a homeland for themselves, their traditions and their posterity. And we demand and strive for that same basic human right for the native English, Scots, Welsh, Irish and Ulster folk who together make up the British.

Strangely, whilst focusing on the 'green menace' – which the Sikh and Hindu fringe groups agreed was a significant threat – the BNP overlooked identifying their newfound partners as 'British'.

Islamophobia, with strong South Asian flavours, has fuelled the BNP's recent growth. Entirely as a result of the successes gained through openly anti-Muslim campaigns in northern towns heavily populated by South Asian Muslims – Bradford, Oldham, Burnley and so on – the BNP has found a quasi-legitimacy that since 9/11 has made it a party that now senses a real opportunity in local council elections across the country. Targeting its seats directly and specifically, the BNP now has a previously unprecedented total of 18 elected councillors across the country, from Grays in Essex in the South, through Sandwell and Dudley in the West Midlands, to its stronghold in Burnley in the north, where it holds eight seats on the local council. And on the back of these successes, other far-right groups that for some time have been largely ineffectual have been reinvigorated, adopting an anti-Muslim stance with the same especially South Asian Muslim flavour. Groups such as the National Front, Combat 18, the White Wolves and the White Nationalist Party, amongst others, are now all campaigning and developing on this basis: among the most prominent campaigns are those of the National Front against the building of new mosques in places such as Feltham and Morden.

'I am an Islamophobe and proud': the role of the media

It is no surprise that this reinvigoration, growth and subsequent success of the far right should have occurred in a post-9/11 climate. Language, terminology and ideas widely circulated in the public domain encouraged Islamophobia and acceptance of anti-Muslim negativity. Explicitly commonplace in the BNP's and similar literature, ideas and expressions of anti-Muslim racism have floated to the surface in other, less murky sections of society. And if naturalisation – or taken-for-granted acceptance – of Islamophobia and anti-Muslim ideas, sentiments and attitudes was suggested in the Runnymede Trust report (1997), then the EUMC report's acknowledgement of a greater receptivity to similar expressions may be the latest evolution of this syndrome.

In the aftermath of 9/11, therefore, whilst it has been much easier both to express and to identify anti-Muslimism, particularly towards South Asians, it has also been easier to understand how such expressions have shifted, what their causes have been, how they have located themselves into existing frameworks, and how they have sought the necessary, albeit questionable precepts and justifications: *questionable* because should similar formulations have been made using markers of race or ethnicity, then these same precepts and justifications would have met with societal derision and dismissal.

Immediately following the events of 9/11, anti-Muslim views appeared in a number of publications. Baroness Thatcher's blanket condemnation of Muslim leaders in the *Times*, insisting that all Muslims – as a homogeneous group – should share responsibility for the attacks (4 October 2001), was followed a few days later by an article in the *Telegraph* entitled 'This War Is not about Terror, It's about Islam' (7 October 2001). The article sought not only to praise Baroness Thatcher's stance, but also to confirm that 'Western' fears about Islam were justified because 'some three-quarters of the world's migrants in the last decade are said to have been Muslims ... [these] escapees, victims, scapegoats, malefactors and "sleepers" are awaiting their moment'.

By extension, all Muslims in the West were thus being marked as potential, if not actual, terrorists – both of which are grossly disturbing and Islamophobic claims. The next day the *Telegraph* set out to read the homogeneous 'Islamic mind' ('In This War of Civilisations, the West Will Prevail', 8 October 2001), explaining that while Westerners are honourable, 'Islamic' fighters are not, combining 'crude weapons' with 'appalling violence', preferring 'ambush, surprise, treachery and deceit'. Rooted in Huntington, employing the term 'crusade' and much Orientalist terminology (Said 1979), it described the perpetrators of 9/11 as 'appearing suddenly out of empty space like their desert raider ancestors', the descendants of 'the horse-riding raiders before Mohammed'. Drawing upon the unidimensionality of the Runnymede Trust report, the article depicted Muslims as the backward, barbaric, enemy other of old.

All sections of the media approached the ground taken by the *Times* and the *Telegraph* at times, and while some attempted balance and fairness, much coverage did not. Even in the more liberal newspapers, similar standpoints could be detected. In the *Guardian*, Polly Toynbee reiterated her distaste for Islam and Muslims in 'Last Chance to Speak out' (5 October 2001). Having previously aired her views in the *Independent* in 1997, declaring 'I am an Islamophobe and proud', Toynbee (like the BNP) drew highly selectively on the Qur'an to reinforce her arguments. Having noted the 'bloodcurdling words of the Prophet ..."slay or crucify or cut the hands and feet of the unbeliever" (5: 34)', Toynbee asked how such words could ever be reinterpreted in peaceful or harmonious contexts – making much the same point as, at the opposite end of the political spectrum, the BNP had done. Concluding somewhat unconvincingly that they cannot be so interpreted, Toynbee dismissed talk of Islamophobia as a mere smokescreen to deflect valid and necessary criticism. The *Telegraph* approached dismissing Islamophobia from an alternative perspective: despite overwhelming evidence to the contrary, it offered (reiterating the exact phraseology of the BNP's *Islam: a Threat to Us All*) 'the lie to this imaginary Islamophobia' (12 October 2001), extolling the virtues of the British in actually creating a wave of 'Islamophilia' instead.

With Islamophobia in denial, the centrality of South Asians became ever more relevant and pronounced. Nine months after 9/11, the former Chancellor of the Exchequer, Norman Lamont, wrote in the *Telegraph* of the ills of multiculturalism highlighted by recent events. In his article, 'Down with Multiculturalism, Book-burning and *Fatwas*' (8 May 2002), the immediate association to be gleaned from 'book-burning and *fatwas*' was a direct link to South Asian Muslims. In addition, the article suggested that British youths fighting for the Taliban, together with 'forced marriages, polygamy, burning books, [and] supporting *fatwas*' were the primary factors restricting the success of multiculturalism and 'Britishness'. Whilst these are commonly, if somewhat inaccurately seen as South Asian and Muslim issues, the fact that Lamont went on to congratulate 'West Indians, Africans and Indians' for their sense of being British, further demarcates Bangladeshi and Pakistani (or South Asian) Muslim communities as remaining external to this happy band. By what was not being said, rather than by what he did say, Lamont was able to lay the blame for the failures of multiculturalism firmly at the door of South Asian Muslims.

With similar sentiments, the Home Secretary David Blunkett voiced his concerns at about the same time by verbally attacking South Asian Muslims in Bradford peacefully campaigning against the harsh sentencing of those convicted of involvement in the 2001 disturbances, calling them 'whining maniacs' (Allen 2003). Numerous other public positions taken at this time and reports in circulation highlighted the reflexivity connecting Muslims, South Asian Muslims and 9/11, even if the links were often less than explicitly made. One might include within these Mr Blunkett's widely reported endorse-ment of the more 'rational' standpoint attributed to the assassinated Pim Fortuyn – though this was almost solely anti-Muslim and strongly against any further Muslim immigration to the Netherlands – that Muslims should accept 'our culture' and its ways. This followed on the heels of his equally contentious statement that asylum seekers – a group that had become largely interchangeable and indistinguishable from Muslims in the post-9/11 period (Allen and Nielsen 2002) – were 'swamping' schools, particularly in the north of England. This was a distinct echo of similar suggestions made by the then Prime Minister, Margaret Thatcher, some twenty years before – and Thatcher's comments then were deemed to be a formative moment in the development and transition of 'new racist' ideologies by Barker (1981).

Finally, there was the statement made by Peter Hain MP suggesting that it was South Asian Muslim communities' own isolationist behaviour and customs that were creating the climate in which the far right was able to expand and grow. Perhaps the most amazing aspect of Hain's statement was that he chose to describe Muslims as 'immigrants' – although South Asian and other Muslim groups have been settled in Britain for at least the past three or four decades. If Hain's remarks are taken with the 'swamping' comments of Blunkett, a worrying overlap between such government-led ideas and assertions in the public domain must at least initially, if only implicitly, be identified.

South Asian, Muslim or both? Demystifying the 9/11 fog

While the main aim of this piece has been to consider Islamophobia in the context of the shifting focus of racism – from markers of race to religious equivalents – alongside the increased receptivity of society to this shift and the opportunity for exploiting this seized on by a resurgent far right, there are also clear signals to suggest that the issues since 9/11 should have commanded greater questioning and concern at the heart of the society and in its governing circles. Across Europe, the manifestations of Islamophobia that followed 9/11 mirrored the national, ethnic and cultural characteristic of its various Muslim communities. In Germany, Turkish communities were identified as targets for the backlash. In France, Algerian communities fulfilled this role. It is therefore no surprise that in Britain the backlash was distinctly felt by South Asians. Yet, in Britain, these same communities should have been protected under existing race legislation that makes prejudice, discrimination and racial incitement against Bangladeshis, Pakistanis and Indians unjust and illegal. However, the shifting of prejudice, discrimination and incitement towards religion and religious adherence exposed the loophole in race relations legislation that many had previously identified and campaigned against, recognising its potential for disaster. Such is the contemporary climate, and the evidence offered by repeated rejections of various attempts to close this loophole, that the 'legal' victimisation and vilification of Muslims and South Asians, occurring now, will also continue for the foreseeable future.

The situation since 9/11, therefore, is complex. A dangerous cocktail has been mixed on the basis of a pre-existing phenomenon now shaken with the hyperbolic exaggerations emerging from the fog of 9/11. Other ingredients are the anomalous legislation that was meant to afford adequate protection and the predominance of South Asians within Britain's Muslim communities. The 9/11 attacks themselves were terrible and devastating – there is no disagreement there – but the aftermath and the ensuing processes may well be equally catastrophic, albeit in ways less explicitly horrifying. So far, neither within the wider society nor at the institutional level has the shift from 'race' to religion and the impact of 9/11 on Muslims been accorded any real significance: some awareness, yes; commitment to change, no. Conversely, the impetus and success gained by those exploiting this same transition – the far right, for example – is significant. For Muslims, therefore, and particularly for South Asian Muslims who typically comprise the explicit projection of both 'race' and religious markers, the specifically post-9/11 transition to religion as a marker for hatred and hostility is one that surely will have deep consequences and ramifications for years to come.

In the process of understanding and contextualising the magnitude and ongoing significance of this period of change and aftermath, it is essential that not only the loudest voices get heard: we must learn to listen to the silent, and to make the hidden visible. Islamophobia, already growing before 9/11 and possibly even naturalising, must now be checked so as not to allow any further normalisation. South Asian Muslims, irrespective of applicable markers, must not remain victims of racism and hatred. The legislation that was initially conceived to protect them and others should not be evaded by shifting the markers of difference towards culture or religion. Nor, indeed, should other Muslims now be marked and targeted in similar ways. Despite the repeated failings of this and previous governments to address this situation in a comprehensive way, those Muslim and other groups who continue to lobby for and support the wider calls for change should not be dismissed because of the quickened step of global history and the hyperbolic overstatement that has since been associated with the events of 9/11. Islamophobia is both *not* a post-9/11 phenomenon and also a *distinctly* post-9/11 phenomenon. It emerges from the overlap, blurring, exaggeration and confusion of the bizarre triangle that is held together by the nodes of 9/11, Muslims and South Asian Muslims. Whilst Islamophobia's roots are firmly planted in a pre-9/11 context, a post-9/11 impetus has been the dangerous catalyst driving its evolution, diversification and acceptance – including those manifestations of the phobia that have sought to identify and target South Asian communities in the name of new forms of cultural and religious difference.

Chapter 5
Negotiating British Citizenship and Muslim Identity

RON GEAVES

Introduction

Any analysis of the relationship between Muslim identity and British citizenship amongst communities of South Asian origin first needs to be aware of the pitfalls, in that all three categories lend themselves to being essentialised by the partial and simplistic gaze of the other. Recognising the diverse, tenuous, multifarious and situational nature of diaspora identities, both South Asian and Muslim, it is also necessary to acknowledge that citizenship is also not straightforward. To many white British subjects, participation in citizenship is a non-problematic given, a set of clothing that fits like a glove, put on at birth, taken off at death, viewed uncritically and unchallenged.

However, it is far more likely that both first-generation and British-born South Asian Muslims have been far more conscious of citizenship and identity issues, and, certainly in the case of the first-generation male elders, more involved in the processes of micro-politics than an equivalent proportion of white citizens. British Muslims have had to address citizenship, not only within the frame-work of the legal and political structures of their new home with its emphasis on democracy, secularism, individual rights and pluralism, but also in negotiating and harmonising that framework in terms of *shari'a* and Islamic state discourse. They have had to discover how to be Muslim in a secular society and to develop the appropriate strategies for living as a minority in a non-Muslim society. It has been essential to reconcile faith-based identity and citizenship, individual rights and community rights in an environment where the concept of others has dominated, without retreating into isolationism. Perhaps above all, they have needed to discover how to participate in a society which has no need for Islam in its public life.

In addition, as former citizens of the subcontinent, British South Asian Muslims have inherited the colonial history of their past relations with Britain. When combined with racism, endemic in the new home, this creates an environment of suspicion in which British Muslims may place non-Muslim citizens outside their own communities under the scrutiny of a gaze that oversimplifies and essentialises, reinforcing perspectives of the other. The same gaze, returned, often demands assimilation under impossible conditions. In this essay, I will argue that, since the tragic and traumatic events of 9/11, both exponents of the gaze have had to develop a more penetrating view of each other's presence.

If before 9/11 and its aftermath, the British involvement in the wars in Afghanistan and Iraq, the choices were relatively simple between isolation, rejection and participation, they are now far more complex. New leaderships have emerged, with much greater representation of the British-born generations. They function away from the mosque, which remains the domain of first-generation elder males, engage with the British state and participate in society. New organisations such as the Muslim Society of Britain (MSB) and the Muslim Association of Britain (MAB) have joined in alliances with the Islamic Society of Britain (ISB) and Young Muslims UK, and actively involved their members in issues of living in a plural society; they have opened up new discourses on citizenship that include common values shared by Britain and Muslims.

Although there may still be traditional South Asian religious movements present in Britain that historically have developed strategies of isolation as a defence mechanism in response to Muslim loss of power in India and to protect a vision of 'pure' Islam' when surrounded by non-Muslim populations, isolationism increasingly becomes impossible in a world where the global and the local become inextricably linked. Although isolationism may still be found amongst the traditionalists of Tabligh-i Jamaat or Deoband, others, especially amongst the young, have chosen an oppositional path to British society, rejecting its values and promoting the cause of an Islamic nation or *khalifat*. The minority who have embraced Hizb al-Tahrir or al-Muhajiroun have been influenced by the global rhetoric originating in the camps of Afghanistan and use 'democracy' as a weapon to criticise Muslims who have embraced it as 'running dogs of the West'. On the other hand, since 9/11 those who buy into the rhetoric of the clash of civilisations increasingly use 'democracy' discourse to browbeat Muslim states into a sense of inferiority and a recognition that they need to join the new world order. Whilst this has been taking place, other British Muslims have aligned themselves with democratic values, engaged in inter-faith activities with the Church of England, been invited to participate in government-sponsored conferences and consciously distanced themselves from both isolationist and rejectionist positions. Pnina Werbner (2002: 177) asserts that,

> Some British Muslims may see their redemption as choosing to struggle for individual and communal commitment to the creation of a new unified Islamic empire powerful enough to withstand western domination; however most will be concerned with economic progress, equality and the rights of citizenship over and above the dream of creating a true Muslim state.

I intend to argue that one very significant factor in transforming ideas of citizenship has been the collaboration of the Muslim Association of Britain in the Stop the War Coalition and the participation of thousands of Muslims in a very traditional form of British pluralist dissent – the peaceful demonstration against a single issue that brings together disparate groups and forms temporary alliances based on mutual interest. Such participation marks a sea-change in Muslim participation in citizenship and can be viewed as a form of 'coming out'. In addition, I will draw upon Bakirathi Mani's article 'Undressing the Diaspora' to provide a 'dressing' analogy that helps develop the 'discursive possibility of "coming out" as South Asian' (Mani 2002: 119).

The development of citizenship amongst South Asian Muslims can be seen to have passed through a number of transformations that began with non-conformity and isolation, at which stage citizenship issues were addressed within the context of outsider/other relations. Since 9/11, participation in shared antipathy to the Second Gulf War has given rise to the possibility of a new model for citizenship as shared resistance and indignation. Even the early pioneers, the single men arriving in the 1960s and 1970s as economic migrants with a 'myth of return', transcended passive citizenship by taking on civic responsibility as they negotiated unfamiliar spaces and carved out new territories in which their families could flourish materially whilst maintaining a hold on culture and religion. Werbner (2002: 49) describes this process accurately:

> In Britain these men who arrived penniless and single in the 1960s have become active citizens within the diasporic public sphere and community spokesmen who routinely deal with ministers, MPs, civic leaders, police inspectors, and join forces with or against these state representatives in emancipatory struggles for multicultural or anti-racist citizenship in Britain.

Theirs was a localised politics concerned with the development of anti-racist legislation, the provision of community centres and places of worship, and establishing status within the newly formed communities. This first leadership, localised and dominated by male elders, was primarily concerned to defend ethnic interests and community borders, but developed very little in the way of a discourse of shared citizenship and common values. Local rivalries also made it difficult to create any kind of national leadership in spite of several efforts to create umbrella organisations.

The *Satanic Verses* protests

The turning point and watershed in national Muslim participation has to be the protests, both expressing indignation and as a strategy of resistance against the publication of Salman Rushdie's *Satanic Verses*. The existing leadership, skilled in local ethnic micro-politics, was not able to express the feelings of the Muslim community to the wider British society. Unfamiliar with the symbolic significance of book-burning in a society which still retains strong collective narratives based on resistance to fascism, the Bradford Council of Mosques achieved widespread animosity by their protest. However, the publication of the book, so offensive to a wide spectrum of Muslims, did achieve political mobilisation and the provision of a national voice of protest with remarkable speed. It also provided a platform for various organisations and traditional enemies in the subcontinent's religio-political life to cooperate with each other.

The difficulties generated by the Salman Rushdie affair, the polarised views of a secular liberal society defending the freedom of the individual and the Muslim voice demanding redress for a perceived blasphemous insult to their religion, inclined Muslims towards believing that there were very real limitations on their position as British subjects. At worst presented as a fifth column, undermining British democratic institutions; at best presented as uneducated and misunderstood victims of racism, British Muslims experienced the frustrations of their own limitations in bending British political institutions or public opinion to their point of view.

The discovery of the British blasphemy laws allowed British Muslims a way out of the impasse of a clash of civilisations, providing instead a campaign for social justice and equality before the law. Fighting for a change in the blasphemy laws to include other faiths and an extension of the race discrimination laws to include religion as a category of discrimination allowed Muslims to struggle for the rights of minority citizenship. New political campaigns could be organised both locally and nationally around practical agendas such as the recognition of Muslim schools or a reform of the Race Relations Act to protect religious minorities.

However, one important aspect of the Salman Rushdie affair was to transform the politics of identity from a rallying around South Asian ethnic issues to an overt Muslim religious identity that allowed a bridge between local micro-politics and global Islamicisation. Werbner makes the point that before the publication of *The Satanic Verses*, Pakistanis were virtually absent or invisible as national political players, 'submerged into hidden networks of kin, friends and work or business partners. These networks were sustained by an elaborate ceremonial gift economy controlled by women, and by agonistic rivalries for status and power by men' (Werbner 2002: 62). This has not changed but after the protests South Asian settlers would become more aware of their rights as citizens and no longer satisfied to be a silent and passive presence hidden within their own communities. The Salman Rushdie affair opened up the possibility of active participation in British society in an anti-racist, equal rights discourse that defended the religion of Islam within its new location. As stated by Werbner, 'it liberated Pakistani settler-citizens from the self-imposed burden of being a silent, well-behaved minority, whatever the provocation, and opened up the realm of activist, anti-racist and emancipatory citizenship politics' (Werbner 2002: 258).

If anything, the protests were to demonstrate the need for a new leadership independent of the mosques and the original settlers, and able to engage with British civic society beyond defending localised ethnic interests. This was further demonstrated by international political events after Salman Rushdie. If Rushdie, racism and the politics of equality provided British Muslims with a number of social justice issues, these could be articulated more effectively against the global background of perceived injustices to the international Muslim community. The Qur'an's emphasis on Allah's quality of justice and its framing of human history within a titanic cosmic struggle of good and evil provided Muslims everywhere with a discourse of resistance to express discontent with the international situation. Millennial expectations, combined with conspiracy theories and very real intractable regional crises in Palestine and Kashmir, created an environment in which local injustices and global Islamicisation could be perceived as part of a single struggle in which the discourse of religion was deemed more effective than that of ethnic politics.

Post-Rushdie – the worsening international situation

This sense of Muslim beleaguerment was to become much worse after the collapse of the Soviet Union and the resulting increase in US hegemony. Palestine remained unsolvable and degenerated into a vicious condition of strike and counter-strike against civilians on both sides; the USA, Britain and their allies invaded Iraq and Afghanistan; Kashmir remained a sore point for British Pakistanis in particular. The collapse of the Soviet Union and world communism created armed struggles in Chechnya and Bosnian Muslims found themselves targeted by the horrific ethnic cleansing strategies of primitive Serbian nationalism.

Into this already difficult international scenario, 9/11 came as a catalyst, achieving an iconic status even greater than the cataclysm itself. The worsening international situation, convincing millions of Muslims that they were the new enemy of the USA after the end of the Cold War, was echoed locally by the street riots in several northern cities with large Muslim populations of South Asian origin. Although not connected in any way, both were to act together as catalysts for the British nation-state to close its borders and defend its civic culture. Whilst support for multiculturalism continued, a new language of integration and cohesion was voiced by national politicians demanding controls on imported imams, intercontinental marriages and far more rigid controls on political and economic migrants. While their elders continued with the management of the mosques and the maintenance of traditional cultural and religious domains, young British Muslims were once again being confronted with the question of what it means to be Muslim and British.

New organisations, such as MAB and MSB mentioned above, provided a means for British-born Muslims to create dialogue with local and national government on specific and achievable agendas, while demonstrating that the majority of Muslims in Britain were moderate and peace-loving, duty-bound to respect the law of the land, and able to find creative solutions to the harmonisation of Islamic notions of citizenship based primarily on interpretations of revelation and British democratic institutions based on human rights. These organisations forged new alliances with the New Labour government, realising that, for Muslims living outside *dar al-Islam* – if such an entity was even viable as a concept in the twenty-first century's new world order – none of the traditional interpretations of *fiqh* concerning minority living were workable. Such views were articulately expressed by Tariq Ramadan (2004).

In addition, the new organisations provided British-born generations with their own political space, to include not only the young but women – both traditionally denied access to the leadership of the mosque. As Werbner (2002: 199) puts it:

> Young men [and women] too must fight to create their own spaces, because male elders, who currently control the symbolically prestigious public space of community activities, are unlikely, it seems, to relinquish their hold over this domain without a struggle.

Werbner goes on to argue that if there is a counter-movement against the traditional leadership of male elders centred around the mosque and local ethnic politics, it is in the involvement of youth and women in 'British national and local government electoral politics and the emergence ... of popular forms of public protest and syncretic popular cultural celebration' (Werbner 2002: 249).

If the First Gulf War landed British Muslims in the paradoxical situation of defending Saddam Hussein whilst proclaiming allegiance to Britain, and 9/11 produced a traumatic denial of Muslim involvement and a host of conspiracy theories, the Second Gulf War was to provide them with a firmer platform for expressing their sense of injustice without jeopardising either their sense of Britishness or the recognition of their loyalty by the wider community and the media. The alliance of MAB with the Stop the War campaign was to have profound significance and herald a new stage in Muslim participation in citizenship.

The Second Gulf War and the anti-war protests

The second Gulf War and the culminating invasion of Iraq by US and British forces without the consent of the UN, and the subsequent controversies over the accuracy of intelligence concerning weapons of mass destruction, have led to a widespread disaffection and distrust of government in Britain that goes well beyond the Muslim community. Many British citizens of all shades feel that the nation was pulled into a war by the US, whose own motivations for an invasion of Iraq were deeply suspect. The moral ambiguities of supporting Saddam Hussein in the First Gulf War, or divided loyalties in regard to Osama Bin Laden – whose image as a devout 'desert' Muslim sacrificing his millionaire Westernised lifestyle for the cause of Islam clashes with the traumatic awareness of 3,000 dead civilians of all faiths in New York – disappear in the case of opposing US and British foreign policy on Iraq.

My argument is that joining the Stop the War protests was qualitatively different from previous protests in that the Muslims who participated found themselves alongside a range of dissent from the wider non-Muslim population. Thus they were able to bond with 'communities of suffering' or elements of the population seeking social justice for those who had been violated. Habermas argues that such demonstrations mobilise broad alliances that defend the nation's civic culture (Habermas 1994). Although such alliances may be temporary, as in the case of the American Civil Rights movement and the anti-Vietnam war protests, they can create new moral communities that transcend ethnic or religious differences. As far back as 1958, Gluckman was arguing that violation of the human body, sacred symbols and property or an individual's civil rights can result in a collective solidarity around symbols and images. Such events can lead to emancipatory struggles that can transform society and lead to new freedoms.

Social justice discourse, so much a part of Islam's original message, not only links Muslims in a global resistance to perceived injustices, bringing together disparate alliances of moderates and radicals, but also creates bridges to non-Muslim organisations concerned with similar issues of inequality, neo-colonialism, ecological concerns or other imbalances between the world's powerful and less powerful nations. Addressing this point, Pnina Werbner (2002: 177) points out that

> As long as political confrontations in the Middle East, Kashmir or Bosnia continue, and as long as anti-Muslim or immigrant sentiments

and practices persist in Britain, the conjunction between Islam and social-liberal values is unlikely to be ideologically severed.

Werbner is probably referring more to multicultural rhetoric, or to equal opportunities and the experience of racism, than to participation in the Stop the War demonstrations, but her point is an important one. The demonstrations have forged alliances with social-liberal values and shown many young British-born Muslims that a dissenting voice is also a time-honoured method of showing citizenship. The struggle for democracy itself was achieved step by step, victory by victory, over the voices of powerful establishments that did not want to relinquish their advantages or share privileges with the less powerful. Even those who protested for a wider franchise or the basic rights of workers were regarded as dissenters. Although sometimes imprisoned and deported, the nineteenth-century radicals, themselves often using a language that combined politics with religion, were no less citizens than those they struggled against, even though they were probably accused of anti-social or deviant behaviour.

The political alliances forged by the Stop the War may be typical of modern politics, where a number of identities are fleetingly taken on as alliances are formed that may not survive the particular issue. They are nonetheless significant in that they challenge essentialist thinking regarding ethnicity by exemplifying the creation of hybrid or flexible identities (Kawale 2003). Kawale argues that identity is not only about who you are but where you are, in that space and place are crucial to a sense of identity. If it is true that identity changes when public space shifts, then the new space created by the anti-war demonstrations provides for new possibilities of overlapping and intersecting.

The above views were reinforced by a meeting with several young Muslim women aged between 18 and 22, mainly of Bangladeshi origin, and all studying a variety of subjects at university. All had participated in the demonstrations, either nationally or locally. Interestingly, their age range meant that they had not participated in the First Gulf War demonstrations and were barely born at the time of the *Satanic Verses* controversy. Without exception they maintained that their first loyalty was to their religion but they did not perceive any contradiction between their faith commitment and their 'Britishness'. In fact, it was striking that their British identity was firmly imbedded and provoked little sense of conflict or alienation. The meeting took place in the office of the Women's Officer of the Student Union, and all the participants were active in the union with regard to women's issues. However, their politicisation, both in this context and through participation in the anti-war demonstrations, arose primarily out of their Muslim identity and their sense of injustice. Their 'Britishness' rose to the fore only in the context of their feeling that their nation of birth provided them with the right to be Muslims and publicly express their democratic right to oppose government policy. They were aware of the paradoxical nature of forming alliances with some non-Muslim groups who were probably atheist, such as socialists or communists, and their views confirmed the ideas of Habermas mentioned above. Most striking, however, was their awareness of being second-generation Muslim British women, unencumbered by the identity crisis sometimes apparent in the first generation, and able to handle flexible or situational identities with ease, secure in their primary identities of being Muslim and British. They were also intensely aware of the role of the demonstrations in opening a public political space to young Muslim women.

In a fascinating article, Bakirathi Mani examines the impact of mixing and matching South Asian clothing with conventional forms of western dress in the North American situation. She argues that 'The choice of some South Asian women to wear *Himachali* caps or *kurtas* with their otherwise "Western" clothes, denies precisely those patriarchal attempts to demand perfect reproductions of nation and culture' (Mani, 2002: 125). The mix-and-match clothing of North American South Asians can be seen as a device to both confuse essentialised and stereotyped racial and religious identities, but also to deliberately 'confound neat demarcations of culture and citizenship demanded by the US nation' (*ibid.* 129). Although the British form of multiculturalism is different to that of the US, I would like to suggest that the example of clothing is a metaphor for the mixing and matching of the disparate groups that form the Stop the War Coalition, and that Muslims who participate are equally developing a narrative of participation that 'confounds' the normative language of both assimilation and integration models, and are thus discovering an authentic way of being both true to Islam and sharing in the values of citizenship as emancipatory and essential for the health of a liberal democratic society.

Mani's idea of 'coming out', used to describe the open display of South 'Asianness' in dress behaviour, works no less well for Muslims who participate in the anti-war demonstrations. Kawale (2003) states, in the context of South Asian gender issues, that 'coming out' creates a new space in the sphere of identity politics. Those British-born Muslims who have chosen to 'come out of the closet' of ethnic community politics, the domain of their elders, and participate in national and global struggles for emancipation, have also created a new space for the formation of Islam in Britain after the traumatic events of 9/11. It is a far more public space; they are less invisible than their elders, whose political activities took place in the relatively anonymous realm of ethnic relations and intra-community affairs.

It is not only the British government that needs to be concerned about the alliances, however short-lived they may be, but also those in the Muslim diaspora who strive to maintain 'authentic' reproductions of culture. However, the process of 'coming out' by participating in the demonstrations is relatively non-confrontational, in that elders are likely to approve the tacit support of Muslims against Western domination, and the gaze of outsiders, which might in other circumstances be oppositional, is rendered friendly and safe.

Conclusion

It is possible to perceive a qualitative transformation in identity politics and the formation of a moderate Muslim identity that creatively interacts with British citizenship as a result of the aftermath of 9/11 and the conflicts generated by British and US foreign policy.

The demonstrations after the publication of *The Satanic Verses* alienated the British public, who were not used to such passionate feelings aroused by religion. On the other hand, they reinforced Muslim suspicion of the values of their new home and led to increased isolation and ghettoisation. The demonstrations against the First Gulf War led to the paradox of Muslims supporting Saddam Hussein. However, the Stop the War campaign has involved Muslims in emancipatory discourse that is historically part of British democratic processes. As a result there has been a shift from notions of a fragmented self torn between culture and religion and ethnicity and 'Britishness' to that of a multi-layered self that lies outside the traditional/modern dichotomy so often presented in right-wing minority discourse when speaking of Muslims. Pnina Werbner (2002: 249) observes:

Young men simply avoid the mosque altogether, finding the sectarian arguments and factional fights incomprehensible and unpleasant. A few join youth associations, the majority inspired by Islamist ideas and promoting global versions of Islam. For all these young men Islam seems far from being a religion of peace.

I would suggest that the Stop the War Coalition can help young British-born Muslims to find a way to reconcile the values of Islam with those of their nation of birth while at the same time providing a vehicle for activism that will turn out to be more fruitful than the anti-West rhetoric of the 'Islamicists', and at the same time reinforce convictions that Islam is a force for peace. The anti-war demonstrations have accelerated a process whereby British Muslims are more able to engage in their society with an increasing emphasis on mutual interests and commonalities with the wider non-Muslim population. In the words of Manazir Ahsan, Director General of the Islamic Foundation (2003: ix),

> when British Muslims disagree with their governments on issues of political, moral or religious values as with the *Satanic Verses* affair, the Gulf War or the bombings and invasion of Afghanistan, their contentions should not be viewed in terms of their specific loyalties or belonging to Britain. Rather, their alternative views should be interpreted as an expression of their democratic right to oppose government policies.

Chapter 6
In the Shadow of September 11:
Multiculturalism and Identity

STEPHEN LYON

In a review of a recent anthropological conference on Pakistan, Iqbal asked how one promotes 'notions of cultural blending and "melting" in the face of fundamental differences in values between post-Enlightenment Europeans and revivalist Islamist populations around the world?' (2003: 24). The question is not academic, in the sense that the answers matter to all of us both in and out of the academy. Nevertheless, anthropology is particularly well suited to try and discuss the question. This chapter addresses this question by examining different approaches by two British Muslim Pakistanis, examining ways in which multiculturalism may be achieved. The first example clearly conforms to the model that Tony Blair and some of his ministers seem to have in mind. Islam is an important aspect of this man's personal self-representation; however, it is restricted to a fairly banal set of activities that do not impact on his primary economic activities. The second man poses a challenge to the model in which we all share universal values. As a Muslim cleric, he represents ideas and values that question the merit of so-called universal values. Despite the differences in their willingness to adopt Blair-like Western values, both men have had cause to question their own place in British society in the post-September 11 world; both have had to consider the extent to which they may need to accommodate the new world order.

This chapter presents two very different men and a glimpse into some of their ideas and their attitudes to the global events that have engulfed us all. They were chosen not because they represent all Muslims in Britain but because they represent some of the boundaries of the range of experience. There are of course people who represent more extreme positions than either of the men I will discuss here; my objective, however, is to offer a voice to men who have been caught up in turbulent times and who must somehow find ways to give meaning to things happening both far away and very close to home. They were selected from a larger group of British Pakistanis with whom I have conducted formal and informal interviews since late 2002. The two men discussed here, like all of my informants, presented a complex set of ideas and experiences, yet between the two of them they seem to offer a microcosm of the total set of narratives that form the basis of my ongoing study. The main aim of the project is to produce and analyse a wide selection of narratives from Muslims in Britain today. The stories that people tell themselves and others reveal cultural patterns of meaning that help us to understand why people make certain decisions and hold certain beliefs.

Equally importantly, I wish to highlight pervasive ambiguities in terms often used by politicians recently but rarely defined. These terms lie at the heart of how some people have come to view multiculturalism. Watson (2000: 3) suggests that multiculturalism requires the state to endorse difference and enhance people's desire to 'join in common citizenship with members of other cultural groups to protect the liberal tolerance which is so important for them'. If the state fails to endorse and protect different values and practices, then that desire to be part of a common citizenry is at risk. By invoking poorly defined terms to justify a remarkable array of activities, and, further, by suggesting that we all must share in these values, the state puts at risk the very concept of multiculturalism.

September 11 and the rise of universal values

Prior to the horrific events of September 11, questions of multiculturalism were important but perhaps less urgent. The riots of the summer of 2001 in northern England did underscore the need for greater understanding of the tensions between whites and Asians in Britain, but those events could be understood, in part, as expressions of economic competition for poorly distributed resources. The cultural differences between British Asians and British whites did not seem as pressing as a fundamental examination of employment and educational opportunities and how these were distributed across Britain's ethnic populations. When 19 Muslims hijacked four commercial jets in the United States, Huntington's (1993) appalling thesis of civilisation clash was brought to the fore. The notion that there is somehow a fundamental incompatibility between Muslim civilisation and Western civilisation, or rather between key 'values' embedded within the cultures of those civilisations, poses a very threatening and depressing challenge to those who like the idea of living in a multicultural Britain.

The New Labour government (or certain spokespersons within it), having embraced something called multiculturalism in Britain, appears to want this concept defined in ways that sanction the imposition of more rigid notions of acceptable behaviours and attitudes on minority ethnic communities. There is an explicit declaration that our values are in fact not Western at all. They are 'universal' after all. The problem is not Islamic 'culture' but that too many Muslims around the world have either been 'duped' into not opting for the universal values or are being actively constrained from making those choices. Huntington's clash of cultures is explicitly sidelined for a number of reasons and in its place is a poorly formed hypothesis that Muslims around the world all want what we want but they are the victims of oppression or false consciousness. Since September 11 there has been a massive expansion of British and American military activity in the Muslim world. Tony Blair, in particular, has gone to great lengths to avoid alienating Muslims by arguing that 'a fanatical strain of religious extremism has arisen, that is a mutation of the true and peaceful faith of Islam' (Blair's speech to the US Congress 2003). Blair has apparently done his homework and discovered that much of the doctrine of Islam, as in Christianity, promotes peaceful solutions to conflict. Those Muslims who are not 'peaceful', therefore, must be heretically subscribing to this 'new and deadly virus' of a mutation. The new version of multicultural society consequently implies that ethnic differences must be embodied through colourful wedding outfits or quaint dances that ethnic folk do at the weekend. The core values underlying peoples' economic and political activities on the other hand, are universal. 'Ours are not Western values,' Blair said,

> They are the universal values of the human spirit and anywhere, any time, ordinary people are given the chance to choose, the choice is the same. Freedom not tyranny. Democracy not dictatorship. The rule of law not the rule of the secret police.

Elsewhere Blair stated that 'the values of liberty, the rule of law, human rights and a pluralist society are universal and worthy of respect in every culture' (2002: 120). With these statements Tony Blair reassured the American Congress and the world that imposing democracy, freedom and the rule of law as defined by some people in America and Britain is neither cultural imperialism nor capitalistic thuggery. It is rather Mr Blair and Mr Bush giving all the underprivileged, downtrodden, oppressed masses of the world the opportunity to live the way they want to if only they had a truly free choice. David Blunkett's statements in the *Independent on Sunday* on 9 December 2001, about 'norms of acceptability' and 'our home', localised Blair's notions by suggesting that it is acceptable to impose certain values on anyone who enters Britain (whether they share them or not). The problems inherent in such positions do not only apply to British South Asian Muslim migrants, of course; it is dubious whether one can indeed talk of British and American understandings of these values as one and the same thing. These concepts are suspiciously prone to re-interpretation and manipulation even within a single culture group. The odds that non-Muslim British and American speakers talk past each other when using terms like 'freedom' seem to have become increasingly good in the aftermath of the invasion/liberation of Iraq.

The New Labour think-tank, the Foreign Policy Centre, has produced a series of publications of varying quality exploring issues of multiculturalism that have the benefit of being more substantive than most political speeches, but sometimes potentially more alienating. Michael Wills, Member of Parliament for North Swindon, in an attempt to define British values, begins by asserting that September 11 resulted in an 'expression of the Atlantic identity of this country, rooted in our own unique history and culture' (2002: 15). For Wills, the riots of the summer of 2001 and the alienation of young British Muslims amount to a failure to secure a sense of British identity. For him a large part of the problem lay in economic and social exclusion. Therein lay an important stumbling block. The economics may eventually take care of themselves as they have with past waves of migration (albeit often unacceptably slowly and with little comfort for those generations who must endure economic exclusion). But what if the social exclusion emerges in part from an inability to embrace much of Wills's shared sense of belonging to a Britain that takes a critical part of its identity from an Atlantic connection to America? America and Britain severed colonial ties well before the British East India Company gained effective control of the Moghul Empire in 1857–8. The great wave of South Asian migration to Britain was a post-World War II phenomenon, so one might forgive a young British Pakistani or Bangladeshi who felt no ancestrally inspired emotional tug towards Washington DC, and indeed may have some antipathy to that sense of Britishness. Under British values, Wills (2002: 19) cites

> creativity built on tolerance, openness and adaptability, work and self-improvement, strong communities and an outward-looking approach to the world – all of which flow from our unique island geography and history, all rooted in a deep sense of fairness and decency.

We are back to more of the hard-to-define batch of shared values, only this time they are a collection of adjectives that are often used to describe the stereotypical Briton. One could argue that the Pakistanis who came to Britain following the war typify Wills's notion of British values – only they might not agree that these are typically British values. In the same volume, Francesca Klug offers a more carefully considered examination of shared standards and values. She questions the government White Paper proposition that the Human Rights Act of 1998 should stand as the 'key source of values that British citizens should share' (2002: 25). Klug rightly points out some of the inherent contradictions of the Human Rights Act as a 'statutory expression of historic British freedoms and rights' alongside other British symbols such as the 'Monarchy, the Anglican church and the Empire'. She cites, for example, the way in which the 'loss of empire ... is still routinely portrayed as a trauma ... [but] for about a third of the population of London this loss was their liberation' (2002: 27). Klug suggests that Blunkett, rather than calling for greater allegiance to British values, should instead call for Britons to be united by human rights values. She criticises the government for not expanding on the Human Rights Act to lay down in law a set of values for modern, multicultural Britain, which, she argues, could be accepted by all religions.

A survey of government statements on shared values would be lengthy and no doubt disturbing. Few if any of us would argue against giving people some control over who will represent them, or what laws should be passed. Who would dispute that everyone should obey the same set of laws, once these have been accepted? Most of us think that the ideas underlying such terms as democracy and freedom are good. They are at least good for *us*, if not for special cases of others (many societies have provisions for disenfranchising individuals without jeopardising the basic principles of democracy and freedom). Nevertheless, the degree of implementation of such principles and how one goes about 'exporting' such notions leads to some rather dramatic differences of opinion.

As an anthropologist and someone who is fundamentally attached to notions of democracy and freedom of expression, I only wish the message that Tony Blair delivered to the American Congress was not quite as loaded with Orwellian double-speak. I cannot recall ever meeting someone who argued that they did not deserve the right to express their opinion. Nor can I remember meeting anyone who thought it appropriate for the state to arrest them without cause and torture them until they confessed to a crime they did not commit. I think it goes without saying that those women tragically and brutally executed by the Taliban certainly did not feel that the punishment fitted the crime. Nevertheless, from those 'universal' truths I am unable to say categorically that my friends in Pakistan and I share a common understanding of the terms 'freedom', 'democracy' or even 'rule of law'. And while we do at some point probably share similar basic notions of what these terms mean, that does not mean that we necessarily relish them with the same zeal as Mr Blair, or agree on the best method for their implementation. This chapter is not a systematic attempt to address whether or not Pakistani Muslims understand these terms as Mr Blair does, nor even if they would adopt them based on that understanding (which is itself somewhat fluid and contingent on time and place). It is rather a vignette of two British Pakistanis with very different strategies for living in a world where Orwellian newspeak seems to pervade the political élite's vocabulary. This is an attempt to demonstrate that while there are some 'universal' values that are not Western in either origin or presence, they are mediated by culture, society and an alarming brand of political zeal. This mediation means that notions of 'multiculturalism' that assume universality are risky at best.

There are very serious problems with the idea that our values are universal: for some people, freedom would include the right to protect one's children through controlling their choice of spouse, occupation and place of residence. Or freedom might include the right to avenge a grave affront to one's reputation in ways that ordinarily are proscribed by the law. And notions of justice and fairness, indeed, might dictate policies that contravene a blind adherence to something called the rule of law or even democracy. To complicate matters further, Watson (2000) reminds us, yet again, that 'culture', which informs and makes sense of 'values', is (like ethnicity, identity and religion) a dynamic process. So, just as the first generation of any migrant population may hold cultural values profoundly incompatible with those of the succeeding generation, so too might the values that Tony Blair hails as 'ours' become incompatible with future generations. These values in which we place so much faith are negotiated in specific historical and cultural contexts. It seems clear that there is variation in how people make sense of particular value notions at any given time.

The Blair multicultural project in action and the clash of civilisations

I have known Jahangir Choudry[1] for over 20 years. We met as adolescents in Pakistan. His parents had sent him 'home' to get more Pakistani and I was a dependent teenage ex-pat in Lahore, Pakistan. He was born in Glasgow to first-generation Pakistani migrants. His history offers a clear example of one of the 'types' of British Pakistani, while simultaneously defying the more pervasive stereotypes. His father owns and runs several 'corner shops' thanks to several decades of perseverance, hard work and canny business sense. Jahangir married young to a white British woman. Despite a great many positive aspects of the marriage, it was not easily accepted by Jahangir's family. Three children with Muslim names eased some (but not all, by any means) of Jahangir's parents' displeasure. Educationally, Jahangir underperformed for a variety of reasons. Although he was considered very clever by his peers and his teachers as an adolescent, his temper occasionally got him into minor trouble at school. He largely resisted, in interesting ways, his parents' attempts to make him more 'Pakistani'. He participated in important cultural events such as Eid-al-Udha and was courteous and attentive in mosque, but he periodically posed legitimate yet subversive questions to those in positions of authority. Now in his mid-thirties, Jahangir has divorced his first wife and remarried another white woman (a continental European this time). He is now managing director of a media organisation, based in London, that caters for ethnic minority business people in Britain.

Throughout our long friendship, Jahangir and I have had countless occasions to argue and squabble over any number of issues; however, I cannot recall us ever having an argument about religion. Each of us has quizzed the other about logical contradictions in Islam or Christianity, but always in a good-natured, non-combative way (whereas our arguments about computers, stereos, cars or music always have the potential to get quite heated). The first indication I had that Jahangir and I might fundamentally differ in our values arose during the *Satanic Verses* affair in the late 1980s. I was visiting Jahangir and expressed my dismay that Muslims were so outraged by a book that hardly any of them had read. He was initially adamant that Salman Rushdie should be killed. As our argument became increasingly strained he assured me he was joking about killing authors, but thought this author was insensitive to how cherished and important the Holy Prophet is to Muslims. Our friendship survived the joke and the minor disagreement over Rushdie.

The next time we fundamentally disagreed over something related to Islam was in the aftermath of September 11. I believed, then and now, that the invasion of Afghanistan was a brutal act of retribution against some of the poorest and most miserable people on the planet. I found myself in the odd position of having to defend the Taliban (a group with whom I think I share almost no common vision of the 'perfect' world). Jahangir agreed with me that the Afghan people were not responsible for the September 11 attacks, but argued that the Taliban were implementing a perverse version of Islam which discredited Muslims the world over. After more than two decades of friendship, there is no longer any danger that we will sever all communication over such a disagreement; indeed, I found the disagreement instructive. Jahangir had never before demonstrated an affinity with those in the West who might want to attack a Muslim country. What had happened on September 11 to make him side against Muslims, when just over ten years before he had clearly opted to side with his Muslim brothers against the imposition of liberal European values related to free speech?

To be fair, a great many people felt that the invasion of Afghanistan, although regrettable and costly in human lives and livelihoods, was justifiable. And while I do not agree with them, I respect both those people and their arguments for such an attack. When it came to Iraq, I felt certain that my Muslim friend Jahangir would revert to type and be against the war. Surprisingly, I was wrong. Jahangir, an avid follower of the news and a well-educated man with his finger on the political and economic pulse of Britain, supported the British government's decision to invade Iraq. I was puzzled and intrigued.

Shortly before the Iraq war began in the spring of 2003, I asked Jahangir why he supported a potential invasion. He produced a list of reasons, including: 'Saddam is a bastard'; Saddam is a dictator; if he does have weapons of mass destruction, then he could certainly use them against his Muslim neighbours some day (Iran, presumably, being high on the list). Significantly, after discussing this list for some time, Jahangir said: 'Bush and Blair are going to do it no matter what you or I think – just let them do it quickly so we can get back to normal.'

Although Jahangir did not cite a desire to return to 'normality' as a primary justification, it loomed ever present in our discussions. He is a businessman. His economic values are eminently compatible with Blair's (although he is far less of a religious zealot than Blair). Subsequent conversations revealed minor incidents which caused Jahangir to confront his own difference within white Britain. His name, for example, proudly proclaims him a South Asian Muslim. His skin is dark. He speaks Punjabi and Urdu fluently and knows what to do when he goes inside a mosque. He does not feel threatened by the call to prayers and men in beards are not menacing to him. He prefers Pakistani food and believes that *halal* butchers provide better-quality meat. In his work he capitalises on his specialist knowledge of Islam and South Asia. Prior to September 11, this was an asset about which he was proud and vocal. Today, there is a reserve. He is no longer confident of white people's perception of him. He mentioned the looks that liberal-looking white people gave him when he was near a mosque (wearing a suit and tie). He said he could tell that they felt uneasy. They looked uncomfortable because they were no longer sure that underneath that Western veneer there was not some incompatible fundamentalist Islamist ready to set off a suicide attack. Jahangir strives to be British but since September 11 a whole new barrage of obstacles has emerged to maintain those boundaries between him and white Britain. Jahangir is not alone in perceiving a greater sense of unease among his white neighbours. While my research on this topic remains tentative, every one of my Muslim informants has reported the same phenomena. They report that non-Muslims seem more nervous and anxious when confronted with possible Muslims, especially in the vicinity of mosques.

Had Blair, in his declaration that this violent brand of Islam was a 'new deadly virus', a mutation from the 'true and peaceful Islam', given Jahangir a way out? Had the newspeak of freedom, democracy and the rule of law as universal values offered Jahangir a way of appealing to Muslim friends and relatives and whites simultaneously? Could he be British and Muslim at the same time if only he subscribed to the idea that underneath all the hype about cultural differences 'ordinary' people the world over really subscribed to the same values and wanted the same thing? It is far too early to say whether Jahangir has been able to accommodate his Islamic values with his British values. For now, he has managed at least to provide a Muslim face that is more amenable to his white customers. He offers proof that Blair is correct and that ultimately we are all 'good, right-thinking' people living in a mutually compatible multicultural society. What seems evident, however, is that September 11 represents a watershed for him as a British Muslim. Following September 11, Jahangir feels more compelled to adopt the values of Tony Blair in order to retain what is precious to him – Britishness – where before he had more liberty to be British and contest some of the 'universally' held values of Western Europe.

In many ways Jahangir's story reflects the experiences of many second-generation British Pakistani Muslims. He is caught between competing models of appropriate action. Some people around him expect him to support his religious brethren while others increasingly expect him to vocally and visibly distance himself from perceived anti-secular, anti-liberal forces within British Muslim communities. Jahangir represents an important minority voice within the British Muslim community that requires considerable care in analysing. Anthropological studies of individual identity reveal the need for more nuanced factor analysis when trying to understand the choices that people make. Jahangir and others like him express views that are contrary to what is perceived to be the dominant British Muslim narrative for a number of reasons related to class, education, occupation and place of residence. While these factors fall outside of the restricted ethnographic and biographical scope of this study, they are nevertheless important in understanding the ways in which Jahangir represents one response, possibly an extreme one, of the British Muslim population to the increasing demands for visible conformity to certain values.

Unlike Jahangir, Imam Haji Asif is neither British-born nor secular. He is a professional Islamic cleric who came to Britain at the age of 25 to preach in a mosque in an industrial city in the north-east of England. After nearly 20 years in Britain he is a prominent member of the local community. He represents local British Paki-stanis on the city and county councils, and British Muslims at conferences around the Muslim world. His identity lies somewhere within the myriad Islamic identities present in Britain and Pakistan.

He is Sunni, Barelvi, an adherent of the Hanafi school of thought, Pakistani, Punjabi, male, father, member of a patrilineage, member of a Punjabi caste and, of course, after 20 years in Britain, he is also British. He is multilingual and multicultural in many ways yet he is firmly rooted in a community that, at first glance, looks somewhat incompatible with Blunkett's multicultural Britain.

He believes in a rigid segregation of Muslim men and women after puberty; he believes that Muslims should not engage in the sale of alcohol, even to non-Muslims. He believes that one of the biggest problems facing British mosques today is the friction between mosque committees and imams, which, notably, is partly the result of the democratisation of British mosques. He believes that Saddam Hussein is (or perhaps was) an evil man, not because he had weapons of mass destruction (he points out that such weapons are held by both Britain and the United States) but because he is an enemy of Islam. Moreover, Saddam Hussein is evil because he was the agent of the United States against Iran, which was attempting to create an Islamic state for Muslims (of which he approves).

Imam Haji Asif challenges notions of multicultural Britain as a place with a universal set of shared values underpinning all communities. Interestingly, Haji Asif said that prior to September 11 he thought that most Muslims agreed with Blair's definitions of democracy, freedom and rule of law. Speaking about democracy in particular, Haji Asif stated:

> British Pakistanis understand democracy and what the Prime Minister talks about, but I think after 11 September, this time is a turning point for Islam and the entire Muslim community throughout the world ... when they are saying now, 'democracy', before 11 September, our thinking about democracy was the same, but after 11 September our thinking is different.

Specifically pointing to Saddam Hussein's role as American proxy in the war against Iran, Haji Asif asked how dedicated America really is to the rule of law and democracy. Nevertheless, he did not argue that Muslims had distinct values from those of British people; indeed he sounded eerily like Tony Blair when he suggested that many white British people shared his values. It is Mr Blair and Mr Bush who display a lack of commitment to democracy, freedom and rule of law when they first sponsor Saddam Hussein, then attack him. Haji Asif was acutely aware of the lack of democracy in the

Muslim world: he asked how Blair and Bush can continue to support the Saudi Arabian regime, with its blatantly separate legal codes for citizens and foreigners (even Muslim ones), or Pakistan, whose current leader General Musharraf assumed power in a very undemocratic coup in 1999. Haji Asif seems to be suggesting that British and American leaders share a belief in their own self-interest: when it suits those interests, they will invoke a collection of terms that most people associate with something good.

Haji Asif offered a further example of differences in definitions of democracy in an unrelated conversation, when discussing the problems of democratising mosque committees. There are no elections for mosque committees in Pakistan, he said. The people who do all the work are not elected and receive no formal title or office. They donate their time to the mosque voluntarily and are self-selected. In Britain, on the other hand, mosque committee members are accorded respect and privilege by local city and county councillors; this has led to competition for the positions, not out of duty to Islam or God, but rather out of a desire to establish personal relationships with prominent individuals in the area. The factional violence that erupts around mosque politics[2] in Britain is deeply troubling to Haji Asif, and whether or not he is correct that the root causes are linked to democratisation, he believes this to be the case. Democracy at this level, it would appear, can lead to a degradation of people's dedication to Islam and to the mosque community.

Haji Asif and individuals who agree with him presumably have the right to dissent from Blunkett's or Wills's definition of British identity, yet this dissent raises the spectre of a clash of 'unshared' values between groups in Britain. Haji Asif has profoundly different expectations and ideals of gender roles and relations from many in Britain (though not all, by any means). His opinions on democracy are contradictory and reflect the drawbacks of democracy, on which many have commented (including seminal advocates of modern democratic institutions like Thomas Jefferson). Prior to September 11, many of these unshared values might have remained unchallenged and unnoticed. In the aftermath of September 11, however, the British Labour government and the American Republican executive are declaring a set of ill-defined terms to be universal and 'core'. Anyone not sharing those values is an enemy. Suddenly, differences in values have become tantamount to treason (or terrorism?) in the new world order.

Conclusion

Perhaps it does not need saying, but it is probably easier to be friends with someone who basically agrees about the kinds of entertainment that are permissible (going to a pub, for example), or the ways in which one should relate to women, both in and out of the home. This does not mean that I am not friends with people like Haji Asif, nor does it mean that I do not like or respect these people. Indeed I both respect and like many devoutly religious people. Nevertheless, there are barriers to these friendships that must be accepted even if they are not usually explicitly acknowledged. My friendship with Haji Asif is not the easy casual relationship that I share with Jahangir. It is more formal, more stylised and more controlled. We may not share a common vision of the kind of world in which each of us would like to live. Fortunately, both Haji Asif and I share a common faith that our worlds can coexist within this larger domain of what we call British multiculturalism. We negotiate neutral arenas for communication in which we can get to know and respect each other without forcing our differences to the surface. Where differing values emerge and prove incompatible, we negotiate viable strategies for coexistence.

As a migrant to Britain myself, it is easy for me to accept that it is incumbent on me to make compromises to get along with my neighbours in this country. I recognise that this notion of compromise may be harder for indigenous white British people to accept. Prior to September 11, my informants imply that the compromise was happening – slowly but surely. The attacks on the World Trade Centre and the Pentagon in the United States, the invasions of Afghanistan and Iraq, the bombings in Indonesia and the heavy-handed treatment of Muslims suspected of terrorist activities by the United States seem to have hardened a great many people's hearts. Where compromise and accommodation appeared to be on course before September 11, they seem sporadic and uncomfortable today. Where some people might have been able to turn a blind eye to profound differences in opinion on the importance of elections in some organisations, or the roles and relationships attached to gender, for example, now these must be scrutinised as potential indicators of 'terrorist' sympathies. Some secular British Muslims, like Jahangir, have become hawks, fully adopting the universal values defined by Blair and Company (regardless of inconsistencies or contradictions), while Haji Asif has come to the conclusion that Britain's leaders no longer understand or care about values at all.

The world is *not* a safer place as a result of the war on terrorism. Pushing the likes of Osama bin Laden (and Saddam Hussein until he was caught) into hiding does not seem to have reduced the number of politically violent events or made people feel more comfortable boarding jumbo jets. The capture of Saddam Hussein does not seem to have reduced the violence in Iraq. If this escalation of tension, violence and bloodshed were to defend a set of values that we all shared against a small number of radical followers of a 'mutation' of Islam, then perhaps those values should have been a little more explicitly defined so that people like Jahangir wouldn't feel the need to go along with everything and people like Haji Asif wouldn't feel so betrayed by words and ideas he thought he knew all about.

Notes

1 The names of the two participants cited in this chapter are pseudonyms. This is not to deny their voices, but rather to give their voices the freedom to contradict both local and national 'wisdoms' and 'values' without fear of repercussions.
2 See especially Werbner's account (2002: 233–50) of how mosque elections in Manchester in the late 1980s and early 1990s were plagued by factional violence.

Chapter 7
Lobbying and Marching: British Muslims and the State

JONATHAN BIRT

Introduction

Much has recently been written about 'Islamic terrorism' and its emergence in Western Europe, particularly 'Londonistan' (Thomas 2003), but little attention has been given to how it catalysed the mainstream British Muslim response to the attacks in New York and Washington. By lobbying and marching, the vast bulk of British Muslims sought to confute their stereotyping as a violent 'fifth column', operating as critical citizens within the norms of democratic dissent. British Muslims mobilised to defend what they saw as the civilised nature of their faith, to take a stand against their own extremists and to prevent the logic of revenge dictating an approach that would claim innocent Muslim lives with no connection to the original crime. The public defiance of radical Islamist groups like al-Muhajiroun or figures like Abu Hamza al-Misri, or the revelations about 'British Taliban' and 'British al-Qa'ida' on each occasion produced genuine spasms of angry and heartfelt denial from British Muslim leaders, who were aware that patient bridge building after the political isolation of the Rushdie affair years was in grave danger.

In other words, the most salient point about the radical fringe in relation to the British Muslim mainstream was its role in provoking widespread political mobilisation as Muslims among an ethnically disparate set of communities. At the same time, the government expected mainstream opposition to the radicals to translate into support for its policy in Afghanistan, a translation they attempted unsuccessfully to direct throughout the campaign in the autumn of

2001. This essay intends to concentrate upon the substance of the mainstream response, which might be summarised as lobbying and marching, and to outline how the British government attempted to manage British Muslim opinion during this period.

The government's management of the Muslim lobby

Prior to the start of the bombing campaign in Afghanistan in October 2001, the government's strategy with regard to British Muslims, seen as a key domestic constituency in this instance, was simple. The first aim was to defuse any rise in anti-Muslim tensions at home by making a clear distinction between Islam and terrorism, and by maintaining that this war sought to combat the perpetrators of the original attacks, al-Qa'ida, and the Taliban regime that supported them. There were certainly grounds for concern over an anti-Muslim backlash in the weeks following the attacks: mosques were vandalised, there were some violent assaults and Islamophobic verbal abuse (EUMC 2002: 29–30). There was a broad cross-party consensus on the need to distinguish between Islam and terrorism that was rigidly held to. When Baroness Thatcher flouted this by remarking that she 'had not heard enough condemnation from Muslim priests', the Conservative Party wasted no time in distancing itself from her comments. Its Vice-Chairman remarked that, 'Her comments were unhelpful. I'm afraid it's a voice from history. It doesn't speak to modern Britain' (*Guardian*, 4 October 2001).

However, this politically expedient distinction between Islam and terrorism was barely tenable after the start of military action, with widespread scepticism being expressed by most British Muslims. Faisal Bodi summed up the feeling well:

> Of course, that's not how Bush and Blair want the world to see their new double-act. Indeed the prime minister has gone on a charm offensive, turning itinerant imam in his quest to woo Muslim opinion. None of it washes except with the stooges who dutifully march down to Downing Street every time Mr Blair wants to suggest that since British Muslims are on side this cannot be a war against Islam. Since September 11 my imam has extended Friday prayers with a special supplication reserved for times of affliction, imploring God to annihilate Islam's enemies, to "rock the ground underneath their feet". [...] For the rank and file believer, a drawn-out military offensive against terrorist groups and those that harbour them can only mean one thing: the extirpation of

Islam as a political threat to the west's exploitation of our countries (*Guardian*, 17 October 2001).

The government's second aim was to highlight the condemnation of the attacks by Muslim leaders in order to isolate the radicals, and to gather Muslim support for the coming military effort. It expected that its chief ally in delivering these aims would be the Muslim Council of Britain (MCB), the largest national umbrella body with around 380 affiliates, which had been patronised by New Labour since its official launch in 1998. The day after the attacks, the Prime Minister, Tony Blair, highlighted his close connection with the MCB, and shared his conviction that common outrage at the attacks was sufficient for all to agree on a unified course of action led by the Western powers:

> I was pleased to see the very strong statement of condemnation from the British Muslim Council [*sic*], echoing that of the American Muslim Council. As Muslim leaders and clerics around the world are making clear, such acts of infamy and cruelty are wholly contrary to the Islamic faith. The vast majority of Muslims are decent, upright people who share our horror at what has happened. People of all faiths and all democratic political persuasions have a common cause: to identify this machinery of terror and to dismantle it as swiftly as possible (*Guardian*, 13 September 2001).

Behind the scenes, Downing Street promised the MCB that it could have easy access through the Prime Minister's Assistant Political Secretary, Razi Rahman, to express its concerns. It was also promised that the government's spin machine would be used to influence the press, which already was expressing scepticism at the uncoupling of Islam and terrorism, to put out positive pieces. The most notable success in the first week was the *Sun's* agreement to feature a centre page spread entitled 'Islam is not an evil religion' on 13 September. Top-level meetings were arranged over the following week with the relevant ministers to discuss Muslim concerns over foreign policy, protecting Muslims from harassment and on what was seen as divisive press coverage.[1]

For its part, the MCB worked to bring together rival Muslim leaders to sign a joint letter outlining their concerns. In addition to the ritual demand for legislation on religious discrimination, the letter stressed the need to keep any response within international legal norms, and that talk of war would have a divisive impact on

British Muslims. With an eye to Muslim public opinion, it emphasised that 'further indiscriminate violence where ordinary people are the victims ... is neither civilised, nor a long-term answer to the problem of international terrorism'.[2] It asked for a proportionate and moderate response that looked for long-term solutions. By the end of the first week, the MCB was also sending out the same message publicly that 'the world powers must not respond with military action'. (MCB Press Release, 19 September 2001). Yet despite these private and public reservations, the government remained confident that community leaders could deliver domestic Muslim support for the war.

This tension was apparent in the meeting between the Prime Minister and Muslim leaders on 27 September. At the photo call, Baroness Uddin quipped, 'It looks like we're all [being] lined up here to be shot' (*Guardian*, 19 June 2002). Alastair Campbell, Downing Street's Director of Communications (2001–3), advised Muslim leaders privately at the meeting that, 'You guys have got a selling job to do' (*Daily Telegraph*, 19 October 2001). According to government sources, the MCB's Secretary-General, Yousuf Bhailok, in his public statement, appeared to give unreserved support: 'we are united in the campaign against terrorism and, indeed, we have made this quite clear universally' (10 Downing Street Press Release, 28 September 2001). But in its own gloss on this statement, the MCB called for the pursuit of 'justice, not vengeance' (MCB Press Release, 28 September 2001) and warned that any 'collateral damage ... [was] totally unacceptable' (*Times*, 28 September 2001). Adequate pressure still had to be applied by government.

The government expected that the MCB and other Muslim representatives would either support the war, or, at the very least, keep quiet about their opposition, and pressure was directly applied on them to do so at a special meeting convened at Number 10 just after the start of the bombing campaign (*Guardian*, 13 November 2001). Thus, the MCB publicly noted its 'grave concern over military action' and expressed the hope that Britain would move immediately to non-military strategies (MCB Press Release, 7 October 2001). However, the MCB's affiliates warned that it would lose the support of most British Muslims, who were opposing the campaign, if it did not clearly condemn the action. Indeed, the MCB's own council of *ulema* had earlier decreed that bombing would be unlawful (MCB Press Release, 29 September 2001). Two days later, it declared its public opposition to the war, much to the chagrin of Blair who had

Razi Rahman ring Bhailok (then in Qatar) to tell him that the Prime Minister was furious (MCB Press Release, 9 October 2001; Radcliffe 2003: 74). Number 10 stopped returning the MCB's calls, and the Council later sought to gloss over its vacillation by claiming that it was obliged to represent the views of the Muslim majority (*Guardian*, 19 June 2002). The MCB then withdrew its support for the first anti-war march to placate the government, even though a number of its affiliates were involved, but, fearful of being outflanked, it publicly endorsed subsequent demonstrations (*Guardian*, 13 November 2001). It was also careful to maintain the line among all its spokespersons that the Afghanistan campaign was not part of a general war against Muslims and Islam (Radcliffe 2003: 73).

The moment of crisis after the initial attack did little to overcome the deep-set antagonisms that persisted among the small circle of Muslim lobbyists on the Westminster and Whitehall circuit. This circle was divided into the MCB and a loose anti-MCB grouping, united in preventing it from monopolising government attention. After the start of the bombing, when the Prime Minister could not find a prominent British mosque from which to continue pressing home the line that the 'War on Terror' was not a war on Islam, he was opportunistically granted a platform on 25 October by the small Iraqi Shiite umbrella body, the al-Khoei Foundation, which only had around 15 members, at a conference on 'Islamic Responses to Terrorism', attended by a select number of diplomats, academics, journalists, human rights activists and colonial creations like the Raja of Mahmudabad.

After the failure to keep the MCB on board, the government then made various attempts to produce statements of public support from among its own Muslim Labour supporters. It turned first to its Muslim parliamentarians, who were called to Downing Street on 18 October and told to sign a statement in support of military action. Despite deep reservations, they agreed to sign a modified statement that backed military action as unavoidable but necessary (FCO Press Release, 18 October 2001; *Sun*, 19 October 2001). However, all the parliamentarians, with the exception of Khalid Mahmood MP, subsequently disowned the released statement, saying that they had been the victims of government spin. In a private letter written to the Prime Minister, which was then leaked, they argued for a cessation of the bombing. They were reportedly told to keep quiet out of fear of protests from British Muslims (*Mail on Sunday*, 4 November 2001). To counteract the failure of the parliamentarians to remain 'on message', fifty Muslim Labour councillors were then drafted in to sign virtually the same statement of support, but this had relatively little impact (*Sun*, 8 November 2001).

Two key articles by Muslim loyalists then set the tone for a new turn in government tactics: to outflank the mosque-based national leadership by finding new, more secular alternatives, and to defend its current domestic and foreign policies. Faz Hakim, Downing Street's former Race Relations Adviser during New Labour's first term, who had been instrumental in promoting the MCB as well as recommending Muslims for the House of Lords, now admitted that this strategy of incorporation had failed.[3] The government had put too much onus on an unrepresentative mosque-based leadership that could not be expected to deal with the problems of a disenfranchised youth, which was seen as increasingly turning to extremism:

> The original fear of many of these community leaders was that young people would become more Westernised and abandon their religion. What has happened instead is that many in the younger generation are attracted by increasingly radical solutions. Faced with this, the leaders feel threatened and uncertain. Perhaps denouncing Western democracy and trying to keep their children apart from other young people is not the best way to encourage a harmonious relationship with other Britons. (*Times*, 30 October 2001)

The solution now was for New Labour to deal with disaffected youth directly through 'mainstream' Muslim politicians, a point that was forcefully argued by Khalid Mahmood MP, the remaining Parliamentary loyalist. In a Foreign and Commonwealth Office-penned article, the substance of government frustration with British Muslim public opinion on foreign policy was revealed in Mahmood's five 'myth-busting' arguments: that the war was not anti-Islamic; that non-military options were debated fully in Parliament; that the proof against bin Laden was adequate; that Muslim concerns over Palestine and Kashmir were being addressed; and, finally, that Muslims were unprincipled in their opposition to the bombing, because they had supported it against Bosnia. While a pacifist position was deemed to be morally consistent, Muslim transnational loyalties were not (*Observer*, 8 November 2001). One of the rebel Muslim peers, Lord Ahmed, who had leaked the fact that this was FCO propaganda, was told that he was now out in the cold. He made allegations that he was being bugged by MI5, which were described by a government source as 'bollocks on stilts'. Clearly, government was disappointed that one of its appointee Muslim peers had now joined the anti-war Labour group: Lord Ahmed subsequently went on a fact-finding mission to Iraq with leading rebel Labour MP, George Galloway (*Guardian*, 13, 21 November 2001; 17, 21 December 2001; *British Muslims Monthly Survey*, 11 (12) 2001: 12). At the same time, government ministers and advisers and other public figures expressed coded disappointment at the failure of Muslim leaders to challenge 'radicalism' among British Muslims. The Foreign Secretary gave the clearest official statement in January 2002:

> Some Muslim leaders in Britain, and international figures like President Musharraf in Pakistan, took an honourable and courageous stand. But not everyone in the Islamic world shared their view. For many, outrage, or perhaps more commonly plain unease, were the prevailing reactions to the international coalition's military campaign against Al Qa'ida and their protectors in the Taliban regime. Some in positions of respect and authority in their communities were all too ready to play on this unease, and to stoke up extremist feeling.
>
> By now, I hope that the gradual establishment of a broad-based, multi-ethnic government in Kabul, and the wholehearted support which we are providing for it, have convinced many of the doubters about our intentions. I know that mainstream Muslims do not feel they have more in common with Usama Bin Laden than with people of goodwill in other faiths. But I know from my own Muslim constituents that many mainstream Muslims can feel awkward about speaking out. I understand that the reasons for this are complex.
>
> Particularly communities of recent immigrants may feel the need to be defensive when some others in society still find their presence hard to accept. But it is important to avoid giving the impression of monolithic Muslim support for extremism, which plays right into the hands of those who would stir up hatred against Muslims.
>
> So, with great respect, speaking as a non-Muslim, but as one who has watched Islam for many years, I want to suggest this evening that all of us have an interest in promoting a more robust, open, explicit debate and marginalising the extremists.[4]

Faz Hakim was more explicit about the disappointment in government circles that British Muslim leaders had not been the moderating influence they had looked for. She voiced the view that the government had been unaware the MCB's Secretary-General had shared a platform with Hamas, Islamic Jihad and Hezbollah at an international conference in Tehran in 2001 whose communiqué had promised 'unlimited support for the Palestinian uprising'. She asserted that the government had recognised that it had been mistaken, and that all Muslim organisations had similar sentiments and probable links to terrorist organisations, and that this now constituted a 'problem'. Faz Hakim called upon Muslims to reassess their position: 'are they bringing kids up to be anti-British and anti-Jewish? They have to think.'[5]

Taken together, the government's basic analysis conflated the conclusions of a series of official reports after the summer disturbances of 2001 in the North of England – mostly involving Asian Muslims – with the events of September 11, by multiplying together the consequences of inner-city self-segregation and the spread of oppositional Islamic discourses. The MCB and, by extension, all other Muslim leaders were effectively accused of having exacerbated religious separatism and inadvertently laid the grounds for a further youthful radicalisation that they neither condoned nor could control, which in turn had fed the rise of anti-Muslim racist politics with the local electoral success of the BNP in recent years. Any meaningful analysis had collapsed: British Muslims, and in particular disenfranchised young Muslim men, were viewed almost exclusively through the lenses of social disorder, self-inflicted isolationism, racial tension and the security containment of terrorist threats.

The government creation of a unified Muslim lobby

Whilst the MCB gained quasi-official status under New Labour, it did owe its initial emergence to a demand, made in March 1994, for a single body by Michael Howard (then Conservative Home Secretary), primarily on the basis of administrative convenience. Reportedly depressed and concerned at the infighting among Muslim leaders, he said that he would not entertain their concerns seriously until a credible representative body had been formed. This invitation was seized upon by a clique that had first came to prominence in national politics during the *Satanic Verses* affair, comprised of middle-class Islamic activists, intellectuals and businessmen broadly inspired by the South Asian Islamic reform movements, the Jama`at-i-Islami and, to a lesser extent, the Deobandis, although the Council cannot be defined by the ideologies of these movements, as subsequent political praxis has been much more constitutive of its outlook. Informed by a commitment to faith-based political activism and a suspicion of the compromises inherent in party politics, the subsequent actions of the MCB are in practice only explicable as a balancing act between affiliate expectations and the maintenance of favoured access to if not influence with government.

The lengthy consultation process, begun a month after Michael Howard's request, was mostly ineffectual, and designed 'to consolidate a political alliance of mostly like-minded people' (Q-News, March-April 2002). The UK Action Committee for Islamic Affairs, whose leadership and agenda continued to dominate the consultation process (with the declared intention to establish the MCB), led it throughout. The consultation document proposed the simple argument that there was no real alternative to the creation of a new national body, thereby betraying the sentiment that it thought earlier national bodies either too ineffectual (the Union of Muslim Organisations) or too radical (Muslim Parliament of Great Britain) (McRoy 2001: 235–42).

Conceived from the start as an organisation that would remain close to government, the MCB initially operated with the assumption that the mere fact of access to power would bring concessions – although this optimism did not last long – and would allow the organisation to establish control of political patronage for British Muslims, the chief means for the Council to broaden its support. The determination to retain monopoly status was shown by its marginalisation of rival activist Muslim groups or individuals operating in Whitehall and other establishment institutions, and by its intolerance towards public criticism of its role. In 1998, for instance, the Council was quick to compete for the appointment of its candidate for the new post of Muslim adviser to the Prison Service ahead of the long-term campaigner for the reform, the Islamic Cultural Centre[6] (Q-News, October 1998, September 1999). In 2000 the Council pushed aside the initiative of the Association of Muslim Hujjaj to establish an official Hajj delegation to provide support to British pilgrims. As soon as it was granted Home Office funding, the Council was able to dominate the selection of candidates for the Hajj delegation, and succeeded in having its own preferred delegation head, Lord Patel of Blackburn, appointed over the original candidate, Lord Ahmed of Rotherham (Q-News, March 2000; Piscatori 2001: 13) Over time, the MCB was given a role in recommending appointments from the Muslim community to government advisory committees, for instance at the Foreign Office, and suitably moderate spokespersons for BBC programming, although subsequently these privileges have been challenged (*Guardian*, 22 October 2001). From its inception, the Council has been quick to counteract Muslim public criticism of its leadership, for example in the case of the journalist Faisal Bodi, when its Media Committee asked for his removal from regular employment with the *Guardian* and supplied the editor with a dossier of evidence (*Q-News*, May 1998, March–April 2002; Islamic Human Rights Commission, 'ALERT UPDATE: Support Journalist Faisal Bodi', 4 March 2002, e-mail communication).

Popular British Muslim opinion and the rise of new anti-war networks

Overall, government attempts to massage Muslim public opinion by enlisting a succession of groomed but resistant Muslim leaders proved ultimately naïve and ineffectual against a solid block of opposition to the war. The only professional poll of British Muslim public opinion conducted during the Afghanistan campaign broadly showed strong disapproval of the attacks (81 per cent), scepticism over bin Laden's culpability (67 per cent) and broad opposition to the bombing campaign (80 per cent). Those who opposed military action supported alternatives like diplomacy (86 per cent), intelligence gathering (84 per cent) and the seizure of financial assets (74 per cent). A majority (57 per cent) had not believed the government line that this was not a war against Islam (ICM Press Release, 14 November 2001). A less professional poll suggested that some elements of mosque-going male opinion were more adversarial: 11 per cent thought the attacks justified, 40 per cent said that bin Laden had reason to launch an anti-West *jihad* and 40 per cent that British Muslims were right to fight with the Taliban (*Sunday Times*, 4 November 2001). Another poll revealed the fragility of the 'Asian' identity category, when it showed that Hindu and Sikh opinion was much closer to the national average over post-September 11 issues (MORI Press Release, 22 November 2001). A leading 'Asian' radio station, Sunrise, declared that, under pressure from Hindu and Sikh listeners, it would re-brand itself because 'Muslims were bringing the Asian community into disrepute in Britain and [they] do not want to be put in the same bracket as them' (*Q-News*, January–February 2002).

The centrepieces of this popular 'ummatic' protest against the 'War on Terror' were the national marches undertaken in response to the international crisis that emerged after the September 11 attacks.[7] The Stop the War Coalition (SWC), which began in an *ad hoc* fashion, broadened from the 'usual suspects', satirised in some quarters of the press as 'Leftistan', or Taliban and Trotskyists, to include large segments of previously politically inactive Muslims and non-Muslims. What is noticeable about the post-September 11 response was the willingness of younger Muslims to form expedient alliances of dissent outside of their community, which was certainly not true of the Rushdie affair in 1989 or the Gulf War of 1991.

Like all temporary mobilisations, the coalition, or the 'multitude' (Hardt and Negri 2000), formed a temporary, diverse movement that incorporated an incompatible range of political views and agendas. Many of the young Muslim activists saw their coalition partners in simplistic, instrumentalist terms, as non-Muslim compatriots, without consideration as to their differing organisational agendas: the Trotskyite left like the Socialist Workers' Party; the trade union movement; the Campaign for Nuclear Disarmament (CND); the anti-globalisation movement; dissident journalists like John Pilger, Robert Fisk and Yvonne Ridley; and the maverick left-wing MPs on the sidelines of New Labour like Tony Benn, George Galloway and Jeremy Corbyn. The marches also included the broadest possible range of Muslim opinion, covered by the fig leaf of anti-American imperialism: Muslim liberals, like the novelist Kamila Shamsie, demonstrated side by side with fanatics who had, on one Palestine demonstration, marched with fake plastic explosives around their waists (*Guardian*, 1 August 2002).

Among the many, two spontaneous networks proved important in the early period when the MCB and the main Islamist networks did not put their weight behind the anti-Afghanistan bombing marches in October and November 2001. The first was a small network of London-based Muslim professionals, with an avowedly anti-sectarian and multi-ethnic outlook and an agenda of promoting capacity building among British Muslims based on business models and techniques, JustPeace, formed in September 2001. Working closely with the Muslim Parliament of Great Britain (MPGB), which after the death of its founder, Kalim Siddiqui, had moderated its views substantially, JustPeace, along with the more secular Palestinian groups like the Palestinian Solidarity Campaign, aimed explicitly to mobilise Muslims into a political alliance with the fledging SWC. Their mission statement encapsulated a new determination to find allies: 'Muslim participation in movements that campaign for freedom from oppression and injustice'. In other words, they harnessed to oppositional, humanitarian currents the mobilisation under the category 'Muslim' that arises in response to the perceived oppression of fellow believers (a recurrent pattern throughout the 1990s in the wake of the Rushdie affair, see McRoy 2001).

Another larger *ad hoc* network, Islamic Network UK (InUK), which was pivotal in making Birmingham a centre for the SWC, was, unlike JustPeace, based mainly around established Pakistani kinship networks, mobilised primarily through the mosques and the pro-Kashmiri political party, the People's Justice Party, which had won some local council seats. This fledging network, again set up in September 2001, did not fully mobilise existing networks until the second anti-war march on 18 November 2001. As with the Rushdie affair, participation was resolutely cross-sectarian, with the participation of all the main South Asian sectarian groupings. However – and here it was unlike the Rushdie affair – practical political leadership and strategy were given over to the second generation, which was more minded to seek broader alliances. A much-quoted statement by Salma Yacoub, the chairperson of Birmingham SWC, captured the new awareness in Islamic activist circles that this protest could not be seen solely as a Muslim affair:

> If only the leftists had been here today, people would have said we're all lefties. If only CND had been here, they would have said it was the middle-class élite. If it was only the Muslims, they would have called us extremists. If it was only Asians and black people, they would have said it was the ethnic minorities. Tony Blair, we are here united against this war. You cannot dismiss us all. (*Q-News*, November 2001)

Yacoub's own story of instant politicisation was made to stand in SWC publicity for the very ordinariness and spontaneity of the early days of the Coalition, and is a good example of how the Afghan conflict served to create an ephemeral, intensified sense of shared global Muslim victimhood when combined with the threat of Islamophobia at home and the need to absolve Islam from the charge of inherent violence and barbaric terror. A few days after the attacks, when Yacoub, a 30-year-old British Pakistani psychotherapist and *hijab*-wearer, was walking in central Birmingham with her three-year-old son, a man spat on her. Having never experienced such direct racism before, she 'stumbled' into activism by joining the anti-war movement in its early stages. Having never been a member of any political party, she found herself being appointed chairperson of the Birmingham chapter of the emerging SWC (*Independent*, 21 October 2001).

In early 2002 the Islamist Muslim Association of Britain (MAB) took steps to mobilise the first national march on 13 April 2002 in protest against the Israeli incursion into the Palestinian Authority-controlled town of Jenin in the West Bank.[8] This allowed the MCB (because MAB is an MCB affiliate) to take a more central role in the SWC for the first time: it was anxious not to repeat the mistake of initially misjudging the popular Muslim mood over Iraq as it had over Afghanistan. On 28 September 2002 the march against Iraq and Palestine attracted some 400,000 participants, with a full turn-out by the MCB's main supporters.[9] Significantly, Baroness Uddin and Muhammad Sarwar MP also spoke from the platform. By September 2002 there were signs that a wider opposition to the 'War on Terror' was beginning to emerge (*Independent*, 29 September 2002), which culminated in the largest public demonstration in British history, co-organised by MAB and the SWC, of between 1.5 and 2 million on the eve of the second war on Iraq in March 2003. Whereas during the Rushdie affair British Muslims had marched alone, in 2003 they had helped to create a national movement of popular protest that ironically eclipsed the particularities of their own 'ummatic' discourses in favour of the general anti-war senti-ment of middle England.

Concluding remarks

Between September 2001 and 2002 the MCB found that it could not lead Muslim 'ummatic' sentiment either for its own purposes or government's; instead, it struggled to retain its credibility with British Muslim opinion while attempting to keep channels of com-munication open with government. In the view of Yousuf Bhailok, the MCB came close to splitting apart during this period, which would have ended its political credibility (Radcliffe 2003: 83). Through this period, the MCB learned that it could not afford to ignore popular British Muslim sentiment for long, a failing it successfully addressed over the Iraq War by aligning itself with popular Muslim protest through its affiliate MAB – admittedly a less risky option given the greater groundswell of anti-war sentiment. Thus the established Islamic activist circle that came to prominence with the Rushdie affair has reasserted its primacy and eclipsed the *ad hoc* networks, which, after the *fait accompli* of the invasion of Iraq, have struggled like the rest of the SWC to maintain their political impetus. JustPeace has thrown itself into a legal campaign to free the British Guantanamo Bay prisoners and InUK has contemplated joining the new political party proposed by the anti-globalisation movement.

In the short term at least, the MCB has remained 'the only show in town' in the eyes of the government, whether for the symbolic purposes attendant on the 'politics of recognition' (Taylor 1994) or as a means to gauge Muslim reaction to impending policy, in particular to attune foreign policy rhetoric to Muslim sensibilities both at home and abroad (Radcliffe 2003: 81, 85–94). Having groomed and promoted a unified Muslim lobby for nearly a decade, the British government depicted it as part of the problem when it proved insufficiently compliant. In this sense, 'ummatic' loyalties trumped those of long-term political calculation and nationalist sentiment in time of war. In the longer term, it is possible that in the future the government will attempt to promote a secular Muslim leadership through the party political system, which might play the politics of representation in ways more amenable to its purpose.

Notes

1 Muslim representatives met Jack Straw, the Foreign Secretary, on 18 September, and David Blunkett, the Home Secretary, and Tessa Jowell, Secretary of State, Department of Culture, Media and Sport, on 24 September.

2 Unpublished letter to Tony Blair, 18 September 2001, signed by the Islamic Cultural Centre, Muslim Council of Britain, al-Khoei Foundation, Forum Against Islamophobia and Racism, Muslim Aid, Palestinian Community Association in the UK, UK Islamic Mission, and the Council of Imams and Mosques. The second largest umbrella body, the Union of Muslim Organisations, with around 214 affiliates, is noticeable by its absence.

3 The key broker for the MCB's cause outside government in 1998 was the Interfaith Network, as well as Lords Patel and Ahmed from within the Labour Party.

4 Jack Straw, 'Championing Greater Understanding between Different Faiths and Cultures', speech at the Oxford Centre for Islamic Studies, 25 January 2002.

5 Synopsis of comments in *Who Speaks for Muslims*, Channel 4, Friday 15 March 2002. Jamil Sherif, closely involved with the MCB since its inception, argues that these allegations were leaked as part of a smear campaign by the government against the Council after it came out publicly against the Afghanistan campaign (Jamil Sherif, 'The Day

Campbell Tried to Bring Muslims "on Message"', *Salaam*, created 6 August 2003, http://www.salaam.co.uk/themeofthemonth/january03/intelligence06 0803.html, accessed 16 February 2004).

6 In the end, the Prison Service decided to open the post to public competition and to create a Muslim advisory body composed of the original competing organisations.

7 By 'ummatic' is meant the attachment of Muslims to their fellow believers who form the imagined global Muslim nation (*ummah*), an attachment that can vary according to ethnic, sectarian, national and generational proclivities.

8 MAB, which is closely affiliated with the Muslim Brotherhood, was set up in 1997 to address what was seen as the failure of youth mobilisation among Jama`at-i-Islami youth groups like Young Muslims, Young Muslims Organisation and the Islamic Society of Britain, after the death in 1996 of the charismatic leader, Khurram Murad.

9 As is reflected in the line-up of Muslim speakers at the march of 28 September 2002. Trenchant and open critics of the MCB were noticeable by their absence from the platform, like Dr Gayasuddin Siddiqui of the MPGB, who, despite his early and prominent role in the national marches of autumn 2001, was consigned to addressing local rallies.

PART III

Media Representation,
Gender and Radical Islam

Chapter 8
Reading between the Lines:
Muslims and the Media

TAHIRA SAMEERA AHMED

One of the most significant developments for Muslim communities in post-September 11 Britain has been the role of the media. Extending their primary function of reporting the events of the day, the media have increasingly occupied a crucial social and intellectual space through which issues pertaining to a post-September 11 world have been articulated. Increased attention on Muslim populations, particularly those living in the West, has meant that individuals, organisations and community institutions have found themselves the focus of political and public interest and scrutiny. Much of this interest has been evident in the various forms of media in Britain and around the world.

The growing salience of media in the development of attitudes, perceptions and received wisdom is inescapable in contemporary society. Media occupy a more prominent position in our social and cultural landscapes and their ubiquity has become a normal part of our lives. In addition, community or particularistic[1] media are becoming especially important in providing minority groups with their own voices and alternative sources of information. The development of Muslim media over the past decade is testimony to this, and has become especially significant since the events of September 2001, as well as during more recent geopolitical events such as the war in Afghanistan and the invasion of Iraq.

This chapter aims to present a brief overview of the Muslim press in Britain and proceeds to examine response to Muslim print media among young British South Asian Muslims. In order to do so, the chapter combines two data sets:[2] one pertains to Muslim media and the other to a group of consumers. The data on Muslim publications give a brief political economy of the British Muslim press, outline aims and objectives of editors and provide examples from selected Muslim publications of how the events of September 11 were covered. The second data set comprises material derived from interviews with young Muslims and examines how the media are developing a sense of British Muslim identity as well as facilitating other developments in the lives of young British Muslims.

An important issue following September 11 has been the representation of Islam and Muslims in various media channels. Research has suggested that media portrayal after the attacks was responsible not only for generating a negative perception of Muslims but also for perpetuating and helping to legitimise subsequent political ideologies, as well as inciting attacks against Muslims (see, for example, Bunglawala 2002). Though these negative images continue to be of concern to Muslim communities, this chapter does not attempt to provide a description or analysis of media representations. However, mainstream media coverage of Islam and Muslims forms an important backdrop against which the current work needs to be understood.[3]

Britain's Muslim press

The existence of a Muslim press in Britain is a relatively recent phenomenon, although it precedes the events of September 2001 by many years. A small number of publications have been in circulation for many years,[4] but the majority of publications have a shorter history. The events of late 1989 onwards with respect to the Muslim community, specifically the reaction to Salman Rushdie's book, *The Satanic Verses*, and the first military action in the Gulf, were the background events that framed the early life of much of the Muslim press. The demand for print media in English grew as this became the preferred language for an increasing number of Muslims. Newspapers were often written in the mother tongue (for example *The Jang* and *Awaz* in Urdu), effectively cutting out many second-generation Muslims[5] who, although they had a basic command of spoken Urdu, Punjabi or Bengali, were often not fluent in reading or writing these languages. As the Muslim communities developed a more distinctly religious identity, alternatives to mainstream media were sought through which to express this identity, and Muslim media become an important means by which information was obtained and ideas developed. Those with a desire to maintain or even strengthen cultural and religious identities saw strong and vibrant media as one way to achieve this.

In expressing their aims and objectives for setting up publications, editors noted that the intention was to produce a publication – title, content, outlook – that reflected strongly the Muslim or Islamic identity of both its producers and its readers. Editors were also consciously distinguishing themselves from the British *Asian* media. The nature of the British Muslim population meant that a large proportion of Muslims were South Asian, but despite this fact the publications wanted a strictly *Muslim* identity, encouraged by both readers and editors. Certain aims and objectives for setting up their respective publications were shared by all editors: for example, the gap seen in mainstream media in reporting on Muslim issues and the need for a perspective more aware of and sympathetic to Muslims. A combination of the demand from within the Muslim community and editors' own convictions brought about the realisation of Muslim media. One editor said:

> We were aiming our magazine at young second-generation British Muslims and these are the people who have made up their mind that Britain is their country, who want to come to terms with their lives and the fact that they are British and they are Muslims and we wanted to capture the day-to-day struggle about each aspect of their lives.... (*Q-News*)

When the editor of *The Invitation* was asked to describe the magazine he said:

> We started [in 1989] to run a study circle ... with the idea to attract young Muslim boys and to also support them with their school work and with that came other *dawah*[6] opportunities like holding regular quarterly youth camps and from that sprang the idea of actually putting things on paper ... the idea was really to reach the young people who couldn't read *Urdu* ... our priority has always been Muslim youngsters.

And the editor of *Impact International* said:

> This magazine started about 29 years ago so it has evolved over a period of time.... In the beginning, we started with a very basic agenda of trying to remove so-called misunderstanding and present an Islamic viewpoint but I think as we proceeded we realised...what we are trying to do [is] we are trying to equip and educate our readers with facts and information and understanding of what's going on in the world so that

when they go out into society they are able to explain to others, they are wiser than otherwise.

A direct reflection of the changes that were taking place in the Muslim communities in the late 1980s and early 1990s can be seen in trends in the media. Since 1989 there has been a substantial increase in the number and variety of publications. In addition the existing publications have started to discuss topics other than religion, such as politics and social issues.

> Before they would hardly discuss about issues like domestic violence or whatever now they are more open, you will even find religious publications, that is community publications, discussing these issues because they have seen that *Muslim News* and *Q-News* are discussing ... and you've also grown in size and in confidence as well. (*Muslim News*)

The editor of *Impact* predicted that a greater diversity in Muslim media was something to look forward to as the communities themselves contained many different aspects that needed to be expressed.

> I think there is a great proliferation of house magazines, societies have their own journals and magazines and handouts, I think that's a good training ground for people to do their own thing.... It's a factor of time, in the course of time, the Muslim media are also going to be part of the mainstream, I don't think this so-called ghetto situation is a permanent situation, the difference is that Muslim media primarily address a Muslim readership so it creates an automatic division but later on I think this is going to change. (*Impact*)

Clearly the contents and outlook of each publication are determined by its background, the ideological or political stance it takes, its editor/writers and its expected readership. They are also determined by whether the producer's aim is to provide a current affairs (political) source of information or is more concerned to address social and cultural issues. All publications tend to advertise events taking place around the country aimed at young Muslims, to have book reviews and also to publicise charity appeals (mainly by Muslim charity/relief organisations). The range of issues covered by the publications varies and like mainstream media they have regular features: editorials, news, book and conference reviews, profiles, columns, spiritual sections, question and answer forums, matrimonial advice, jobs and community advertising are among these. Most publications (excluding specialist ones) tend to combine current affairs with social and religious issues – the latter category offering faith or belief topics, explanations of the Qur'an and Hadith,[7] 'how to' guides on certain practices in Islam and reminders of special dates in the Islamic calendar. Social and cultural matters relating to Muslims in Britain and more immediate problems in the community were also a focus. The target audience of many of the publications tends to be young Muslims and therefore it is common to find coverage of issues affecting this age group. Frequency of publication (weekly, monthly, bi-monthly, etcetera) automatically influences the currency of topics addressed. At this fairly early stage of development of Muslim media – some publications are barely a dozen years old – much of the focus is solely on Muslim issues. The editors themselves want to expand the topics they cover and to aim at being a Muslim version of a broadsheet or magazine, so that they are not always tackling negative issues or issues of concern to the Muslim communities alone. To this extent the editors are conscious of their limited niche within the media environment – providing news from different sources, and on topics which mainstream media would not necessarily cover, for a clearly defined audience.

Certain publications have arisen out of already established groups or movements – for example, *Crescent International* closely follows trends stimulated by the Iranian Revolution – and the ethos of the publication will reflect its provenance. *The Invitation* ('The Family Magazine'), as its subtitle indicates, is aimed at young families and the simpler writing style reflects this. The niche market of *Q-News* appears to be young, professional Muslims seeking a publication that addresses relevant social and cultural issues. The recent expansion of *Q-News* into the North American market[8] also indicates that it is targeting young diaspora Muslims in the West, presumably having identified a commonality between the European and North American markets.

The diversity of Muslim media, illustrated by the different kinds of publication available, reflects the variety of opinions, organisations and perspectives within the British Muslim population. Identifications with various ways of thinking and approaches to Islam – different political inclinations, *dawah*-oriented outlooks, variants of academic or spiritual Islam – are facilitated and reinforced by different publications. Certain fundamental aspects of identifying oneself with Islam are shared by almost all groups of Muslims, but there is also diversity, as in any other community.

Covering September 11 – the Muslim press perspective

The coverage given to the attacks of September 11 was widespread and diverse in nature, in some places basic and stereotypical and in others analytical and challenging. Following the events there was clearly an intensification in anti-Islamic discourse in both media and academia (Allen 2001). Many of the commentaries which focused on Islam and Muslims were analytical in their nature, debating either the reasons for the attack, the situation in Muslim countries or foreign policy issues which may have prompted the attack. The role of the media cannot be underestimated in these situations: they provide a fair proportion of the understanding people have and, at times when there is such an intense focus on Muslims, the information circulated within mass media is particularly significant in developing attitudes and opinions. Significantly, much of the media negativity was accompanied by verbal and physical abuse of Muslims, including knife and baseball-bat attacks, as well as arson and bomb threats against mosques and Muslim organisations. The Runnymede Trust's Commission on British Muslims and Islamophobia felt it necessary to publish a resource booklet, *Addressing Prejudice and Islamophobia*, as a result of the reactions in Britain to the WTC attacks. It cites examples of Islamophobic behaviour and attitudes in the days after the attack and also provides guidelines and resources on how to deal with the situation and combat prejudice. There has been documentation of the repercussions of the attacks on Muslims here and in other countries, especially the USA (Runnymede Trust 2001; Sheriff 2001a).

The European Monitoring Centre on Racism and Xenophobia (EUMC) analysed the negative impact on attitudes towards Islam and Muslims in the 15 EU member states following September 11; it specifically examined the role of media (Allen and Nielsen 2002). The report found that, although it was difficult to pinpoint with accuracy whether the overall impact of media had been negative or positive (it conceded that the role of the media is always contentious and debatable), it was possible to highlight instances of sensationalism and stereotyping in the media coverage of almost all member states (including the UK) to a greater or lesser degree. As media attention on Muslims was intense, with debates on electronic media and analyses in newspapers, websites and academic articles, keeping abreast was a top priority for many Muslim organisations, who analysed and responded to a plethora of articles and programmes.

Media coverage was extensive not only in mainstream but also in Muslim media, with the cover story of many publications being the New York attacks. The articles in Muslim publications were predominantly concerned with the Islamic standpoint on perpetrating such actions, the condemnation of the attack by British Muslims, the reactions against Muslims in the UK and the US (actual incidents that had taken place as well as predictions of what the events would mean for Muslims in the future) and analyses of the possible reasons for the attack. An important role for Muslim media was to furnish readers with more in-depth and alternative analyses of September 11. Whether the editors felt this would counteract negative portrayals in the mainstream media is difficult to ascertain; obviously, few non-Muslims in the mainstream media audience were likely to access Muslim media. Although the audiences are not the same, the need for balanced reporting of the events remained, with background information and in-depth analyses presenting an alternative discourse to that circulating in the popular domain.

In order to illustrate how some British Muslim publications reported on the events of September 11, a summary of articles and information in issues published following September 11 is given in Table 8.1. Unsurprisingly, almost all media focused on the event of September 11 and Muslim publications were no exception. In fact, it can be argued that Muslim media were particularly concerned to cover the issue because of the immediate focus on Muslims that resulted from the attacks. As Table 8.1 shows, apart from reporting on what actually happened, many articles dealt solely with the response to the attacks from the perspectives of Islam and Muslims. It appears that the press took it upon itself to act as a spokesperson for the Muslim communities in condemning the act and expressing sympathy for the victims. This initiative was no doubt a consequence of genuine feelings about what had happened but perhaps also a result of what editors perceived to be expected of them as voices of their communities. In the same way prominent Muslim spokespeople (including religious and community leaders) came forward to express their regret at what had happened and to clarify the Islamic perspective on such actions; the Muslim media, too, carried many such statements. Indeed, they were among the main vehicles through which the spokespeople expressed themselves and attempted to lessen the damage done to Islam and Muslims by negative reporting.

The role of Muslim press appeared to be of particular significance after September 11. It provided a platform for discussion not only

Table 8.1 Coverage following 9/11 in selected Muslim publications

Publication	Cover	Articles (1)	Articles (2)	General Summary
Q-News (1) October 2001; (2) November 2001)	1 End of Innocence. 2 The Call to Peace.	There Are No Muslim Terrorists. After the Fall. Islam Is Peace, not Terror. What Does Islam Say? A Time for Introspection. The American Tragedy: A Scholar's Opinion. Report from Ground Zero.	War Veterans Fight for Peace. Anthrax a Domestic Crime, Say US Officials. Q-Poll: Readers' Survey. Ready for Jihad: Young, Muslim and Angry. A United Call for Peace, Anti-War Movement.	1 Editorial dedicated to the event and its impact. Almost entire first issue dedicated to 9/11 analyses. 2 Rather fewer pieces looking at 9/11 but still a feature.
The Muslim News (1) 28 September 2001; (2) 26 October 2001	1 Outpouring of Muslim Grief. 2 Mosques Firebombed, Muslims Assaulted, British Muslims under Siege	Outpouring of Muslim Grief. Mosques Firebombed, Muslims Assaulted, British Muslims under Siege. The Good, the Bad and the Ugly. North American Muslims Face Backlash. Trapped in Manhattan. Terrorism Alien to Islam, says Blair. The USA, Israel and the 'War on Terrorism'.	The War to Win Hearts and Minds of Muslims. Israel and UN Resolutions. Demonstration against [Afghanistan] Bombing. Healing the Wounds. Casualties of War. Incitement to Religious Hatred May Be Used against Muslims. A war on Terrorism? But What Is Terrorism?	1 Editorial asks: is war on terrorism or Muslims? Backlash against Muslims in the aftermath of NY attacks (letters). Almost every page (12 page newspaper) featured articles about 9/11. 2. Considerable number of articles on 9/11 but also focus on Afghanistan and implications of 'War on Terror'.

Publication	Cover headline			Coverage
Crescent International (1) September 16–30 2001; (2) October 1–15 2001	1 Whoever Committed the Crime, Muslims Face the Consequences. 2 Afghanistan and the World Await US's Response to Air Attacks	[Edition was printed after 9/11. However a special editorial supplement was attached which analysed the attacks]	Analysing the Aftermath of the American Attacks. US Anger Turns to Blatant Strategic Opportunism. Palestine 'Ceasefire' as Arafat Buckles under Israeli Pressure. Muslims Come under Attack as Islamophobic Bigotry Sweeps US.	1 Various articles on international geopolitical issues. 2 Wide coverage of international issues but with several articles discussing the attacks on 9/11.
Impact International (October 2001)	Tyranny of Terror	A Terrorist Disaster. War against Civilisation. Most Hideous, Most Spooky. Who Done It? Who Knows Who? Understanding Afghanistan.		Extensive coverage of international issues and regular features. Analysis of Afghanistan.
Khilafah 1. October 2001; 2. November 2001	1. [No words, just image of burning WTC] 2. Terror War	USA – Pirate of Land, Sea and Air. The Politics of Terrorism. The Treachery of the Muslim Rulers. How Should Muslims View the Attacks in America? Where Are the Terrorists?	The Truth behind US Colonialism in Central Asia. Musharraf's Choice. The Campaign to Subvert Islam. What Can Muslims in the West Do to Establish the *khilafah*? Elections in Bangladesh.	Summary of world events. Critical articles about geopolitical situation especially focused on 'Western domination' of the world.
The Invitation (October 2001)	Muslims Against Terrorism	Rioting Asian Youth. Hope, not Bullets. Drugs – a Growing Problem. From the Ashes.		Only one article relating to 9/11. Greater focus on riots in North-West in 2001. Regular features such as Q & A, Qu'ran and Hadith, letters, poems, etc.

Note: 1 and 2 – First and second issue following 9/11

within the established readership but arguably opened new avenues for debate amongst those who would not normally access ethnic or religious media. The exchange between mainstream and alternative press was also clear as writers from the Muslim press were invited to write in the mainstream press.[9] Although events in the US were the stimulus and main focus of the media, they also provided an opportunity to consider other matters of significance to Britain's Muslims.

Consuming the British Muslim press

Research has shown that the role and use of alternative and community media amongst minority ethnic communities is considerable under 'normal' circumstances (Dayan 1998; Husband 2002). Such extraordinary events as those of September 11 can only serve to heighten the importance of these media, not only as sources of information but also as channels through which minority communities express their views and anxieties.

In the research I conducted, a number of reasons were given for reading Muslim publications. These are given in Table 8.2. It would be fair to say that the most frequently stated reason (national and international Muslim current affairs) would have increased considerably at the time of September 11, and in subsequent days. The number of non-Muslims accessing Muslim media would also have increased at this time, including the use of Muslim publications by the government to communicate its views and responses to the Muslim public.[10]

Table 8.2 Reasons for reading publications

Reason	Frequency
Muslim current affairs (national and international)	47
Religious knowledge	21
Interesting news/articles	9
Supporting Muslim media	7
News from alternative perspective	5
Sense of community/unity	4
Disillusionment with mainstream media	3
Reviews	2
Academic study	2

Note: Respondents often gave more than one reason.[11]

Accessing Muslim media facilitates the desire to keep informed about fellow Muslims, feel part of a larger group and keep in touch with what is happening in the rest of the Muslim world, all of which leads to a greater sense of belonging to the global *Ummah*. The importance of this belonging and identification with the global community was noticed by Jacobson (1998) and Vertovec (1998) in their studies of young Muslims. Anderson's (1983) concept of an 'imagined community' is also evoked in people's reasons for using the media, and increased awareness means identification with other Muslims is stronger. In this way the media provide a focus that gives a sense of belonging to the British Muslim community, perhaps in the absence of any other focus such as a representative group or person. If a sense of community and belonging existed prior to the advent of media, the media have increased this sense, although it has by no means permeated all spheres of the Muslim population.

In general, there was a consensus among the young South Asian Muslims interviewed in this study that Muslim media had great potential to develop further, encompass more information and appeal to a larger number of people. What already existed was appreciated and it was seen as a positive way to initiate debate within Muslim communities that could also extend into mainstream society. Most young people agreed that there need to be more Muslim media ventures and that those existing currently need more publicity. The purpose of setting up Muslim publications was seen as to educate the Muslim community about Islamic issues as well as giving information about what was happening in the *Ummah* across the world. Another reason was thought to have been to counteract the negative portrayal of Islam and Muslims in the mainstream Western media. It is a reasonable prediction that scepticism about mainstream media may encourage the use of alternative sources, especially Muslim media, by young Muslims.

One young woman commented that because many of the Muslim publications were written by Muslims who were born and brought up in Britain it made it simpler to relate to the issues they had reported. Writers and editors were often second- and third-generation Muslims who were acquainted with the British lifestyle and could communicate with their audience in an effective way. Thus, the appeal to young Muslims seemed greater as people from their generation – with similar experiences, similar aspirations and empathy with the problems and challenges they face – are the ones constructing a discourse on British Muslim life.

Muslim press – not just a good read

What do Muslim media mean to young British South Asian Muslims? Both prior to September 11 and especially following this date, Muslim media appear to be performing various functions for their readers. This was evident in the research study I conducted and can be seen from current developments within the Muslim media environment. Here 'media' are defined in the broadest sense to include, as well as the traditional print and electronic forms, the new audio-visual information technology; social and cultural events and activities; events aimed at learning and acquiring knowledge; the exchange of political information; and expressions of identity. The functions and influences of Muslim media identified in the research include: belonging and identity, knowledge and learning; and 'community' – as well as other aspects of media relating to the lives of respondents.

One of the most pertinent issues that September 11 brought to the fore was that of being *British* and *Muslim*. If this was something that previously had interested academics, policy makers, the general public and the media, now it became more significant as a result of September 2001: the loyalty of Muslims and the security of Britain were being questioned. In order to capture how Muslim media are being used to articulate a Muslim identity, or at least aspects of a Muslim identity, the survey asked specific questions on the sense of belonging gained through media and how this helps readers to think about their own identity. Many respondents noted how the media enabled them to identify with and feel part of a Muslim community, helping to strengthen their identity as Muslims. In some responses there was a clear distinction between feeling part of a British community, on the one hand, and a global *ummah* on the other. The sense from some responses seemed to be that the global *ummah* offered a stronger identity than the local or national community.

> Muslim media have immensely developed my sense of belonging to an *ummah* as articles on Islam are unifying as they entail Islamic beliefs. I don't think the sense of belonging to a British Muslim community is all that evident, as Muslim media are too intent on showing the pitfalls of young Muslims living in Britain.
>
> There are a number of Muslim newspapers I've seen and I feel they strengthen the Muslim community here and inform people about what's happening and what they should do.

The concept of identity linked very strongly to knowing about other Muslims and their conditions of life. Being informed about Muslims around the world seemed to have a direct link to how people identified themselves as Muslims.

> I certainly feel part of an active community. I feel less isolated, better informed about Islamic issues.

> It has helped me to understand a Muslim perspective on issues and made me more confident to be a Muslim and has reinforced my identity as a result.

For many, their identity has been influenced directly by the existence of Muslim media. From the responses it would seem that the Muslim media are indeed playing a role in establishing and developing a sense of being a British Muslim. This sense encompasses beliefs and practices and various elements of socio-cultural, political and economic issues affecting Muslims as citizens of the UK.

Muslim media are also playing a key role in developing and disseminating Islamic knowledge to Muslims, particularly in diaspora communities (Mandaville 2001). Not only have young Muslims utilised Muslim media as an alternative to mainstream media but they are actively seeking out Muslim media to fulfil the requirement of obtaining religious knowledge. Almost every Muslim publication is concerned with imparting some kind of Islamic knowledge to its readers, though the specific outlook varies from one publication to another. For some respondents the presence of Muslim media was essential in providing them with Islamic knowledge, and the easy access to and the informal style of many publications made obtaining information more flexible than through structured learning. Actively seeking knowledge – through literature, electronic sources, events or more traditional styles of learning – is a strong symbol of the assertion of Muslim identity. The emphasis placed on seeking knowledge in Islam manifests itself through this proactive attitude towards learning. This focus on Islamic learning is also visible in academia, with organisations emerging to deal with the roles and responsibilities of Muslim academics, researchers and students.

Apart from reporting on events around the country and globally, Muslim media work to influence and shape the way Muslim communities themselves develop. Not only does the content of a Muslim publication set a particular agenda, but the style of the publication also has an influence on how the readers frame issues. For those readers who are actively looking to Muslim media as their main source of information and as a way through which to measure their own opinions, their presence is vital. Using the media as a stimulus for discussions with other Muslims is one way of developing concepts and issues in the community. As the concept of British Muslim identity is often discussed, readers are automatically focused on this issue and by reading about the experiences and possibilities of being a British Muslim, readers can relate to others in their community. Cases of discrimination, relevant political activity, issues of education, employment and similar concerns are shared, and the media highlight these experiences to reflect the reality of living in Britain as Muslims. The shared experiences portrayed in the media then lead to a perception of shared identity, as Muslims in various parts of Britain are tackling similar issues and facing similar challenges. While raising awareness, the Muslim media are also contributing to a sense of belonging to a particular community, and in this way enhancing a British Muslim identity.

An entire social, cultural and educational infrastructure appears to be developing amongst young Muslims that provides 'Islamic' alternatives in areas of entertainment and social life, but more importantly news and knowledge acquisition. By furnishing themselves with information about fellow Muslims, readers of Muslim publications internalise the feeling of community or belonging thus created (through both production and consumption). This belonging includes local and national Muslim groups but also extends to the global Muslim *ummah*, going beyond simple diaspora connections (mainly to South Asia and other South Asian Muslims around the world for those interviewed in this research).

The use of alternative media was something which gained great significance following September 11, as alternatives to mainstream opinion were sought from various sources, especially the Internet. For many of the reasons cited above (see Table 8.2), including mistrust and cynicism towards mainstream media, young Muslims actively sought alternative sources of information about the events of September 11 and after.[12] Their search took in not only domestic sources but international news media and satellite channels, including *Al Jazeera*. As well as questioning the news media and their coverage of both pre- and post-September 11 issues, Muslim readers were critical of government reactions to the event. A survey conducted by the *Muslim News* following the September 11 attacks highlighted the fact that British Muslims were 'comfortable with being British but not with British foreign policy' (Sheriff 2001b). It asked questions on the reaction to the attack in New York, with 36 per cent saying they thought the attack was a moral outrage and 52 per cent responding to the news with a combination of sadness and understanding. The notion of understanding here is not to be confused with condoning, but points to the argument of commentators such as Robert Fisk that the attacks were 'not mindless and without a sense of cause, however misguided' (*ibid.*: 12). Seventy-nine per cent said they disagreed with the bombing of Afghanistan and felt there should have been a better way to bring Osama bin Laden to justice, following a fair trial. Sheriff (2001b) comments that

> it is clear from the survey, which is at best a 'temperature gauging poll' that most Muslims are comfortable with their citizenship but, like many in the mainstream community, there is a strong element of dissent on the government's conduct of international affairs and this dissent is clearly informed by a perception of the reality of double standards. (*Ibid.*)

Respondents to the *Muslim News* survey said they would support tough action against Osama bin Laden if there had been similar action against perpetrators of atrocities in Kashmir, Palestine and Bosnia.

A similar survey was carried out by *Q-News*. Of 1,312 people surveyed, 29 per cent thought the war against Afghanistan was in fact a war against Islam and Muslims; 44 per cent thought it was an attempt to impose an America-friendly government in Afghanistan; and 18 per cent thought both statements were true (*Q-News* 2001a). Seventy-eight per cent of those surveyed thought the food drops on Afghanistan were part of a propaganda war rather than a genuine humanitarian effort, and there seemed to be a general cynicism about the aims and effectiveness of the war. This was echoed in a series of interviews with three young Muslim men who talked about whether they would go to fight in Afghanistan, whether they thought Osama bin Laden was responsible and how they felt this situation affected them as Muslims (*Q-News* 2001b). Although the men interviewed did not support the attacks in the US and sympathised with the victims' families, they thought the reaction was unjust and that the underlying motives were related to oil resources in the region as well as action against Muslims. The questioning and criticism of official statements and sources of information have encouraged the use of Muslim media as it provides a means through which to articulate alternative perspectives relevant to Britain's Muslims.

Conclusion

The emergence of distinct Muslim media has provided a focal point through which Muslims, and particularly young Muslims, can find expression for their concerns and aspirations. Enthusiasm for Muslim media demonstrates the need for a public discourse on Islam and Muslims and Muslim media; the press in particular has articulated a British Muslimness that readers find increasingly relevant to their lives. The numerous forms of community media, both new and old, are not only enabling Muslims to explore new ways of expressing their convictions on Islam and what it means to be Muslim, but creating new hybrid cultures that merge together aspects of South Asian culture, Islam and British cultural norms. These in turn are being complemented by increasing information about Islam at a global level and giving rise to new relationships between young British Muslims and their environment. The role of Muslim media in articulating the concerns of British Muslims and serving as an apparatus through which to voice the diverse opinions within Muslim communities looks set to increase in significance. Previously this role was about developing and sustaining new identifications with Islam and forming concepts such as the British Muslim identity. With increasing attention now on Muslim publications and other information channels, the responsibility of media as 'spokespersons' for Muslim communities will no doubt become greater.

In the light of the events of September 2001, and indeed more recent events such as the military action in Afghanistan and Iraq and the continuing 'War on Terrorism', the new spaces that are being created by Muslim media are crucial. These spaces are enabling Muslims to express their views and debate issues that are of concern to them, while also anticipating that some of the discourses present in Muslim media may filter through to mainstream media audiences.[13] British South Asian Muslims, especially the younger generation, are using various media channels, including not only new information technologies but also social and cultural activities, to exchange information and disseminate knowledge about their experiences of living as Muslims in Britain. Some of these activities are aimed at including the non-Muslim population with the sole objective of trying to dispel the myths and inaccurate information about Islam and Muslims that has circulated as a result of irresponsible and sensationalist media representations.

Many aspects of life have changed for Muslims in Britain, in the West and indeed worldwide, following the occurrences of September 11. Changes at structural and institutional levels, such as the introduction of new laws and bills, have impacted on the lives of Muslims, but in many ways these have been less intrusive than the overall impact of media on British Muslims on a day-to-day basis. The perceptions and attitudes held by their non-Muslim counterparts, the impact these have had on their relationships, Muslims' own experiences and expectations of living as a religious minority in the West and the future of multi-religious coexistence, are all issues which will continue to be of concern. The media will undoubtedly be one of the most significant arenas in which these concerns are debated and recorded and the Muslim media occupies the primary position in articulating the standpoint of British Muslims.

Notes

1 Dayan (1998).
2 Data collected for doctoral research (Ahmed 2003). This consisted of eight semi-structured group interviews with a total of 27 young South Asian Muslims and editors of five Muslim publications. Interviews were conducted between March and August 2000 and were analysed using Atlas Ti.
3 Various studies have been conducted on the negative representation of Islam and Muslims in the media even prior to September 11, see, for example, Abbas (2000), Poole (2002) and the Runnymede Trust (1997). These were supplemented by a number of other studies following September 11, for example, EUMC (2002) and Runnymede Trust (2001).
4 For example, *Impact International* began in the early 1970s.
5 The majority of my respondents were South Asian Muslims; therefore I am concentrating on this section of the Muslim population whilst acknowledging the great ethnic diversity of British Muslims.
6 *Dawah* is the Arabic word for invitation to or propagation of Islam.
7 *Hadith* literature relates to the sayings and practices of the Holy Prophet Mohammed (peace be upon him).
8 First editions were launched at the beginning of 2002.
9 The editors of *Muslim News* and *Q-News* wrote articles in the *Independent* and *Guardian* newspapers.

10   For example, statements by politicians, including the Prime Minister, in the *Muslim News*.

11   This data was collected from a Muslim media survey distributed through four publications to the interviewees. Of a total of 1,500 surveys distributed, 77 were completed and returned.

12   See *After September 11th. TV News and Transnational Audiences.* http://www.afterseptember11.tv/

13   This is already happening to a degree, with journalists linked to Muslim publications contributing to broadsheets such as the *Guardian* and *Independent* newspapers. In some instances, Muslim media are being reported on by mainstream press (see Vallely 2000).

Chapter 9
Educating Muslim Girls:
Do Mothers Have Faith in the State Sector?

AUDREY OSLER AND ZAHIDA HUSSAIN

In 1998 Islamia Primary School in Brent and Al-Furqan School in Birmingham became the first two Islamic schools in Britain to receive state funding. The campaign for state funding of Muslim schools has received a significant amount of media attention. There has been considerable debate and speculation about the motivation of those who run such schools and about those who send their children to them. Since September 11, a general distrust of Muslims and growth in Islamophobia has made it all the more important that Muslims and non-Muslims engage in a dialogue about what it means to be a British Muslim and about what is an appropriate education for children from Muslim backgrounds (Coles 2004). Our research, which examines the attitudes of Muslim women to their daughters' education in Islamic and non-Islamic schools, is a contribution to that dialogue.

Legislation introduced in 1993 had paved the way for Muslims, non-conformist Christians, and other religious groups running independent schools to opt in to the state sector. The decision to provide state funding for Islamic schools in Britain was not therefore a radical shift in policy. Across Europe a precedent had already been set, with state support already provided in a number of countries, including the Republic of Ireland (Osler and Vincent 2002). The Labour government's more recent commitment to expanding the number of faith schools has, nevertheless, proved to be controversial. Some of the opposition comes from those opposed to the state funding of any faith schools, whether these be Christian, Jewish, Islamic, Sikh or any other religion. Those who adopt this line and who argue for an exclusively secular system rarely address the practical issues arising from the long-standing engagement of the Christian churches in the history of mass schooling in Britain.[1]

The 1988 Education Reform Act (ERA) confirms the 1944 Education Act which requires schools to conduct collective acts of worship, but also allows withdrawal from such worship on conscientious grounds. ERA specified that the daily act of collective worship be 'wholly or mainly of a Christian character' (DES 1989: para 1). This clause and the one requiring that any new syllabus of religious education should 'reflect the fact that the religious traditions of Great Britain are in the main Christian whilst taking account of the teaching and practices of the other principle religions represented in Britain' (DES 1989: para 3) have wide-reaching implications for Muslims and other religious faiths. Although parents can opt for withdrawal or alternative provision, the implied superiority of Christianity serves to reinforce a political climate in which cultural, racial and religious difference is emphasised at the expense of notions of common humanity and shared human rights.

Reports of riots in a number of English northern towns in the summer of 2001 were quickly overshadowed by September 11. Nevertheless, they highlighted the segregated schooling practices that separate white British youth from South Asian British Muslim youth in those towns and the anger that young people from both communities felt at their marginalisation. Equally importantly, they highlighted significant and disturbing levels of Islamophobia within particular white communities. Public and media debate about the state funding of Muslim schools has taken place in a climate where everyday expressions of hostility to Muslims are commonplace.

Education, Islam and women's perspectives

Most Muslim parents in Britain educate their sons and daughters in the state sector. Opposition to Islamic schools has been expressed by those who argue that such schools are likely to offer limited opportunities, particularly to girls. Yet rarely are the views of Muslim girls and women canvassed. This may be explained in terms of the nature of anti-Muslim prejudice, which tends to present Islam as monolithic rather than diverse. If the assumption is made that all Muslims think alike, then there is no need to identify the particular perspectives of Muslim women. Furthermore, if Muslim women are seen as disadvantaged and downtrodden, then it may be assumed that they will not have independent voices worth canvassing. There are some genuine concerns from within the Muslim tradition and beyond that Islamic schools restrict girls' opportunities, but these schools are currently under-researched in respect of the equal rights of girls (Haw 1994). Another, parallel, concern is that some state schools may fail to enable British South Asian girls, particularly Muslims, to fulfil their potential, with some teachers believing that to do so would be to place young women in direct conflict with their parents (Osler and Vincent 2003).

This chapter reports on research into the school experiences of British Muslims. In particular it reports on a study of Muslim mothers and the reasons behind their decisions to send their daughters to either an Islamic or a state primary school (Osler and Hussain 1995). It is informed by life history research on South Asian Muslim women teachers in Britain (Osler 1997; 2003). It considers how mothers' concerns have been influenced by September 11 and its aftermath, particularly by policies and practices that are explained in terms of the 'War on Terrorism'.

A series of interviews were arranged to establish twenty Muslim mothers' views of their daughters' schooling. Half of the women were sending their daughters to an Islamic school for girls; the children of the other half were attending a mixed state primary school. The two schools are situated in a West Midlands city, about half a mile from each other, and all the families in the research sample lived within a two-mile radius of the schools. Mothers of daughters aged seven to nine years were chosen in an attempt to separate out the issue of single-sex schooling, which we believed would be a greater concern amongst parents once their daughters reached puberty (Ashraf 1985, 1993; Sarwar 1991). At the time of our initial study, in the mid-1990s, the school received no state funding.

The Islamic school to which half the mothers sent their daughters was relatively new. At the time of the research there was a total of 75 pupils on the roll. The school catered for children aged four to ten years and had the equivalent of six full-time teachers. All but one of these were qualified; the exception was a teacher of Islamic studies and the Qur'an, who was employed as an instructor since her qualifications, obtained in Egypt, were not recognised in Britain. The school had been subject to government inspection and enjoyed full recognition. It aimed to teach the national curriculum together with Islamic studies, Arabic and the Qur'an. All parents paid fees, although some 60 per cent of families received charitable support and were paying at a subsidised rate. The school brochure outlined the school's philosophy:

> To encourage high academic standards in an Islamic environment so that the girls leave the school with a sense of responsibility towards the Muslim Community and the society at large.

We set out to investigate the factors that influence the choice of school, focusing particularly on the issue of values, the mothers' perceptions of the relationship between the religious education and training provided at home, and the values taught at school. Mothers were asked to comment on the skills their daughters were learning at school and their relevance for life in the twenty-first century. They were also invited to compare their daughters' education with their own and to give their opinions on an appropriate education for life in a multicultural and multi-faith society. We anticipated that parents' own educational experiences would play an important part in the choices they made for their daughters and so mothers were encouraged to talk about their own schooling and, where appropriate, that of their partners.

Education and fundamentalism

Fundamentalists in any religion tend to be viewed with suspicion, but this applies particularly to Muslims. Islamic schools are regularly equated with fundamentalism, and the term 'Muslim fundamentalist' has been used in the British media to represent a range of 'extremist' groups with varied political agendas (Runnymead Trust 1997). Today the term 'fundamentalist' is regularly used both as a form of abuse and as a synonym for terrorist. The tendency to equate Islam as the enemy has grown since September 11 and the development of the subsequent 'War on Terror'. As one education researcher notes: 'Muslims may call themselves "orthodox" or "liberal" but, from my research, never "fundamentalist"'. That word is seen as pejorative, and primarily used by the media in the wake of Islamophobia (Parker-Jenkins 1994). Legislation relating to the detention of suspected terrorists who are not British nationals and immigration and security practices that may disproportionately affect British Muslims have come under criticism. Such practices can undermine the individual sense of belonging.

The vast majority of Muslims, world-wide and in Britain, are Sunnis. One of the central beliefs of Sunni fundamentalists is:

> to recapture the essence of one's faith one needs to return to the source, namely the Qur'an and prophet Muhammad as the perfect model of a Muslim in personal life and public affairs and to reject all historical accretions and contemporary norms as un-Islamic. (Modood 1992: 265)

The headteacher of the Islamic school in this study recognises that ancient religious texts remain open to interpretation. She argues for the individual's freedom to interpret the source and to practise religion according to personal understanding; she sees understanding as the key. It is critical that each Muslim accepts individual responsibility and understanding in order to avoid political manipulation.

In encouraging 'high academic standards in an Islamic environment' the school recognises a responsibility for both the general and the religious education of pupils. It seeks to inform them about the principles of their faith and to offer a broad education that will enhance their future educational opportunities. Some Muslim educators, including the headteacher, argue that Islam offers freedom for women. The school aims to be liberating rather than oppressive, asserting those rights that have long been curtailed by custom and by a lack of understanding of Islam amongst men and amongst women themselves.

Women Against Fundamentalism, which encompasses a range of women's groups and individuals from different religious backgrounds (including Christian, Hindu, Jewish and Muslim), has been active in opposing demands for faith schools. While 'members see the exclusive focus of the media on Muslim fundamentalism as part of the racism of British society' they object to demands for state aid from Muslim and other faith groups, arguing that the purpose of Islamic girls' schools is 'to bring up girls to be dutiful wives and mothers' and that they 'offer inadequate facilities for achieving academic qualifications'. They argue that the British state should be secularised, bringing an end to state support for all religious schools (Yuval-Davis 1992).

Mothers' own education

Of the ten mothers whose daughters were attending the state primary school, all but one was of South Asian heritage, the tenth being African-Caribbean. Eight families originated in Pakistan, and one in East Africa. All but two had completed their secondary education, either in Pakistan or the UK, and three had experience of higher education.[2]

The women who had selected the Islamic school were a culturally heterogeneous group: five of the ten were converts to Islam, some of them quite recent. Of these, three were English and two African-Caribbean.[3] Of those who had grown up in the Islamic faith, two were graduates, two had completed secondary schooling and a third was an East African Asian who had come to Britain as a young woman with very little schooling. In three families one or both parents was of South Asian heritage. The other two families were from South East Asia.

The choice for an Islamic education

Mothers who sent their daughters to the Islamic school were particularly concerned that there should be coherence between the values promoted at home and at school. This was felt particularly strongly amongst recent converts, who suggested they were as yet inadequately prepared to provide their daughters with either the knowledge or the values of their new faith. Zainab, an African-Caribbean convert, was critical of the education her older children had received within the state system, but it was her conversion to Islam and her concern that her younger child should be given an education in keeping with her new faith that propelled her to seek an alternative:

> I'm sending my seven-year-old to an Islamic school now. I had two older children who went to the state school and I worked in the state system myself. I was not completely unsatisfied, but to a great extent I was. Now that I am a revert Muslim I don't feel that my child could actually gain all the knowledge [from me], basic knowledge that is necessary for the child's development.

Tabassam, another convert and a qualified teacher working in an Islamic school, saw learning about Islam as a family venture where parents and children will learn from each other:

> We became Muslims five years ago. We are still learning about Islam ourselves. If we sent our daughter to a state school she would come back asking a lot of questions which we feel we are not equipped to answer yet. We felt that an Islamic school would be the best solution. She will learn about Islam and she will teach us too.

Khadija, who had been educated to degree level in Pakistan, was very clear about her reasons for educating her daughter in an Islamic school and the values she expected the school to promote:

> My brother's daughter ran away from home when she was 18. I didn't want that to happen to me. I don't know what they teach them at school. Back in Pakistan we were taught patience, respect for our elders, sacrifice for the family. Here the only things kids learn is me, me, me ... they are selfish. They may give to charity, but do nothing for their own family. Their parents suffer in old people's homes and they still enjoy life. I want my daughter to learn that she is part of a family. This means she has duties. She's there for them, they are there for her. That's what Islam says, not just me me.

Khadija emphasises the family setting within which a group identity is developed, with emphasis on cooperation and sharing. She expects the Islamic school to reinforce her values, stressing co-operation. This is not to suggest that the cultural patterns of British South Asians are inflexible or incapable of accommodating growing individualism among the young.[4] Khadija's concerns are related to her own family role. She, like many of the women in this study, takes prime responsibility for ensuring the upbringing of her children. If they do not behave 'properly' she fears this will be perceived as a personal failure.

A number of the mothers with daughters attending the Islamic school stressed the importance of partnership between school and home, particularly in the area of values education. It was also pointed out by some mothers that a supplementary school did not adequately meet their needs, as this had the effect of compartmentalising their daughters' education. Supplementary schooling also left mothers with little time to spend with their daughters. This in turn made it difficult to strengthen relationships. These mothers felt the separation of Islamic values from mainstream education might give out wrong messages. Once children were away from home or supplementary school any deviation from Islamic values might be seen to be acceptable. As Nazma explained:

> Children are educated as a whole and not in bits. You cannot say, Qur'an at home, English at school. If you do this you really are saying you are allowed to do what your non-Muslim friends do outside home, but when you come home you behave like a Muslim. You end up with a child who is an actor and who does not really know who she is any more.

Values education in state schools

Those with daughters at the mainstream primary school felt that their children were open to a different set of values at school. Nevertheless, they were generally confident that the school would not harm their daughters, believing that the influences of home and of the broader Muslim community in which they lived were stronger. They also acknowledged that many values were common to home and school. The emphasis that the school placed on honesty and telling the truth, sharing, loving, and caring for others in the community, was both recognised and welcomed. Nevertheless, a number raised concerns similar to those of Shazia:

> My daughter once said to me, 'My friends' mummy and daddy are not married because they say that people who get married argue more'. I was shocked and I told her never to repeat this again.

It worried some mothers that a range of relationships, including having a boyfriend or children outside marriage, were portrayed positively. Another concern was that many children showed a lack of respect for parents and other elders. Some mothers felt that they had very positive relationships with their daughters and a good level of communication between them, so that they were able to ensure that they behaved in an appropriate way at home. Others had to take criticism for failing to ensure that their daughters showed respect to their elders. Shamshad reported how, when her mother-in-law came to visit, she told her son that:

> I was not capable of bringing up my daughter and therefore I should give her to my mother-in-law so she could bring her up properly.

She believed the problem stemmed from a divergence in values between school and home:

> Zulaika does not speak in her mother tongue. Her language sometimes is not good, she uses bad words. She doesn't listen to me. She would answer her granny back, bang doors.... I mean she behaves badly. All this comes from school.

Shama, who was educated in Pakistan to degree level, did not see values education as the responsibility of mainstream schools. The role of the school was simply as a provider of academic skills and knowledge:

> They go there to learn English, maths, science, history, geography, etc. I have told them that anything else you learn at school is rubbish.

She did not acknowledge the complex ways in which subjects like science, history, and geography are value-laden.

Salma, an English Muslim married to a Pakistani, was less concerned about the influence of the state school on her daughter's values, since the child had had plenty of opportunity to experience life in an Islamic context:

> Regular visits to Pakistan give her a regular contact with Islamic values in practice. My daughter is now eight and about five years of her life have been spent in Pakistan. We hope to move there for good before she reaches her teens. During our stay in England she goes to a state school. I don't think that is harmful in any way. It gives her a chance to see British values and compare these to Islamic values.

Mothers who sent their daughters to the mainstream school did not feel that there was any problem in teaching their children that the school's values, when in conflict with those at home, were wrong. One, Halima, saw positive benefits in children coming into contact with value systems that are different from those of the home. She argued that 'you can't wrap children up in cotton wool' and felt that it was important that they should have a taste of 'the real world' and learn how to put their opinions across to other children.

Academic achievement and future employment

The majority of mothers with daughters in the mainstream were content with academic standards. Generally they did not believe they had any real choice of school: taking their children to and from school was largely their responsibility and, since a number did not drive, the local school was the only feasible option. Most felt the school offered an education as good as or better than their own. As one mother commented: 'State school was good enough for me, I turned out OK. Therefore it is good enough for my daughter.'

Those few who expressed reservations about educational standards compared their own achievements with those of their children. They were concerned that, for example, they knew their times tables rather better than their daughters at a comparable age. Many mothers expressed the wish that their daughters would be able to take their education further than they themselves had done and most stressed the encouragement they gave their daughters with regard to school work.

Shazia pointed out that not only was there little real choice within the mainstream but that when her daughter started school there was a Muslim school in the neighbourhood: 'I didn't know they existed.' At primary school her child's happiness, rather than standards, was her priority. A number of mothers felt that they would take more account of academic concerns at secondary level. In this respect the Muslim mothers in this study appear to have similar priorities to other parents of primary-aged children; they are concerned with issues such as proximity and their child's happiness, rather than 'educational content or method' (Petch 1986).

While Sakina, who had finished her own education at sixteen, talked in terms of her daughter having the chance to go on to university and get a good job, others hoped that their daughters' education would enable them to 'fill in forms', make good marriages and be good wives and mothers. None of the state school mothers were in paid employment. Shama, for example, had been unable to get work as a teacher as her qualifications were not recognised in Britain. By contrast, half of the mothers sending their children to the Islamic school were in paid employment.

Research into the educational and occupational aspirations of South Asian girls and young women suggests that most place considerable emphasis on educational qualifications and expect to be economically independent (Brah 1988; Basit 1997). The majority of mothers in this study, particularly those who had chosen an Islamic education, expected that their daughters would gain appropriate educational qualifications to enable them to establish economic independence. None saw this goal as being in conflict with Islamic values. Their understandings of Islam accommodated equal educational and employment opportunities for girls and women at the same time as promoting a 'different but equal' role for women in the domestic sphere. Only a minority of mothers (all with children at the state school) saw the primary purpose of education as enabling girls to make good marriages and become good wives and mothers.

Salma, an English Muslim whose daughter attended the mainstream primary school, felt that Islamic schools were too new and experimental for her to have full confidence in them. She appeared to put academic considerations before questions of values, although she conceded that this was a compromise. Her preference was to bring her children up in Pakistan, but her Pakistani husband argued that the family should spend part of their time in England so that the children were aware of their dual cultural heritage:

In Pakistan the schools reflect the religion, the morals, the culture of the home. In this country this is not the case and it could confuse the children. The reason I spend part of a year here is because my husband feels my children should get to know my parents too. He feels that this is important if our children are to really know themselves. I feel this will confuse them, but again my husband feels that, provided we give our children the right education and answer all their questions logically from an Islamic viewpoint, there is no danger of that. I'm not sure, but time will tell.

Children's identities in a multicultural and multi-faith society

A number of mothers felt that their daughters would only be able to achieve success if they knew who they were and were confident in their Muslim identities. Interest in an education that offered children a clear and positive sense of identity was most strongly expressed by mothers whose daughters attended the Islamic school. For Tazeem, who had converted to Islam some ten years before, the issue of identity was a priority. Her original intention was to send her daughter to a state school. She reported that when she visited prospective schools, 'I didn't feel comfortable in these schools, I straightaway felt different.' She believed that it was therefore likely that her daughter would have to change in order to fit in. She looked to an Islamic school which would 'make my daughter proud of being a Muslim, give her confidence and accept her the way she is'.

Zainab also felt that an Islamic education was important in building a genuine partnership between school and home:

> My daughter liked looking at books, she was good at making things, she enjoyed praying with me, she enjoyed reciting surahs with me, and always played peacefully. I expect the school to build on these things, even praying and surah recitation. This would mean that she could take all of herself to school and not leave bits of herself at home .... This is why I went for an Islamic school.

Many mothers felt self-esteem and confidence were critical to their daughters' futures as Muslim women in British society. Without it the girls would be ill-prepared to make a useful contribution to the wider community. Khadija suggested that life in Britain was inevitably a compromise. While she did not mind compromising aspects of her Pakistani culture, she was anxious that her daughter should not have to compromise her faith. She felt the

Islamic school had a critical role in helping her daughter to prepare for life as a Muslim woman in a secular society:

> I hope that the school will help my daughter according to the Islamic values within a Western setting because, as far as I am concerned, this is my country and my daughter's country. I would like her to be a useful member of this community. She can only be this if she is at peace with herself. Understanding her place in this society is the most important skill I would like her to gain.

Some mothers who had chosen the Islamic school shared a concern that the environment of the Islamic school might be too protective to enable their daughters to cope with prejudice and discrimination. Nurida, an English convert, expressed it like this:

> I worry if my daughter will be able to survive in the outside society. The school teaches her to be nice and she comes across nice girls in school. I wonder how she will cope when she is called a Paki or a traitor like I am sometimes called. I pretend it hasn't happened, but it has and it niggles me and several days later it is still going round my mind. This bothers me and I wonder how a 16-year-old is going to feel.

Nurida's experience of discrimination and abuse came as a shock. Halima, who was also a relatively recent convert, had first chosen a state school for her daughter, believing that children should come into contact with others of different backgrounds:

> I sent my daughter to a Church of England school. This had good academic standards, but then harassment started. Kids used to pick on the child calling her Paki because she wore a scarf. [I] told the teachers lots of times, she's no Paki, she's a Muslim. Do they do anything about it? Nothing! She made all kinds of excuses in the morning because she doesn't want to go to school. It's doing no good to her. She's a Muslim and that's where she belongs.

Persistent bullying and racial harassment caused Halima to transfer her child to an Islamic school. Failure of mainstream schools to challenge racism effectively is a key reason for the growth in demand amongst black communities for alternative educational provision (Troyna and Carrington 1987).

Preparation for living in a multicultural and multi-faith society was the key reason some mothers felt their children should attend a mainstream school. Many felt that the best preparation was learning to value themselves. For some this could best happen in an Islamic school; for others the type of schooling was largely irrelevant, as the main responsibility lay with the parent. Noreen stressed the importance of teaching a child to 'respect her parents and other older people and love younger people'. She believed such an education would enable a child to live anywhere. She pointed out that merely being together does not equip people to live in a multicultural society, for 'if this were the case there would be no racism in Britain whatsoever'. Thus, she argued, mainstream multicultural schools do not necessarily equip children to live together.

Tabassam, whose daughter attended the Islamic school, suggested that

> An Islamic school is multicultural and multi-ethnic anyway. If Islam is taught properly, religions like Christianity and Judaism are talked about, both in terms of their similarities and their differences. As far as I know Islam clearly states that we must respect people of all faiths and not pass judgements. If Allah wanted everyone to be Muslims all he would have had to do was to will it and it would have happened. If Allah himself has allowed humans to make their own choices, then our responsibility is merely to share with other human beings what we know, and to respect their decisions in terms of their belief.

Nurida expressed a similar view, drawing on Qur'anic teaching to emphasise the equal human rights of Muslims and non-Muslims:

> If you look at the Qur'an a great portion of it is dedicated to the rights of human beings, for example, parents, children, neighbours, guests, relatives, and so on. Nowhere in the Qur'an as far as I know is it mentioned that these rights should be given to these people if they are Muslims only. To the contrary, if one looks at the life of the prophet (peace be upon him) whose example we are to follow, a woman went to him and asked 'Oh prophet, my mother is coming to visit me. She is not a Muslim, but I am. How should I treat her?' The prophet (peace be unto him) replied, 'Exactly the same way as you would have treated her if she was a Muslim'.

This theme, the importance of Muslims being able to turn to the Qur'an to guide them in securing human rights and peaceful coexistence within a multicultural society, was also highlighted by Khatoon as a fundamental capacity she wished her daughter to acquire:

> We need to practise true Islam which is simple, peaceful and gives all humanity and living creatures their rights, and in which there is no

hatred or prejudice. I hope that the school will teach my daughter that whenever she wants guidance she should go back to the sources; this is the most important skill.

What do Muslim women want?

The research set out to capture the perspectives of British Muslim women, largely those of South Asian heritage, on the education of Muslim girls. Their concerns focus on four key areas: the development of Islamic values; educational qualifications and future economic independence; identity, self-esteem and confidence as Muslims; and preparation for life in a multicultural society. All these concerns have been heightened to various degrees by September 11 and its aftermath.

The majority of Muslim parents do not face a choice of whether or not to send a daughter to an Islamic school. Most Muslim children will continue to be educated in the state sector in non-Islamic schools. However, there are questions about what Muslim and non-Muslim children should be taught about Islamic values, particularly in a society in which, post-September 11, expressions of Islamophobia in schools, communities and the media have become commonplace. In Britain, the US and other parts of the world Muslim women and girls who choose to wear the *hijab* (and indeed others assumed to be South Asian or Middle Eastern) are particularly vulnerable to hostility and abuse (Amnesty International 2001; *Independent*, 4 January 2002). Schools need to include in their equality policies specific guidance on responding to (and challenging) racist and religious harassment. Faced with abuse, violence or threats of violence, as well as images of Islam 'as violent, aggressive, threatening, supportive of terrorism, engaged in a clash of civilisations' (Richardson 1997) many young people may need considerable support at school in identifying Islamic values and understanding their relationship to human rights. This implies an inclusive curriculum, including a citizenship curriculum that consciously sets out to promote a common civic culture and participation of all, Muslims and non-Muslims alike, in the economic, social and public life of the nation. Given the primary responsibility that many British South Asian Muslim women have for children's upbringing, a dialogue between Muslim women and schools will be critical to the success of any programme of values education.

Mothers placed emphasis on the need for their daughters to achieve appropriate qualifications and thereby secure their future independence. Official statistics indicate that, on average, children of Pakistani and Bangladeshi heritage[5] perform worse than most of their peers[6] in tests taken at the end of primary school in English and mathematics. A similar pattern emerges at GCSE level. In 2000, just 35 per cent of Pakistani heritage students and 37 per cent of Bangladeshi heritage students gained five or more marketable A*–C grades, compared with 47 per cent of students overall (Tikly *et al.* 2000). Although the attainment gap appears to be closing, this remains a cause for concern. Given the link between school performance, disaffection and longer-term social exclusion, these outcomes suggest an urgent need for greater collaboration between school authorities and Muslim parents.

Educators have long stressed a link between school performance and a sense of positive identity and self-esteem. Some mothers in this study also made connections between a strong and positive Muslim identity and success. Post-September 11, faced with hostile media presentations of Muslims and Islam, schools are faced with the challenge of reinforcing a positive identity in their Muslim pupils. Muslim women student teachers and teachers are also very conscious of their Muslim identities within their professional lives and are aware of the need to promote a strong sense of identity among Muslim children (Osler 1997; 2003). Among these teachers, the choice of whether or not to wear the *hijab* was as often related to identity and to self-confidence as to concerns about modesty.[7] For many girls, a decision to wear the *hijab* is a positive assertion of Muslim identity, often in the face of hostility. From the mothers' perspectives, the Islamic school was doing much to confirm their daughters' identities as Muslims. The challenge is for all schools to address this issue in a context where young Muslims may find their identities undermined, marginalised or ridiculed.

Finally, mothers were concerned that their daughters be prepared for participation in a multicultural and multi-faith society. Some felt that a good Islamic education that explored human rights and responsibilities was likely to be a far better preparation for life in a pluralistic society than some of the more tokenistic approaches they had experienced. They were critical of a multiculturalism in which difference and diversity (in relation to clothes, food or music) was celebrated but human rights and equality were not emphasised. Failure to address the issues raised by these mothers undermines the future of our multicultural and multi-faith society. Since most Muslims are educated in mainstream schools it is in these schools that the academic, religious, cultural and pastoral needs of young people must be met.

Post-September 11, members of Muslim communities find that the media spotlight is focused on them. Their loyalty, identity and sense of belonging have been challenged and sometimes undermined. Muslim women, particularly those who choose to identify themselves by wearing the *hijab*, find themselves at the centre of these controversies. This research reminds us that Muslim women are not a homogeneous group, but have a range of opinions and perspectives. The challenge facing schools is to listen to the views of Muslim women and girls and to build on them so that they are inclusive communities where all children can belong and feel secure. This is a critical first step in developing a multicultural and multi-faith society where the twin principles of equality and diversity are upheld.

Notes

1 The Christian churches continue to exercise considerable influence at school level, not simply owning buildings and land but also engaging in policy development, as employers and within school governing bodies.

2 One was born in the UK, had completed her primary and secondary schooling here, and married a UK-educated Pakistani. A second had come to England aged five and had attended school until the age of 13, when she had returned to Pakistan for three years to complete her schooling; she had married a Pakistan-educated man. The third was an English woman married to a Pakistani man who came to Britain to complete his higher education. The other five women had been born and educated in Pakistan and had come to the UK after marriage to men who had been at least partly educated in British state schools. Three had grown up in rural areas; one had only had a few years of primary schooling and the other two had attended secondary school, from which one had matriculated. The other two Pakistani-educated women were from urban areas and both had experience of higher education. The East African Gujurati had attended a *madrassa*, a religious school where only the Qur'an was taught, until the age of eight.

3 Of the converts, one English woman was brought up a Catholic and met her Muslim husband in Malaysia; she had converted to Islam some ten years previously. A second English woman had converted to Islam with her English husband five years before. Both these women were graduates; the second was a qualified teacher. A third English woman, a teacher working in the state system, had converted with her English husband two years before. Of the two African Caribbean converts, one had converted with her

husband. The other was a social worker whose husband had been unwilling to accept Islam. The couple had since divorced.

4 All too often black and minority ethnic families have been pathologised by focusing on breakdown or generalising from particular instances (Bhachu 1985).

5 No breakdown of statistics is available according to the religious affiliation of students. However, the majority of Pakistani and Bangladeshi students are of Muslim heritage. There are no statistics that show the breakdown by gender and ethnicity.

6 Students of black Caribbean heritage perform better than Pakistani but worse than Bangladeshi heritage students in mathematics tests at the end of primary school. At GCSE level both Pakistani and Bangladeshi students outperform black Caribbean heritage students.

7 A strong sense of identity and self-assurance led women to make different decisions in this regard. The views of British South Asian Muslim teachers are, in this respect, confirmed by reports from Muslim women in Morocco (Brown *et al.* 2004) and Egypt (Abdou 2003).

Chapter 10
Attitudes to Jihad, Martyrdom and Terrorism among British Muslims

HUMAYAN ANSARI

Since the attacks in New York and Washington on September 11, a vision of Islam and Muslims as 'fanatical' and 'violent' has again hit the headlines in the West. Reports of 'suicide bombings', hostage taking and harsh punishments have deluged the media. The attention of the world has been refocused on Islamic extremism. Thus recent global events, some undoubtedly dramatic, have deepened popular perceptions in the West that there is 'something' in Islam, more than other faiths, which condones political violence. How accurate and valid are these perceptions? Exploring this question historically, there are many instances when Islamic ideas have been drawn upon to justify violent activity. On the other hand, ideas regarding *jihad* have also been invoked that have stressed peaceful coexistence and toleration between Muslims and non-Muslims (Streusand 1997). Indeed, as religions go, violence is not unique to Islam. Examples of religiously instigated violence abound not only in the history of Christianity but in all other major organised religions. And secular movements have been no less culpable in this respect than religious ones, and frequently more so.

By analysing British Muslim responses on *jihad*, martyrdom and terrorism, it is possible to go some way towards questioning the popular beliefs about Islam and Muslims that have filtered into Western academia and policy-making arenas, and which, in turn, have given them sustenance (Silverman 2002). Furthermore, given the emotional discharge that questions of identity and citizenship aroused post-September 11, it is useful to explore connections between attitudes towards acts of terrorism and religious martyrdom, and the issue of identity formation, as well as any changes of feelings noted by respondents since September 11.

The research for this study was conducted by circulating attitudinal questionnaires to a random sample of volunteer respondents. A proportion was then followed up with in-depth interviews. Participants were predominantly of South Asian descent, identified through a network of contacts in three distinct communities. Efforts were made to gather views from a wide range of people – men and women from different age groups and socio-economic and educational backgrounds. There was quite an even split in terms of gender. The most represented age group in the sample was the 16–24 year olds. Eighty per cent of the sample was in the 16–44 year age range, making it a relatively young group of Muslims, and therefore likely to be more acculturated into the British environment. Occupationally, a sizeable minority attended school, college or university; many were professionally or self-employed. The majority of the respondents were from relatively affluent backgrounds and had attained high standards of education with reasonable chances of occupational success.

Can any inferences be made about how strict Muslims in the sample were in terms of their religious practice? Dassetto in the early 1990s estimated that up to 60 per cent of the 15 million or so Muslims living in Western Europe could be called 'Muslims' on the basis of their ethno-historical roots, with identities not strongly influenced by Islam (Mandaville 2001: 111). The level of religious observance among our sample, however, appeared to be relatively strong: 50 per cent of the respondents said that they regularly prayed five times a day (only ten of the participants said they 'almost never' prayed); 86 per cent fasted in the month of Ramadan; and 69 per cent said that religion was 'very important' to them. The sense of Muslim identity among the majority appeared to be extremely strong, with 85 per cent indicating that they were 'very proud' to be Muslims. The fact that these findings contrast with Dassetto's observation makes it unlikely that our respondents could be taken as entirely representative of the British Muslim population as a whole, something that needs to be factored into any assessment of the sample's responses.

Jihad

Much confusion exists about the concept of *jihad*, among both Muslims and non-Muslims. The Western media refer frequently to *jihad*, usually, if misleadingly, translating the term as holy war

(Lewis 1988: 71). Many Western journalists, politicians and indeed scholars, have tended to reify the notion of *jihad* and so have not only rendered it ahistorical but also validated understandings of *jihad* as synonymous with violence. Barber interprets *jihad*, 'in its strongest manifestation', to mean 'bloody holy war on behalf of partisan identity that is metaphysically defined and fanatically defended' (Barber 1996: 9). For Pipes, *jihad* is 'holy war' (Pipes December 2002), or 'warfare against unbelievers to extend Muslim domains' (Pipes November 2002): 'it means the legal, compulsory, communal effort to expand the territories ruled by Muslims at the expense of territories ruled by non-Muslims ... *Jihad* is thus unabashedly offensive in nature, with the eventual goal of achieving Muslim dominion over the entire globe (Pipes December 2002). Likewise, MacArthur claims that war is a legitimate means of converting non-believers, and that while not all Muslims are terrorists, support terrorism or rejoice when terrorists strike at their enemies, 'nonetheless violence against infidels and the concept of *jihad* are fundamental to Islam and an inescapable fact of Islamic history' (MacArthur 2001: 32–3).

Among Muslims too the notion of *jihad* has been debated and contested right from the time of the Prophet Mohammed. Indeed, as Esposito (2002: 26) puts it, 'If you were watching a television special on *jihad*, with four Muslim speakers, you might well hear four different responses to the question: "what is *jihad*?"' An historical review of *jihad* would illustrate that there has been no single doctrine of *jihad* that has been always and everywhere accepted in the Muslim world. Its meaning has changed over time as diverse individuals and religious authorities have interpreted and applied in specific historical and political contexts what they have found regarding *jihad* in the Qur'an and in the practice of the Prophet Mohammed. According to Euben (2002: 12–21), '*Jihad* is less a fixed set of rules for violent, fanatical conquest than a category that refracts changing understandings about the scope and meaning of worldly action given radical political and social change': in his view, *jihad* (derived from *jahada* meaning 'to exert', 'to struggle' or 'to strive') literally involves the use of 'one's utmost power, efforts, endeavours, or ability in contending with an object of disapprobation' or 'striving toward a worthy goal'.

Even in the Qur'an, the concept of *jihad* seems to develop over time in divergent, and in places apparently contradictory, fashion. Muslims were at various stages commanded to be peaceful in their persuasion of non-Muslims, to fight in self-defence, and to fight unbelievers in general subject to certain conditions (Firestone 1999). These differences may suggest modifications of policy resulting from particular circumstances as well as diverse and conflicting tendencies and positions in the Muslim community during different and early stages of its development. Ambiguities in Qur'anic references to *jihad* have led Muslim scholars to emphasise either the peaceful or the violent character of *jihad*, depending on their own understandings of the sacred texts as well as the circumstances in which they have wished to apply the concept. Some Muslim scholars have privileged *al-jihad al-akbar* (higher *jihad* or the struggle against one's own desires and temptations) over *al-jihad al-asghar* (lesser *jihad* or armed fighting in the path of Islam), while many classical jurists certainly felt that the Prophet considered the greater endeavour to be 'the struggle against one's self', of which *jihad bil qalam* (struggle against ignorance through knowledge) and *jihad bil nafs* (struggle against one's own destructive tendencies) were a part (Al-Hujwari 1976: 200).

During the medieval period, given the parlous state of the Islamic *ummah* (community), various legal scholars advocated a militant view of *jihad* to resist subjugation by non-Muslims and to overturn the accelerating decline of the Muslim polity. For them, *jihad* was not merely an internal struggle to be a good Muslim, but also an external fight in order to protect Islam from non-Muslim aggression: to defend life, property, wealth, land, independence and principles. For Ibn Taymiyyah, (1268–1328 CE), fighting in a *jihad* constituted a higher obligation than *hajj* (pilgrimage) and *som* (fasting) – two of the five key pillars of Islam, which do not include *jihad*. His advancement of a militant strand in Islam was given a more rigid and puritanical twist by the Saudi Arabian theologian Muhammad al-Wahhab (1703– 92 CE), who advocated the need for armed *jihad* against all infidels as well as against Muslims who did not subscribe to his views. From the middle of the twentieth century, Muhammad Abdus Salam Faraj (1952–82 CE), Hasan al-Banna (1906–49 CE), Sayyid Qutb (1906– 66 CE), Abu al-A'la Mawdudi (1903–79 CE) and Ayatollah Ruhollah Khomeini (1903–89 CE) further elaborated these doctrines, by arguing that *jihad* is an urgent imperative applying not only to relations between Muslims and the 'unbelieving' West, but also to those between Muslims and so-called Muslims who aid and abet Western supremacy by betraying the precepts of Islamic sovereignty and opening the door to foreign corruption (Euben 2002: 19).

Thus, for modern militant Islamists, *jihad* is a means of challenging oppression and establishing the rule of Islam. They contrast *jihad* with other forms of war pursued for purely worldly concerns, and describe it 'as the act of supreme sacrifice to preserve human rights bestowed by Allah', portraying it as a struggle 'to help the oppressed against atrocities committed by the aggressors' (Sikand 2001: 225). Even Hizb al-Tahrir, a radical Islamist organisation operating in Britain, prescribes *jihad* as the primary duty only for Muslims living in Palestine, who face Israeli occupation directly: for those who live in Britain, the primary duty is to work for the establishment of the caliphate. Since Hizb al-Tahrir insists that the caliph is the exclusive prosecutor of *jihad*, Muslims in Britain are instead enjoined to fulfil the secondary duty of *jihad* through means other than actual fighting. Another militant Muslim organisation, Al-Muhajiroun, has gone further, welcoming Hamas's suicide bombings and reportedly urging its followers to offer financial support 'to fight the occupiers, and to recruit mujahideen to drive them out of Palestine' (Taji-Farouki 2000: 34). Al-Muhajiroun was also enthusiastic in its support for the efforts of 'Shaykh al-Jihad', the 'lion' Osama bin Laden, to expel 'the American occupation forces' from the Middle East, congratulating him on the US embassy attacks in Nairobi and Tanzania, and declaring American forces to be legitimate targets (*ibid.*: 36–7).

While the doctrines of militant Islamists[1] have gained increasing leverage, the idea of the 'higher *jihad*' postulated by the Sufi tradition, calling for a spiritual struggle for purification against one's baser instincts for moral self-improvement and the reform of society, remains part of the discourse on *jihad*. Muslim politicians have attempted to address issues of economic development, illiteracy, poverty, hunger and disease through appeals to this 'higher' *jihad*. Muslim scholars, too, have construed *jihad* as a fight for justice using all one's wealth and material resources.[2] However, these modernist thinkers and their precursors such as Maulvi Chiragh Ali (d. 1895), Sayyid Ahmed Khan (d. 1898), Muhammad Abduh (d. 1905) and Rashid Rida (d. 1935) – who sought to show that 'a religious war of aggression' was not 'one of the tenets of Islam', that it was not 'prescribed by the Qur'an for the purpose of proselytising or exacting tribute' (Moaddel and Talatoff 2000: 71), and that peace rather than enmity was the normative state of affairs between Muslims and non-Muslims in Islam – remain, for Islamists, apologists of the West and imbued with false consciousness (Alsumaih 1998: 6).

Clearly, therefore, Muslims (and non-Muslims) can mean different things by *jihad*. Differences in interpretation are deeply rooted in Muslim history and reflect the diversity of Islamic thought. Under these circumstances, it is not surprising that our survey included a variety of responses regarding *jihad*, with roughly half the respondents considering it to be important.

A large proportion understood *jihad* to mean either a 'holy war' or a 'Muslim war', fought for Allah against 'those who threaten the existence of Islam'. Another common understanding was of *jihad* as a struggle against oppression, which could be 'the oppression of the Muslim people', or, equally, the oppression of their beliefs. In one way or another, *jihad* was interpreted as a fight for Islam primarily against 'non-Muslims', a 'fight for justice', a 'fight against those who deny Muslims their rights' and 'treat [them] unfairly'. In the absence of the community taking responsibility to counter this unfair treatment, some respondents felt that individuals could 'take matters into their own hands'. A small minority, however, did not see this 'fight' in physical terms, but described it instead as a mental or emotional one, which helped to 'purify' someone for Allah. Many respondents also referred to *jihad* as 'a struggle', not necessarily implying physical violence or death but rather a constant striving for faith. Some viewed *jihad* in terms of an inner struggle for the sake of peace and truth within oneself. For them, there was more to *jihad* than a 'war' in the crudest sense. Instead, this 'war' or 'struggle' could be a personal 'inner struggle'. One respondent introduced the concepts of 'lesser' and 'higher' *jihad*, and argued that the concept is often manipulated for political ends by Muslims and non-Muslims alike. Indeed, several respondents hinted at this 'higher' *jihad*, which they referred to as a series of challenges such as 'trying to better yourself', 'not committing sin' and 'increasing your faith'. They described it as a 'personal' and 'daily' struggle, whose ultimate aim was 'self-purification', or reaching a state of 'peace and truth within oneself'. Another, more general definition of *jihad* involved 'keeping Islam alive' or 'spreading Islam'. Likewise, three respondents emphasised that *jihad* was an 'effort for justice' and that this effort should be a conscious effort to speak, understand and practise truth.

Thus, the respondents in our sample provided a range of meanings for *jihad*. Many possessed a wider, more encompassing interpretation of *jihad* than the commonly understood 'holy war', associating it with violence. Some described *jihad* essentially as a 'struggle', which did not necessarily imply fighting or dying, but rather a constant effort to 'struggle in your life to do right things'. Some, however, confused *jihad* with martyrdom, since, for them, it meant dying for one's religion, dying to protect other Muslims, dying for a particular cause or belief, or being able to sacrifice oneself for that belief. To some extent, this confusion is understandable since, when *jihad* is invoked to urge Muslims to fight, the main motivation is the belief that if they die on the battlefield, the reward will most likely be immediate Paradise at the highest level.

Martyrdom

The Arabic word *shahid* (martyr) does not mean sacrificing one's life. Instead, it literally signifies 'being present', or an 'observer', in the sense of 'a person who bears witness' to the truth. A martyr is an exemplar and *shahadat* (martyrdom) need not be viewed as a death that is imposed by an enemy. Rather, martyrdom for a Muslim can be a choice – between accepting 'disgraceful death of a humbled people' and a 'desired death when confronted with the destruction of one's freedoms and rights'.

For Muslims, martyrs occupy a special status akin to prophets, righteous men and just imams. In the eyes of many ordinary Muslims, a martyr endows his entire community with grace and purity. His immediate family becomes the object of admiration and support, and its members are given similar privileges – including being spared the pain of death, remission of sins, exemption from the punishment of the tomb and the final judgement, intercession on behalf of their co-religionists, marriage to *houris* and a place in *Jannat al-Firdaws* (the highest level of Paradise). And martyrs live on not only in the afterlife but also in the memories and thoughts of the living community through repeated remembrances and retelling of stories, endowing their deeds with a measure of immortality.

Yet the category of martyr in Islam stretches beyond those who die on the battlefield. Hence, even lifelong worship may qualify one for martyrdom; those who die protecting their property, or while travelling, or working, or even as the innocent victims of accidental building collapse, may also enjoy the rewards of martyrs. On the other hand, those who just happen to die in battle, but who are not fighting in God's name, may not. Therefore, the perpetrators of September 11 might or might not be considered as 'martyrs' depending on their 'purity of intention'. Similarly, the people who died on the planes as passengers or who were working in the Twin Towers might or might not be considered as martyrs, again depending on one's understanding of intention. Since they died going about their business, this means that for some Muslims their deaths certainly represented a form of 'shahid'. Can non-Muslims, however, be considered by Muslims to be martyrs? Again the response to this question depends on how one sees non-Muslims. For militant Islamists, *jihad* as armed struggle provides the basis for the ideology of martyrdom, in which violent death on the battlefield, and not the inward sacrifice of the believer, occupies a central place. And it is these ideas of martyrdom that have acquired salience among, in particular, young British Muslims.

In the Qur'an there are twelve verses that deal directly with the concept of martyrdom. They imply that a person who becomes a *shahid* does not really die; in fact he or she receives an excellent reward in the afterlife. As a result of what these verses reveal, one of the greatest Western misconceptions about Islamic political behaviour can be resolved. This is that those Muslims who participate in self-martyring operations are not committing suicide by doing so, and, therefore, do not receive the Islamic stigma associated with suicide. Ahmed Ibn Naqib al-Misri, for instance, writes that 'There is no disagreement among scholars that it is permissible for a single Muslim to attack battle lines of unbelievers headlong and fight them even if he knows he will be killed' (Silverman 2002: 88). In effect, the stigma of suicide is removed from the *shahid*, who becomes a model of Islamic behaviour. However, others would argue that this comes very close to the Kharajite practice of *talab al-shahada* (seeking of martyrdom) that was roundly condemned by classical scholars.

How our sample understood the meaning of the term 'martyrdom' was explored by asking the respondents to provide a brief description of the term. Their responses ranged from the specific to the more general: from dying for Allah (a specific), to dying for Islam and Muslims, and then moving on to encompassing a more general viewpoint, such as dying for a faith or a particular belief, and ending up with a more universal definition of sacrifice. For the vast majority, understandings of martyrdom centred round aspects of death and dying for a specific reason.

Eleven respondents specifically stated that martyrdom meant death or dying in the name or cause of Allah. They saw it as defending the cause of Allah, thus 'protecting the faith and those who practise it'. One respondent suggested that by doing this 'we will have paradise'. Another stated that dying for Allah's cause meant dying 'in battle against non-Muslims'. Thus martyrdom meant giving one's life in the name of Islam, including dying while fighting for the right to be a practising Muslim and to be recognised as one. A willingness to die for the sake of religion meant one was dying 'in true faith'. One respondent, however, stressed the difference between dying for your beliefs in war and suicide killings, which were considered to be 'very wrong'. Another said that this action was very important but added 'only in extreme circumstances'. A third respondent understood this act as giving one's life a sense of justice. Some respondents understood and described martyrdom in terms of it being the 'highest sacrifice'. This sacrifice could be in the physical form, such as sacrificing one's life for one's beliefs, for 'the Islamic cause'. It could also imply a more spiritual or mystical meaning such as 'sacrificing one's belongings', the killing of 'the ego' or 'eternal spirit within the human being'. Indeed, many confirmed that dying in this way represented the ultimate form of martyrdom, a response that suggested a more holistic understanding of martyrdom that did not necessarily mean physical death.

Some also raised questions as to the theological or conceptual aspects of the term 'martyrdom', and implied that, though it was a significant concept, it was not necessarily important to them in their everyday lives. They were more critical not only of the term but of how it was being misrepresented. One respondent blamed 'shrewd politicians disguised as clerics' for misguiding people. Another argued that martyrdom 'represents a theological justification for extreme actions that ultimately prolong the injustice that provokes those actions in the first place'.

Meanings of martyrdom thus varied, ranging from dying while literally 'fighting' through to 'dying while undertaking an action for the sake of God and God alone'. For these respondents, martyrdom resulted from a form of *jihad* that did not necessarily involve physical violence or combat against an enemy.

Circumstances when acts of violence can be justified

Given the diversity of views on martyrdom within the sample, it was decided to explore perceptions regarding violence and, more specifically, how far suicide attacks or 'martyrdom operations' might be justified within Islam. It might be argued that just posing this question means that we, as researchers, have fallen into the trap of linking 'Islam' intrinsically with 'violence'. Is there an underlying assumption in the question itself? One of our respondents challenged the whole notion of raising the question of the justification of acts of violence with Islam. In her view, this could be considered as actually falling in with a predominant mindset that there is such a thing as 'Islamic terrorism'. All the same, respondents were asked if there were any circumstances where they felt that acts of violence could ever be justified within Islam.[3] Fifty-eight per cent of the sample argued that acts of violence against Muslims could not be justified within Islam. Forty-seven per cent said that violence could not be justified against non-Muslims, either. Similarly, only 19 per cent agreed that the use of violence could be justified against Muslims, whereas 26 per cent justified the use of violence against non-Muslims. Overall, the sample justified the use of violence against non-Muslims rather than Muslims.

Some respondents gave a 'religious' justification for the act of violence. One suggested that it could take the form of 'permissible acts of war according to the *Sunnah* [the practice of the Prophet Mohammed]'. Some shared the view that 'if they do it, you reply back', and confirmed this with quotes from the Qur'an, such as 'an eye for an eye, a tooth for a tooth', and 'if anyone commits transgression against you, return the transgression in the same way'. They interpreted this to mean that 'if Muslim civilians are targeted, then that transgression may be returned, thus targeting civilians'. Two respondents explicitly stated their belief that it was justifiable to commit acts of violence against non-Muslims, in particular if they 'oppress' or are 'hurting Muslims – physically' such as 'raping' and 'killing'. One respondent justified acts of violence against Muslims, particularly 'rebellious Muslims living under the Islamic state' who are 'working to overthrow the state without justification'. Four respondents, however, stated outright that there was no justification for acts of violence in Islam. While one respondent was sympathetic to the conflict in Palestine and to the Palestinians, he stated that violence was 'still wrong from *both* sides'. Similarly, another respondent agreed that there was no circumstance in which violence can be justified within Islam. This point was further stressed with a religious justification: 'Suicide is against Islam, so contradicts the purpose of Islam ... Islam condones peace'.

At the same time, some respondents questioned what was being asked as well as the context in which it was being asked. One stated that it 'depends on circumstances' whether or not acts of violence are justifiable. Another stressed, 'It's very difficult to say 'yes' or 'no' unless you're in that situation'. In particular, it was highlighted that one's justification or viewpoint towards acts of violence was dependent on how the various terms are defined: 'Islamically we will be judged by our intentions. If our intentions are truly for the sake of Allah and Allah is Peace, Truth, Mercy, Justice, then many things could be justifiable under the right circumstances.'

For the majority of the respondents, violence was not justified, whoever the target. For others, there could be circumstances when it could be justified. With regard to suicide bombing, nearly half the sample felt that this was justifiable or 'possibly' justifiable. In general, those respondents who identified strongly with being Muslim (as opposed to being British) were more ready to feel that, in some circumstances, Islam could justify acts of violence. Twenty-nine per cent of those for whom being Muslim was very important indicated that there were circumstances when they felt that acts of violence against non-Muslims could be justified within Islam (23 per cent also justified actions of violence against Muslims). This contrasted with only 13 per cent of those for whom being British was very important. Twenty per cent of those for whom being British was very important felt that acts of violence in the form of suicide bombings against military targets could be justified in Islam, again contrasting with a higher percentage (36 per cent) of those for whom being Muslim was very important.

Those respondents who indicated that they thought of themselves as British were much less ready to say that violence could ever be justified within Islam. Regarding violence against non-Muslims, this was 10 per cent, as against 52 per cent of those who said they did not think of themselves as British; likewise, regarding suicide bombings against military targets, this was 13 per cent as against 66 per cent of those who did not think of themselves as British. Those who participated more frequently in religious observance indicated a higher level of agreement that there were circumstances in which acts of violence could be justified within Islam. Fifty-five per cent of those who attended a place of worship on a weekly basis (or more frequently) justified acts of violence, under some circumstances, against non-Muslims. Sixty-three per cent justified violence within Islam in some circumstances by suicide bombings against military targets. This contrasted with 44 per cent (against non-Muslims) and 41 per cent (suicide bombings against military targets) of those who attended on a monthly basis or less frequently, including never. The view from those who attended a place of worship was that the justification within Islam for acts of violence was not there to the same extent for violence against Muslims, for suicide (harming oneself) or for suicide bombings against civilian targets.

Thus these findings revealed that views regarding suicide and martyrdom are complex and variable, and very much depend on factors such as the context and the target of attack. One of the points repeatedly made by our respondents was that Muslims suffered from oppression throughout the world, and that, when this is the case, violence is sometimes justified. Some suggested that this had little to do with a religious viewpoint and thought that it was a position with which even non-Muslims could agree. Unsurprisingly, many respondents cited the Palestinian–Israeli conflict as a case in point.

Suicide and suicide bombings

More specifically, the sample was asked whether acts of violence in the form of suicide could be justified within Islam. Could 'suicide bombings' be perceived as 'martyrdom operations'? Suicide might be defined as the act of a person who intentionally kills him or herself, or the act of taking one's life (Reber 1985: 745). But how do Muslims engage with the notion of suicide? An examination of their sacred texts would suggest that Islam upholds the sanctity of life and expressly forbids suicide. Accordingly, those who commit suicide or try to commit suicide are committing a major sin, a crime that, it is believed, will be punished severely by eternal damnation. There are clear references in the Qur'an prohibiting taking one's own life and the Prophet Mohammed condemned suicide unambiguously.[4]

Hence, unsurprisingly, suicide, defined as taking one's life for personal as opposed to political or ideological reasons, was viewed as *haram* (prohibited) by most of our respondents. Indeed, a large part of the sample (76 per cent) agreed that suicide in the form of self-harm is not justifiable within Islam. Their response, however, was more ambiguous in the case of whether suicide bombings are justifiable within Islam, and it was even more blurred when respondents were asked whether it was justifiable for suicide bombers to aim for military targets or civilian targets. The sample's order of priority regarding when violence is not justifiable was, first, suicide (76 per cent), second, suicide bombing civilian targets (68 per cent), and, third, suicide bombing military targets (42 per cent). While the majority of the sample agreed that suicide was not justifiable in Islam, a substantial minority of respondents thought that suicide bombing could be justified by Islam. Thirty-two per cent said it was justifiable for suicide bombers to target military targets. Fifteen per cent justified the targeting of civilians. The order of priority regarding when violence is justifiable in Islam was, first, military targets (32 per cent), second, civilian targets (15 per cent), and, third, self harm (8 per cent). If any respondents answered 'possibly' to any of the above, they were asked to explain their views. The 32 explanations given highlighted various degrees of justification for acts of violence. Only one respondent said that suicide bombing was justified.

The most common view of the sample was that violence could be justified only in self defence or out of desperation. But, while some respondents stated they 'abhorred' the 'killing of civilians', or 'the idea of a suicide attack', and that this could 'never be justified', they then seemingly contradicted themselves by saying that violence was justifiable in self-defence or desperation. It could be argued that the respondents' empathy with this feeling of desperation must be high in order for them to be able to justify an act that they abhorred. Similarly, many respondents, while claiming that 'Islam categorically forbids any violence against civilians', went on to assert that 'when a situation leaves Muslims no other means of resistance, suicide bombing against the oppressing military forces is justifiable'.

Again, the boundaries of what was justifiable were blurred and religious rights and wrongs could change according to people's interpretation of a situation. This was especially true of reactions to events in the Middle East, particularly Palestine. Some people indicated that they empathised with the 'oppressed' Palestinian people who were 'seeing daily atrocities being committed against their communities', and had 'no army/weapons to fight back'. In essence the Palestinian people were seen as the 'victims rather than the perpetrators of crimes'. Thus, an act of violence carried out by such 'victims' was looked upon as an act of self-defence, retaliation and desperation rather than an act of crude violence or murder. In the words of one respondent:

> If they see their only hope to effect change through killing themselves, then one has to look beyond the simplistic categories which equate such acts to murder and look at the deeper significance of such acts, which are not necessarily linked to religion but more to the daily oppression of their right to exist and therefore their humanity.

The oppressor was viewed as 'America', 'Israel', the 'West' in general or the 'UN'; all were blamed for 'ignoring what is going on' and were accused of having 'double standards'. In this way respondents justified the violence carried out by the Palestinians who 'defend their land by sacrificing their life'. Indeed, one respondent described this as 'revenge' rather than *jihad*.

Several respondents felt it would be possible to justify 'suicide bombings' against military targets: 'When a situation leaves Muslims no other mean of resistance, "suicide bombings" against the oppressing military forces are justifiable'. Respondents seemed to have reflected on the motivation of the suicide bombers, and in such instances did not view them as having committed suicide. However, what was meant by the term 'military target' also varied – for some respondents, civilians could be 'military targets' because of their complicity in supporting oppression.

So were the perpetrators of the events of September 11 'suicide bombers'? Could such people be considered to be 'soldiers in a legitimate conflict'? Did these so-called 'suicide bombers' have anything suicidal about them? Or were they, in fact, closer to the Japanese Kamikaze of the Second World War in their motivation and organisation, in their ideology and in the execution of their task? The responses from our sample suggested that the distinction between suicide and martyrdom seemed to be largely in the eye of the beholder. Martyrdom, they tended to feel, reflects situations of persecution, opposition and resistance. There was the belief that it would result in some vicarious benefit; there is expectation of vindication and reward beyond death. In this sense, some respondents considered 'suicide bombing' to be 'martyrdom operations'. Others, though, were more sceptical, and while they did not use the word 'terrorism', they certainly implied it.

Terrorism

So, did those British Muslims taking part in our survey view acts of terror as part of the Islamic strategy of resistance in the face of extreme oppression? Before exploring this question, it is necessary to establish a general definition of terrorism and compare it with what Islam has to say on the subject. This task is made harder by the fact that there is, as yet, no universally accepted definition of terrorism, in part because there is genuine scepticism about what constitutes it. The term 'terrorism' is nowhere fully defined as a legal term, though the Legal Committee of the United Nations General Assembly issued a rough draft of a convention which 'reiterates that criminal acts intended or calculated to provoke a state of terror in the general public, a group of persons or particular persons for political purposes are in any circumstances unjustifiable, whatever the considerations of a political, philosophical, ideological, racial, ethnic, religious or other nature that may be used to justify them' (Roberts, 2004). Recent legislation in Britain, however, has defined acts of terrorism as the 'use or threat, for the purposes of advancing a political, religious, or ideological cause of action which involves serious violence against any person or property, endangering the life of any person, or creates a serious risk to health or safety of public or a section of the public' (*Muslim News*, 28 July 2000).

Does Islam have anything to say about terrorism? If one examines Islamic legal texts, then the category of *hirabah* or *qat'al tariq* does seem to offer an analogy with the term 'terrorism'. The classical Islamic law of *hirabah* possesses several salient features that correspond to those on domestic terrorism in Western legal systems, though it appears to be a broader category covering crimes ranging from breaking and entering to 'hate crimes' to rape and terrorism proper. An agent of *hirabah* is considered to be 'anyone who disturbs free passage in the streets and renders them unsafe to travel ... killing people or violating what God had made it unlawful to violate' (Jackson 2001: 295).

According to Rashid Rida, *hirabah* is 'the commission of acts in the lands of Islam that threaten the security of life and property and honour, while seeking immunity in the power of one's group and refusing to submit willingly to the religious law'. *Hirabah* is distinguished by its connection to the spreading of fear and helplessness and the fact that no effective security measures can be taken against it. It is the most severely punished crime in Islam. Those convicted are required to be 'executed or crucified or that their hands and feet be amputated from opposite sides or they be banished from the earth' (Jackson 2001: 296–303).

As far as many of the respondents in our survey were concerned, acts of violence against innocent people were included in their definition of terrorism and they were to be condemned: 'Killing innocent people who have done absolutely nothing wrong to you. That's what terrorism means'. Some referred to the generation of fear in people through indiscriminate violence and its detrimental effect on their lives: others made references to a distinction between 'terrorists' and 'freedom fighters'. The concern about linking terrorist acts specifically with Islam figured largely in the respondents' comments:

> A terrorist is a person who terrorises other people, whether it's a Muslim terrorist or a Christian terrorist. Not so long ago we had the IRA terrorising us here, but they were not classed as Christian terrorists, they were 'IRA terrorists'.

While the strong condemnation of terrorism by our respondents echoed the findings of an opinion poll conducted by the BBC programme Eastern Eye in November 2001, which showed that British Asians seemed to be overwhelmingly (both young and old) loyal to the country in the action against terrorism, the 'War against Terrorism' by George Bush and Tony Blair was not widely perceived to be fair and equitable by the vast majority of our sample, but was seen as being directed not only against terrorists but also against Islam. Hence, the growth in the appeal of radical Islam, with the rhetoric of *jihad* and the idea of creating a global Islamic state perhaps offering some young Muslims in Britain a means of reconciling apparently contradictory religious, cultural and political loyalties.

Change of feeling since September 11?

The impact of the events of September 11 was obviously felt worldwide by Muslims and non-Muslims alike. In the case of British Muslims, this event seems to have forced numerous issues into the limelight, in particular those involving questions of identity and loyalty. In effect, the event highlighted the complexity of being a 'British' 'Muslim' – one description appearing to be almost in conflict with the other. From our questionnaires and interviews, it was clear that the overwhelming view among Muslims was that the events of September 11 were terrorist acts and wrong. However, the perception of wider society was that British Muslims did not condemn the atrocities unreservedly or sufficiently. Even liberal voices felt that Muslim criticism of 'Islamic terrorism' had been muted.

So, is this perception true? It would be easy to dismiss it as anti-Muslim propaganda, but there could be an element of truth in some of the criticism. Muslims cannot escape blame entirely. Their initial reaction to September 11, for instance, appeared ambivalent. The acknowledgement that something terrible had happened was not only grudging but came with the suggestion that, viewed in a certain context, it could be explained. At the same time, it should be noted that Muslims were not alone in suggesting an 'explanation' for these events. Many non-Muslims, including United States citizens, believed and argued that the roots of such virulent anti-Americanism around the world lay in US policies. The European Left was particularly sharp in calling for self-introspection by US policy makers and, though it was attacked for saying this, nobody accused it of actually supporting terrorism. Moreover, there is some evidence to suggest that Muslims were not against tough action against terrorism but instead demanded even-handedness. The perception among many British Muslims seemed to be that the United Nations and the West had double standards in dealing with injustice in the world, with large numbers agreeing that they would have been more supportive of tough action against al-Qa'ida if the West had been more tough and exacting against Israel (Palestine), India (Kashmir) and Yugo-slavia (Bosnia).[5] It is only Muslims who, for the media at least with their focus on the most extreme and provocative voices, were deemed guilty of being al-Qa'ida supporters until proved innocent.

Nevertheless, our sample's findings also confirmed that British Muslim condemnation of the terrorist events was in the majority of cases qualified:

> I don't support *any violence*, [however] we have to face the facts that the USA is involved in the politics [of] many countries ... which creates a lot of hatred towards Americans.

The comments of our respondents provided insights into their understanding of why it happened:

> Perhaps it was not an act of madness, as the American administration wanted the world to believe ... it wasn't just an attack on democracy, it was an attack against what many people regarded as American imperialism and American oppression, and their support for Israel in the Middle East. And that was the reaction of most of the people I met in my community after the incident.

There was also some questioning of exactly who had perpetrated the acts, with various conspiracy theories put forward. Moreover, respondents recognised the difference, in general, between the react-ions of Muslims and the reactions among non-Muslim British people. One respondent described the different values that Americans seemed to place on individuals' lives. Bitterness as a result of this perception was frequently expressed:

One American probably is equal to ten British people. And one American perhaps is equal to 100 or maybe 1,000 Pakistanis ... if hundreds of us are killed, it is probably equal to one-fourth of one American.

Changed feelings as a result of September 11 included comments along the lines that 'people are very prejudiced against Islam', which even suggested that 'they hate Muslims'. Outward signs of being Muslim (beard, *hijab*) were perceived to be more of a challenge to Western values. There seemed to be an increase in hostility expressed in offensive remarks, intimidating behaviour and a massive escalation in racist abuse:

Before I could walk through the street without people taking a second look – now the case is different. People stare, make comments and whisper.

Indeed, the events of September 11 had resulted in some of the respondents feeling that they had been 'treated differently'. For example, they felt that other people might consider that they looked like a terrorist simply because they were Muslim or dressed as a Muslim.[6] A broader effect of such reactions seems to have been a rise in anti-Islamic feeling in general. Respondents reported a general lack of tolerance, a greater distrust, and a greater display of ignorance and narrow-mindedness, suggesting that there was 'no understanding of Islam'. The overall effect was to highlight a general distrust of anything linked to Islam or being a Muslim. It was this lack of understanding of which the sample spoke that exacerbated this kind of behaviour and meant that Muslims were perceived as a 'challenge to Western values'.

Concluding thoughts

What emerges from the analysis of our survey findings is that most of our respondents had reflected in only a relatively superficial way on issues connected with martyrdom and terrorism. Our findings supported the conclusion that, at the popular level, most religious belief is not very theological. As expected, the majority of our respondents were not profound analysts of the Qur'an. For a vast proportion of these 'believing' Muslim men and women 'Islam' tended to be important in a rather jumbled, half-examined way, with the result that many possessed conflicting understandings. For example, on the one hand, many believed that they understood why some people might be driven to commit acts that were viewed by others as acts of 'terror'. At the same time, they denied that such acts could be the work of Muslims, that indeed Muslims were even capable of such horrific deeds.

Similarly, our survey also revealed a continuing significant gap in perception between Muslims in Britain and wider society. This was reflected in the fact that news stories produced by the BBC and CNN were received with a great deal of suspicion and distrust.

> I don't trust the Western news coverage. I've never had a problem with that in the past. But these days I watch the news and wonder just exactly how much truth they are telling us – and remember, I have grown up watching the BBC.

In part the Western media versions were distrusted because they were challenged by alternative accounts produced by other sources – Middle Eastern television channels such as Al Jazeera. Increasingly, media coverage had come to be regarded as Western propaganda for consumption by its own public. This perception helped to legitimise radical messages that drew on empathy based on personal experience and heightened awareness of the international socio-economic and political situation.

Moreover, the gap that still exists for many Muslims between their lives and concerns and those of wider British society played its part in fashioning the standpoints of our respondents. For many migrant South Asian Muslims, for example, adapting to life in Britain has not meant severing ties with their countries of origin – Pakistan, Bangladesh or India. On the contrary, most have retained strong connections there. For instance, the bodies of the older migrants are still returned to South Asia for burial, and, likewise, ties are continually renewed through marriage. Improved global communication has also helped to raise awareness of connections between local, national and international issues, and has directly helped to shape the differences between non-Muslim and Muslim perceptions regarding events such as September 11 and the more recent Iraq War.

As the findings of this research suggest, Muslim suffering and grievances elsewhere are deeply felt by Muslims in Britain, and influence their attitudes towards the issues that have been under discussion here. Their understanding of the role of violence, together with their interpretations of Islamic texts in resolving conflicts, would seem to be shaped in complex and fluid ways. In essence, they would seem to be influenced more by individual and collective experiences and perceptions of the political contexts, both domestic and international, than by acceptance of some reified and homogeneous prescriptions from the past. At the same time, interaction between past and present practices, ideas and realities forms part of the attitude-framing process. As the responses of our sample highlight, interpretations and understanding of issues such as *jihad* and martyrdom must be located in the context that exists at any given time for their impact to be properly and fully understood.

Notes

1 It should be noted that 'Islamism' itself is differentiated, with strands advocating social and political reform at one end of the spectrum and, at the other end, factions exhorting revolutionary armed struggle.

2 One such scholar, Khalid Masud, has argued that *jihad* needs to be revived as a doctrine of peace and security against prevailing concepts of violence and aggression.

3 The ICM survey conducted on behalf of the BBC revealed that 44 per cent said attacks by al-Qa'ida or similar groups are justified because Muslims are being killed by the Unites States or its allies ... while 46 per cent said such attacks were not justified. Only 8 per cent said attacks by al-Qa'ida or associated organisations against Britain would be justified.

4 'O ye who believe! ... [do not] kill yourselves ... If any do that in rancour and injustice, soon shall We cast him into the Fire ...', Qur'an 4: 29–30.

5 A voluntary survey conducted by the *Muslim News* between 13 November and 4 December 2001. See *Muslim News*, 21 December 2001.

6 That these perceptions were not wholly inaccurate was corroborated by a recent poll that showed that 80 per cent of Britons believed that suspicion of Muslims had increased since the September 11 attacks, though 84 per cent of those polled agreed that Muslims and non-Muslims could live peacefully together; see V. Dodd, 'Muslims Face More Suspicion', *Guardian*, 5 November 2002.

Chapter 11
'(Re)turn to Religion' and Radical Islam

PARVEEN AKHTAR

Introduction

On 24 August 2003 Hizb al-Tahrir organised a conference entitled, *Are You British or Are You Muslim?* Seven thousand, mostly young, participants attended the conference.[1] It was a heavily publicised event which secured much press attention, including a Newsnight report linking Hizb al-Tahrir to terrorism. The message at the conference was bold: the rejection of British identity and the promotion of a single united *ummah*. This is a view that appears frequently on the Hizb al-Tahrir web page and its glossy monthly magazine, *Khilafah*.[2] On 11 September 2002, the anniversary of the World Trade Centre bombings, Al-Muhajiroun, an extremist Islamic group, organised a rally in Finsbury Park, London. Posters and stickers advertising the events appeared in inner city areas with large Muslim populations. They carried pictures of the nineteen hijackers around a backdrop of the World Trade Centre in flames and a smiling Osama bin Laden. The posters stated: 'The Magnificent 19 that divided the world on September 11'. More then 150 people attended.

These are just two examples in what appears to be a growing trend in the revival of Islam. The actual figures are, of course, difficult to report – a situation not helped by the tendency for such organisations to regard membership as a closely guarded secret. However, an examination of the literature probing the subject leaves one with the impression that adherence to an Islamic creed may be intensifying just as much as the debate surrounding the reasons *why*. The explanations most widely cited for the turn to religiosity vary in their emphasis. To explain Islamic regeneration in the West, economic and social exclusion are most often alluded to (Cesari 1998; Kepel 1997; Munoz 1999); to explain the phenomenon in the 'East' (that is, the Middle East and beyond), Kepel, like many others, puts forward a view of Islam as a response to oppressive regimes. Although this suggests a dichotomy between East and West, the underlying thrust of both arguments is the same: the return to Islam is a response to certain structural constrictions.

In this chapter, I shall look at the key reasons why young Muslims are turning to religion. I shall examine the structural arguments and show that what in the literature is taken to be a return to religion is in fact a more complicated phenomenon: one that offers individuals who feel in some way constrained by their circumstances an alternative ideology, a sense of belonging, solidarity, and a means of political mobilisation. I contend that radical groups are able to utilise this turn to religion to their advantage by uniting all the disparate issues faced by Muslims across the globe and building up a simple parable of oppressors and victims. All Muslims everywhere are depicted as the victims of one credible oppressor. Oppressive regimes and social, economic and symbolic exclusion are merged together under the banner of discrimination against Islam from the 'West'. Using the example of Hizb al-Tahrir, I shall demonstrate that September 11 and, in particular, the subsequent wars in Afghanistan and Iraq have provided the context in which radical groups are able to openly challenge not only the 'West' but, more importantly, moderate Islam. Radicalism is thus presented as the only alternative enabling individuals to influence power structures and, in so doing, better their life chances.

'Radical' or 'political Islam' refers to the use of the religion as a means to overthrow the dominant socio-political systems of a particular country and replace them with a new system based on the teachings of the Qur'an. Thus a 'return to religion', as defined in this chapter, does not denote the idea of a religious revival in traditional terms. It does not necessarily refer to an increased adherence to the Islamic code – the practical commitments of prayer or piety – but, instead, refers more to individual empathy with a religious identity; an identity that provides group solidarity and belonging.

Accordingly, let us be clear from the outset: the increased visibility of Islam does not necessarily correspond to a return to religion. Events and debates generally taken to be examples of a return to, or a change in, the intensity of Islamic practice, can sometimes be more accurately described as a change in the *relationship* Muslims have with their 'host' society. Viewed in this way, the building of mosques in France since the early 1980s represents a new stage in ethnic integration, rather than a rise in Islamic practice *per se* (Cesari 1998: 27). The nature of Islamic involvement in a particular society is, it seems, always symbiotic. Thus any serious examination of Muslim integration that does not consider the attitudes of the host society is fundamentally flawed. Take, for example, the acceptability of headscarves across Europe. On 17 December 2003, the French President Jacques Chirac delivered a speech arguing that the proposed law to ban headscarves in schools goes to the very heart of the French conscience. It concerns national cohesion, the ability to live together, to unite on what is essential.[3]

How was he able to make such a claim? In France, headscarves are associated with a philosophy that rejects secularism, oppresses women and, according to some, promotes terrorism. Since secularism lies at the core of France's national identity – the division between church and state is even enshrined in law – the wearing of headscarves has connotations that attack the very 'pillar of [the] constitution' (*ibid.*). By proposing a law banning headscarves in schools, Chirac is in fact following (and so reaffirming) a key ambition of French society: 'secularism', he says, 'is not negotiable'. This is in contrast with Britain, where headscarves lack quite the same connotations. Even if they had, it is difficult to see how they could cause the same furore, given Britain's tradition of multicultural inclusion. The sophistication of this explanation requires viewing the *dominant representation* of Islam within its wider national and international context and discourse. It is important, then, not to conflate symbolic acts of negotiating identity with a return to religiosity, just as it is essential to disassociate the Muslim identity from political developments around the world.

The increased visibility of Muslims in the West, coupled with the increased attention given to Islam in the media, does not itself confirm an increase in adherence to Islam. Indeed, some authors go so far as to suggest that religious affiliation amongst some young Muslims in the West is actually in decline. Leveau (1992) claims that 71 per cent of 18–30 year old Maghrebis in France feel closer to the culture of France than to that of their parents. Similarly, Hargreaves and Stenhouse (1995) report that between a fifth and a third of young people from Muslim backgrounds in France regularly say they are not Islamic believers (Hargreaves and Stenhouse, 1995 cited in Vertovec 1995: 3; Leveau 1991). Nevertheless, Vertovec goes on to contend that European youth identities are often forged in reaction to negative and essentialist representations of both Islam and migrants (1995: 15). Taking this as our premise, the affiliation with Islam amongst young Muslims in Europe would have increased in recent years. I deal with this later, in discussing symbolic exclusion.

The turn to Islam in the West

The notion of exclusion dominates explanations of a return to religion amongst minority populations settled in Western countries. I will offer brief overviews of these explanations, which I have divided into the two distinct types of exclusion – economic and cultural – that come under emphasis. Of course, these facets of exclusion are not mutually exclusive (it is important to note that I am artificially creating boundaries when I separate out two different spheres). Normally, of course, commentators juxtapose different elements from both spheres when explaining Islamic regeneration in the West: invariably, individuals' experiences of cultural exclusion do not take place independently of their experiences in the economic sphere. By separating them out, however, I hope to clarify the basis from which these arguments stem.

Muslims in Britain find themselves at the lower end of the social spectrum. The majority of Pakistanis live in cheap, terraced housing, with a sizeable proportion living in the economically stagnant 'mill towns' of Lancashire and West Yorkshire. Many Muslims living in these areas feel themselves to be the victims of underfunding and a lack of investment (*Guardian*, 12 December 2001). In such a situation, it is common for individuals to look for a collective identity that enables them to negotiate and improve their position (Kepel 1997). Such a view is taken by Munoz (1999), who suggests that Islam can provide a vector for protest against people's social conditions, offering alternative methods of social or political actions. Islam is appealing because it offers a structure to individuals' lives at a time when they feel their life chances are determined wholly by external forces over which they have no control (Poston 1991: 129).

'Symbolic exclusion' is my term for a range of disparate phenomena which, up until now, have lacked the conceptual cohesion of the previous two categories. Drawing upon the notion of the other – prevalent in discussing Islam in the East – we discern a similar idea that applies, with some modification, to Muslims in the West. The notion of the other is, of course, much used (and abused) in discourse today. For the sake of brevity, we will focus on just two important components that are relevant here. First is the assumption, according to Said (1985), that the creation of an Oriental other requires that there is an immutable dichotomy between the West and the Orient. However, Islam is by nature a supra-national institution: it transcends geopolitical boundaries by stressing the importance of membership of the *ummah*, the global Islamic communion. Hence, many Muslims in the West naturally feel a kinship to their Eastern counterparts which negates this supposed dichotomy. The second issue is one of violence. According to Said, the Oriental other is subjected to 'political' violence, being, as it is, marginalised, belittled and dominated. Whilst we may not agree that the West promotes a narrative that does in fact marginalise its resident Muslim population in this way, the issue we are in fact concerned with is the extent to which the indigenous population *perceives* itself as discriminated against in this way.

Accounts of the situation of Muslims in a wider context have an influence on the development and substance of global Muslim solidarity. It has been argued, for example, that the Yugoslavian crisis in the early 1990s precipitated a sense of community that came to include people who previously had not even been considered Muslims (Ahmed and Donnan 1994). In the popular Muslim conception, Bosnian Muslims were 'Europeanised' – they drank alcohol, ate pork, married non-Muslims and so on. Nevertheless, they were among the first victims of the Serbian atrocities, a fact attributed by Muslims to their cultural and religious identity. A similar conviction is evident in Muslim attitudes to conflicts in Chechnya, Kashmir and Palestine. Bosnia, like all these conflicts, has shaped and honed the sense of polarisation in Muslim societies while at the same time increasing the sense of being 'a Muslim'. There is a genuine sense of persecution: that the enemies of Islam will victimise Muslims whatever they do, and that it is therefore important to rally around Islam. In this sense, the return to religion is more psychological, built upon resistance to a perceived scapegoating of Muslims. The demonisation of the Muslim image, presenting it as backward and anti-modern, symbolically sets Muslims apart from all that is progressive and 'Western'. This results in the symbolic exclusion of minority Muslims in the West. The turn to religion, in this sense, could be seen as active resistance to symbolic exclusion.

The Rushdie affair in Britain (1989), the first headscarf affair in France (1989)and the first Gulf War (1990–1) helped people who prior to these events had not paid any great attention to that part of their identity to discover that they were Muslim. They attempted to realise their solidarity with fellow believers whom they saw 'demonised' by the Western media (Kepel 1997). This example demonstrates the distinction between Muslim and Islamic identity. Young people suspected that, as with the demonisaton of Islam during the Rushdie affair, their Muslim communal identity was again under attack from negative media coverage. This observation however, did not translate into prayer (Lewis 1994: 178). Embracing what Vertovec terms a 'cultural Muslim' identity often signifies an equal or greater commitment to a path of resistance. There is doubtless at present growing anti-Muslim sentiment in many quarters of Britain, particularly expressed in local spheres: many youths consequently take up a publicly expressed 'Muslim' identity purposefully, to fly in the face of this growing racism. Other young Muslims, of course, do indeed maintain a more religion-oriented identity (Vertovec 1998: 101). The point is an important one. The popularity of politicised Islam does not imply a strict adherence to the religion's practices and rituals, precisely because what is important is not spiritual or moral guidance. Instead, what attracts is the idea of resisting the dominant, negative hegemony. Islam provides the vehicle for political mobilisation in relation to economic exclusion, and group solidarity in connection with social exclusion. In neither case does the turn to religion have to be accompanied by an acceptance of actual religious practice.

The turn to Islam in the East

Explanations for the turn to religion amongst minorities in the East differ from explanations of the turn to religion amongst minority groups in the West. The rise of Islam in the Eastern region is most often explained with reference to oppressive political regimes and the stifling of political opposition.

Islam has demonstrated itself as a key force in the public life of Muslim societies since the 1970s. For some, Islamic movements denote a genuine alternative to corrupt, exhausted and ineffectual regimes (Esposito 1997: 3). Indeed, one can identify Islamic organisations that were founded specifically to promote liberation and democratisation. Since the late 1980s and early 1990s, Islamic groups have succeeded in winning parliamentary seats, secured portfolios in cabinet and emerged as notable oppositions in countries such as Tunisia, Algeria, Lebanon, Yemen, Kuwait and Pakistan.

By oppressive regimes I refer to the despotism that reigned almost without relief across much of the Middle Eastern region until the 1970s. Absolutist monarchies and authoritarian single-party regimes dominated the landscape. The rare exceptions such as democratic Lebanon did not last long, soon collapsing into civil war. Turkey, too, from time to time practised democracy, lapsing into periods of military intervention. By and large, the single-party regimes degenerated into tyrannies of personal rule (Anderson 1997: 20). Roberts (1991) and Kapil (1991) contend that much of the support for the Front Islamique du Salut (FIS) in Algeria was, in fact, a protest against a single-party regime. This regime had by the late 1980s deteriorated into an inflexible, avaricious establishment (Anderson 1997: 24). Regime decline led to a worsening economy with soaring unemployment, housing scarcity and corruption; ultimately, this gave rise to a crisis of legitimacy and the growth of Islamic opposition (Vandewalle 1997). Much of the Muslim world, having achieved independence as nation-states, now confronts a second transformation: that of national identity and religious reform. The lack of trustworthy, transparent institutional structures for political opposition to work within has provided the context in which religion increasingly has become the official opposition in much of the Muslim world (Anderson 1997: 19). The Islamic political party Hizb al-Tahrir, for example, has one of its largest followings in Uzbekistan, despite its members being prosecuted there for 'civil disobedience'. The country's leader, President Karimov, has been known to torture and even kill his political opponents. People turn to Hizb al-Tahrir because they use religion as a political substitute.

In societies where political opposition is lacking or subdued by governments, Islamists have often emerged as an effective force in both mobilising their own following and appealing to those opposed to the prevailing regime to register their opposition (Esposito 1997: 68). As Hoveyda (2002: 135) notes, the emirs and princes of the Persian Gulf are profoundly despised by the masses and challenged by their own people. Nonetheless, this political use of Islam does not inevitably lead to an increase in Islamic practice. Indeed, research in Algeria suggested that although most people were in favour of the FIS, they did not agree to the Islamicisation of the constitution.

The rise of Islam as a response to oppressive regimes is well documented, so we need not examine any further. We can note, however, that the premise underlying such explanations is similar to those that we have seen for economic and cultural exclusion: namely, the *structuralist* nature of the exposition. In as much as they claim that the current situation *necessarily* leads to a search for belonging or political mobilisation, all such theories are deterministic. They therefore describe Islam as a vehicle for mobilisation or solidarity. If we refer back to a point made at the beginning of the chapter, Muslims are perceived *as* Muslims more at certain moments of political and historical development than at others (Yalcin-Heckmann 1998: 168). Similarly, Muslims emphasise their Muslim identity more at some points than others – points at which they feel excluded socially, economically or symbolically, or indeed, when there is no other way in which to view their opposition to political process.

The question we are now faced with is *how* radical Islam uses and manipulates this dissatisfaction and unites Muslims globally.

Radicalising Islam

Radical Islam, sometimes referred to as fundamentalism, indicates, as Geaves (1999: 375) argues, that religion can be the corporate public action of religiously motivated individuals to change the social system on behalf of what they perceive to be their deepest spiritual loyalties. In trying to achieve social change some forms of radical Islam resort, ultimately, to the notion of sacrifice and terror:

> It's as if a very high impenetrable wall separated you from paradise or hell, Allah has promised one or the other to his creatures. So, by pressing the detonator, you can immediately open the door to paradise – it is the shortest route to heaven. (Quoted in Hassan 2001, cited Jewett and Lawrence 2003: 20)

The simplified moral outlook is evident here. Indeed, radical Islamic groups can capitalise on the social and economic disaffection of individuals, or political grievances, and unite these together in simple moral terms. The world is clearly divided into black and white: a dichotomy necessary for any group claiming ultimate moral truth. But of course, for Islamic radicalism to work there has to be this distinct simplified notion of Islam. There may not be one single Islam, just as there is no single America or Europe or the West (Lawrence, 1998), yet any endeavour to unite a diverse number of people requires the formulation of simple dichotomies. This can be seen also in the rhetoric of the American executive post-September 11 – the 'War on Terror' couched in the language of good versus evil, hero versus villain. Werbner (1994) in her work on the Gulf War, describes this process as 'fabulation' (Werbner 1994). It is simply an interpretation of history from a certain standpoint. Lawrence (1998: 5) argues that in the 1990s most Euro-American journalists propagate one message, 'Islam is one, and Islam is dangerous'. In similar terms Hizb al-Tahrir propound an equally reductive view of the West: the West is one and the West is attacking.

It is important to note that this notion of Islam is divorced from more moderate versions. Reactions to Hizb al-Tahrir amongst the older generation of British Muslims can be negative since they fear the influence such groups have on their children. 'We're extremely worried about young people being susceptible to their message,' says the general secretary of the Pakistani Community Centre in Derby. Groups like al-Muhajiroun, he claims, 'present themselves as positive role models – they make you want to participate and be part of something'. Whereas moderate Islam allows Muslims to negotiate and advance their position within the political structures of the country they live in, the very point of political Islam is to demolish all structures that are not Islamic. It *has* to set itself up as a complete ideology in opposition to the dominant structures to work. Islam cannot be adhered to because of the need to belong, for solidarity or even for political mobilisation. It is a distinct alternative to the current system.

I will turn to the case of Hizb al-Tahrir and show how after September 11 and the subsequent wars in Afghanistan and Iraq the group is able to construct a particular notion of crisis and present itself as the only force for change.

Contextualising Hizb al-Tahrir

Hizb al-Tahrir is a group that presents itself as moderate in its views and denounces all forms of violence. However, the group has recently been criticised for the radical and contentious writings on its website. Hizb al-Tahrir was founded by a Palestinian, Taqiuddin an-Nabhani al-Falastani, in 1953. Although today still headed by a Palestinian, Abd al-Kadim Zallum, the group has expanded across

borders and, indeed, continents, with significant pockets of membership in countries as diverse as England and Indonesia. The group's
aim is to re-establish the Islamic state, called the *khilafah*, which, it
argues, is a central tenet of the Muslim faith. Its eventual utopian
goal is to unite Muslims wherever they may live. To this end, the
group attempts to educate people about the dangers of Western
secular government, which it sees as actively trying to divide the
Muslim *ummah*.

The present political situation in the Middle East allows Hizb al-
Tahrir to construct a particular notion of crises, one that offers its
preferred narrative of the world. Its central message is the
importance of the *ummah*, the importance of a community that is
not shaped by national boundaries nor localised traditions. It
characterises a communal identity that is not context-specific, but
universal; not set by the laws of men, but by divine power. It seeks to
provide social solidarity for those Muslims in the West who feel
excluded.

Hizb al-Tahrir suggests that not only are nationalist boundaries
illegitimate and unimportant, but they also allow for the
suppression and subjugation of Muslim people across the world.
This appeals to those who feel that their political regimes are
oppressive. For Hizb al-Tahrir, nation-state boundaries are illegitimate constructs that serve only to divide people superficially along
nationalistic lines. Indeed, a recurrent theme in many of the articles
featured in the *Khilafah* publication is that the Muslim *ummah* has
been politically divided into 55 entities, and pumped with the
pernicious concepts of independence and nationalism.[4]

I will focus on two main aspects of the Hizb al-Tahrir cause: first,
the role of ideas in shaping the discursive aspect of the group and,
second, the context within which Hizb al-Tahrir has to operate. An
analysis of these suggests a complex interaction between ideas,
agents and structures in a global arena.

The importance of ideas

If we are to examine the reasons why Hizb al-Tahrir appeals to
young Muslims in particular, we must consider the ideas the group
supports. At the level of ideas Hizb al-Tahrir is an extremist rebuttal
of the more mainstream Muslim parties. The primary strategy of the
latter is to show the dangers of the Western democratic path by
analysing political situations, using an Islamic perspective. Hizb al-
Tahrir advocates instead a highly distinctive approach to politics,

bypassing an incongruous assemblage of ideas put forward by the mainstream Islamic groups. Hizb al-Tahrir argues that

> the only correct course of action and political activity is solely upon the Islamic basis, that is, the Qur'an and the *Sunnah*. This is the pathway that the Muslims in the West must all unanimously align themselves to, in rejecting all that is un-Islamic and undertaking only that which is allowed.

These ideas are not original. What gives them such cultural import is the appeal of their advocates, coupled with the current political climate. Hizb al-Tahrir members are well-educated, well-spoken university graduates and professionals: they produce a glossy magazine and make articulate appearances on *Newsnight*. This, it appears, has made an impact on some British Muslims. British intelligence officials suggest that about 1,000 individuals have been recruited in Britain over recent years to fight for the Taliban in Afghanistan. Some of those graduated to al-Qa'ida training camps.[5]

The Islamic identity presented by Hizb al-Tahrir cannot be accepted alongside that of, for example, a British or a Welsh identity. It cannot be reduced to a part-identity or one aspect of identity. Hizb al-Tahrir argues that, 'many times in our enthusiasm, Islam is reduced to a host of rituals and spiritual worships that can live comfortably with Western thought, side by side in perfect harmony'. However, their argument is that 'such a conveyance reduces Islam and falsely accepts the dominance of Western Capitalism'. Islam is, Hizb al-Tahrir contends, an alternative – and this should be demonstrated by 'conveying Islam intellectually, through thoughts'.

Studying the group in isolation cannot account for why its qualities suddenly appeal to a generation of British Muslims in particular. Furthermore, even a strong-willed group such as Hizb al-Tahrir cannot simply impose its will on events and shape the political attitudes of British Muslims, just as it wishes. In this sense, a tight focus on Hizb al-Tahrir fails to take into account the context within which the group has to operate. Howard Gardner (1995) argues that vital to the success of a leader is the skill of being able to 'tell a story' about the past and then to show how only the leader will be able to bring about change (Gardner cited in Seldon 1996: 275). Hizb al-Tahrir's rhetoric portrays itself as a legitimate political alternative, and by doing so presents itself as a challenge to moderate Islam. However, having an ideological space does not necessarily mean being able to push through change without negotiating constraints.

The importance of context
The context is the political, social and cultural arena within which events take place. The context can constrain some forms of participation or facilitate others. In many instances it is heavily influential, indeed indicative of a certain course of action. The war in Iraq (seen as a response to September 11) was the turning point: that was when participating within the mainstream political system became delegitimised. Hizb al-Tahrir, for example, argues that 'the recent aggression against the people in Iraq did not only demonstrate a local reaction from the Muslims of Iraq but invited the expression of others who were not from that region'. The point is essentially that 'the reality of the emotions of the Muslim *ummah* towards issues that may not affect some of them directly ... nevertheless ... reveals that they have taken it as their issue'. And therefore 'the Muslims of Pakistan, Nigeria, Malaysia, Indonesia, Europe, Britain, Turkey, in fact all of them, came out with their unanimous support for the Muslims of Iraq and nothing but repulsion towards the West and the Muslim rulers'.

Hizb al-Tahrir's leaders can always revert back to what happened in Iraq. They can set up a binary opposition with democratic participation and the Islamic way. Their ability to implant their ideas of global brotherhood, of a single united *ummah,* in the public psyche is a key to discrediting democratic participation and gaining the space to advocate change and pacify any discontent by reverting to the idea that there is no alternative. They argue that the Muslim way is the only way for two important reasons. First, and from the point of view of Hizb al-Tahrir most importantly, 'to advocate and undertake such political actions is forbidden in Islam, and contradicts many clear Islamic evidences'. Second, Hizb al-Tahrir contends that attempts to participate in the Western political system have borne little fruit and are therefore futile:

> The futility of such attempts by Muslims to influence Western foreign policy aggressions against the Muslim *ummah* has been reinforced time and again. For what influence can they think the Muslims can exert upon Western politics, when all and sundry were against the British political decision for war against Iraq, and still the decision to go to war was executed?

For Hizb al-Tahrir, participating in democracy is only to serve the West, as in the case of Iraq, 'so the purpose of implementing democracy is to serve the interest of the colonial powers'.

The importance of the war in Iraq in legitimising the course of political Islam should not be underestimated. More important than Western occupation of Muslim land was the failure of the US and the UK to listen to democratic protest, allowing capital to be made of the futility of trying to work within the Western system.

Conclusion

If the return to religion amongst minority groups in the West is most often explained in terms of exclusion, the rise of Islam in the East is largely explained with reference to oppressive political regimes and the stifling of political opposition. Although the emphasis is clearly different, the thrust of the arguments is essentially the same: religion is a response to *structural* constraints, be they economic, social or political. Islam, then, is seen as a vehicle for political mobilisation, it offers a sense of belonging and solidarity. As a consequence of this view, a return to religion does not necessarily correspond to a rise in the adherence to Islamic practice. My argument is essentially that after September 11 and the wars in Afghanistan and Iraq, radical Islamic groups are able to utilise this return to religion by uniting the various grievances of Muslims around the world. A very simple dichotomy is created between 'Muslims' and 'the West'. Using the example of Hizb al-Tahrir, I have demonstrated how moderate Islam, or Muslims groups desiring to work within the Western political system, has been delegitimised. The reference point now is the war in Iraq – where, as Hizb al-Tahrir argues, democracy was ignored to achieve the aims of the West. Radical Islam is thus able to present itself as the *only* alternative to 'the system'.

Notes

1   The figure estimated by Hizb al-Tahrir was 6,000–7,000.
2   The information on Hizb al-Tahrir in this research is taken from the group's website and the *Khilafah* articles on the website www.khilafah.com (5 September 2003).
3   Jacques Chirac, speech on La Chaine Info TV, 17 December 2003.
4   These articles are available at the following website: www.khilafah.com.
5   *Daily Telegraph*, 11 September 2002. This is not, of course, to suggest that all 1,000 were Hizb al-Tahrir members, but merely that the influence of political Islam runs far.
6   A course of action that involves entering the Western political system.

PART IV
Temporal and Spatial
Ethnic and Religious Identities

Chapter 12
All Quiet on the Eastern Front?
Bangladeshi Reactions in Tower Hamlets

HALIMA BEGUM AND JOHN EADE

British Muslims reacted in different ways to the September 11 attacks on New York and Washington and the subsequent attacks on Afghanistan and Iraq. The diversity of reactions – from condemnation, fear and horror at the sheer scale of the terrorist attacks in the USA through to organised street-level protest at the wars in Afghanistan and Iraq – points to a complex collective response from British Muslims. These reactions concur with the Runnymede Trust's report (1997), which called for a broad definition of Muslim identities and a flexible understanding of the circumstances of Muslim communities in the UK. We find that the street-level or grassroots response of Bangladeshi Muslims in Tower Hamlets following the events of September 11 agrees with the broad tenets of these early arguments, which have become marginalised in current analysis of Muslims and September 11 in media, policy and academic circles. September 11 is partly to blame because of its cataclysmic impact in shifting public attention to global Islam *vis-à-vis* the rest of the world through a quintessentially cinematic gaze (Davis 2001). Yet it is also the case that researchers, politicians, experts and other stakeholders have been willing accomplices in the September 11 industry, which constructs hegemonic tropes around demonic Islam.

We bear in mind the multi-faceted dynamics of circumstances and social contexts in which identities operate. We hope to unpack some of these issues by focusing on 'everyday urban' life in Tower Hamlets. We will focus on the daily negotiation of mobile Bangladeshi identities and the politics of the lived experience (that is, the role of micro-publics of opposition and dissent) during the period leading up to the US-led invasions of Afghanistan and Iraq. Bangladeshi

Muslims in Tower Hamlets did not find themselves in political isolation on the Iraq issue; rather, they joined the majority of the local population, across ethnic, religious and age divides, in opposition to the borough's political leadership, which supported the national government's stance in the 'War on Terror'. As a result, Bangladeshi Muslims had at their disposal a wide choice of outlets for popular protest, which did not conform to rigid group identifications on the basis of singular religious or cultural identities. Instead Bangladeshis were able to draw upon secular and religious outlets to articulate their dissent. This response echoes the political roots of Bangladesh and the country's emergence as an independent state from contestation between the religious and secular politics of nationalism. It also reflects the way in which Bangladeshis have interacted with local representative structures and have partly ensured that the population has a strong voice or a plurality of voices within political structures. The local government machinery therefore facilitated widespread opposition to the 'War on Terror', thereby putting protest and opposition at the centre of political discussion.

All these modes of expression were powerfully mediated by local and global projections of vulnerability and fear, to which Bangladeshis responded in different ways, utilising different tactics and acting as a diverse rather than a unified group in order to maximise their collective power to challenge and subvert official narratives concerning the 'War on Terror'.

Tower Hamlets and urban struggles

Tower Hamlets is part of London's East End, which has long been associated with both political and social struggles and with immigration. The area lies just outside the City of London's eastern boundary and by the end of the eighteenth century it had already acquired the reputation for poverty, noxious industries, turbulence and immigrants that was to acquire mythical status during the nineteenth century. Spitalfields, a locality on the eastern border of the City, was occupied by Irish Catholic settlers whose chapels became the target of London's worst spate of urban violence during the eighteenth century – the 'Gordon Riots' of 1780. Spitalfields had been settled by another immigrant community – Protestant Huguenot refugees from France – during the late seventeenth and early eighteenth centuries, but the more prosperous settlers had departed by the 1780s as the locality joined other neighbourhoods in a downward spiral of poverty that led to Victorian middle-class fears about a dark and dangerous East End – London's disturbing Other in respectable bourgeois narratives of place and people. Moral panics concerning East European Jewish settlement during the late nineteenth century were typified by media treatment of the Jack the Ripper murders in Spitalfields and nearby Whitechapel, and by the local political agitation against 'aliens' that resulted in the first twentieth-century attempt to control immigration – the 1905 Aliens Act.

The social and economic reality, of course, differed from these powerful urban myths. Despite the intense poverty and social dislocation evident in the East End's worst slums, occupation, income and various forms of formal and informal education stratified the emerging local working class. There was also a small but highly influential lower middle class of traders and shopkeepers who played a key role in the emerging political organisation of the area. As social and economic conditions improved during the 1920s and 1930s, so the political life of the East End became increasingly dominated by trade unions, political parties and ethnic (primarily religious) organisations in which a diverse working-class culture overlapped with ethnicity (Jewish and Irish Catholic, in particular). Although such urban confrontations/riots as the famous battle of Cable Street in 1936 helped to promote the image of a multicultural, anti-fascist East End working class, the reality was more complex as Knowles (1992) among others has pointed out. The Cable Street confrontation involved a wide range of local activists whose unity against a common foe very briefly overlaid their diverse political agendas shaped by the divisions of religion, education and occupation.

Bangladeshis in Tower Hamlets

Tower Hamlets is a multi-ethnic neighbourhood in the East End of London in which diversity, difference and inter-group conflict has still not resulted in far-reaching social unrest. It is, therefore, an interesting case study of an urban neighbourhood in which social cohesion has prevented a breakdown of trust and law and order. The situation in Tower Hamlets, therefore, suggests that ethnic diversity *in itself* does not offer compelling evidence for the kinds of social breakdown seen in Bradford and Oldham during the summer of 2001. We argue that the Bangladeshi Muslim population in Tower Hamlets is firmly entrenched in local civic structures and political institutions and, therefore, exercises some influence on the borough's political life. It is a highly visible population and its expression and valorisation of culture (through increasing visibility of religion and Islamicisation) is a vital sign of confidence and acceptance in the public sphere and in local democracy. This self-confidence enabled Bangladeshi Muslims to ask searching questions concerning English identities during the devolution of regional structures in the UK and the longer-term shifts in the construction of Britain as a multicultural nation. What were the differences between Englishness and Britishness, for example? How could popular interpretations of Englishness be articulated in ways that included Bangladeshi Muslims and other minorities? Was England a Christian country? If it was an increasingly secular country and an un-Christian land, where would Muslims fit in? This process is what the Parekh report (2000) has called 'multicultural drift', and underwent several crisis points at which the right of minority groups – the Other – to challenge their subordination in the public sphere exposed them to public scrutiny of their right to citizenship in Britain. The constellation of leftist and British Islamic voices over the 'War on Terror', therefore, can be read as another point of renegotiation – this time of the Self (or the majority), fractured and meeting the Other in solidarity. Thus identities are formed, negotiated and renegotiated to produce new social movements. The realignment of new and old identities points to a politics of resistance and opposition new to Britain and elsewhere, in which social movements have converged to produce powerful statements of protest against aggressive US foreign policies and global capitalism.

Earlier crises – the Muslim Parliament, the *Satanic Verses* controversy and the Gulf War (1991)

The recent response is part of a longer process of Bangladeshi collective mobilisation to campaign for social justice and racial equality by working within the system and attaining representation at the leadership level. Although Bangladeshis have supported public meetings and demonstrations on earlier occasions, they have not played as prominent a role as other British Muslims. This was clearly illustrated in the late 1980s during the uproar that followed the publication of Salman Rushdie's book, *The Satanic Verses*. The burning of his book, which attracted so much media attention, took place in Bradford and was led by Pakistani activists there. Leaders of Bradford's Council of Mosques led the protests and although a Bangladeshi led protests in East London, these were comparatively low-key affairs.

When the Muslim Parliament emerged, Bangladeshis were conspicuous by their absence from prominent positions and the Parliament attracted little interest in Tower Hamlets. This anomaly was a reflection of the relatively weak socio-economic position of British Bangladeshis in the UK compared to other British Muslim groups. During the Gulf War interviews with young university-educated Bangladeshis in Tower Hamlets revealed strong opposition to British military intervention but, again, this individual hostility did not translate into high-profile opposition by large groups of Bangladeshis (see Centre for Bangladeshi Studies 1994, Eade 1992). It is relatively difficult for Bangladeshis to articulate their voices within Muslim representative structures, a situation that has made it easier for the population to take part in wider secular protests. There is reluctance within Bangladeshi populations to participate in larger regional or national Islamic networks where presentation of Bangladeshis in leadership roles is weak. There is less incentive to organise effective Bangladeshi Muslim strategies as the secular sections of the Bangladeshi population have become co-opted into the Council structures and can represent Muslim interests through a proxy 'Bangladeshi' or 'black and minority ethnic' identity.

Explanations

Transnational politics, secularists and Islamists
The reasons for this well-established situation are to be found in political developments taking place in Bangladesh as well as Tower Hamlets. Bangladesh had come closer to other Muslim-majority countries during the late 1970s and 1980s, after the early 1970s reaction to Pakistani domination. However, its political and military élites were less embroiled in Islamic ideological debates than their Pakistani counterparts. Demonstrations during the *Satanic Verses* controversy and the 1991 Gulf War were less numerous and intense than in Pakistan. Islamist organisations – political, educational and cultural – were less influential in Bangladesh and were challenged vigorously by secularist groups associated with the Awami League party and left-wing politics.

In Tower Hamlets and other areas of Britain Bangladeshi political divisions were mediated by the predominance of those who had migrated from one particular district in the country of origin – Sylhet. As with other settlements this localism was made even more local through the process of chain migration. Many Sylhetis came from particular clusters of settlements within the district's subdivisions, such as Sunamganj, Habiganj, Beani Bazar and Maulvi Bazar. The outcome was a complicated interweaving of political struggles between (1) the major parties (Awami League, Bangladesh National Party and Jatiya Party) and Islamist pressure groups in Bangladesh and (2) British political parties. Political struggles between Bangladeshi activists in Tower Hamlets operated at several levels, therefore – at the level of formal British political discourse and practice, as well as at formal and informal levels where Bangladeshi political issues were more important. These different levels influenced elections and debates in the Tower Hamlets political arena, so that support for a particular political party and its policies could not be taken at face value.

Local politics and Islamist organisations
During the 1970s the first generation controlled representation of the local Bangladeshi community to 'outsiders', especially leaders of the dominant Labour Party. However, during the 1980s the first generation's leadership was challenged by a more Anglicised second-generation cohort, which forged highly effective alliances with white radical activists within the Labour party. Second-generation activists gained positions of responsibility not only within the local political apparatus but also in a wide range of public organisations (hospitals, health centres, education, housing, amenities and recreation), development agencies such as Cityside, and community organisations. Certain individuals also operated on a London-wide and national stage: Kumar Murshed was an adviser on race to Ken Livingstone, and Baroness Pola Uddin became the first Bangladeshi member of the House of Lords.

The influence wielded by these second-generation Bangladeshis has been under increasing pressure since the late 1980s from Islamist groups. The arrival of wives and dependants in the 1980s virtually completed the process of family formation and made even more prominent the issue of how family life was to be pursued in a non-Muslim and deeply secular society. A process of Islamicisation emerged that centred around the Islamic education of the third generation, provision at local state schools for their Islamic needs such as *halal* food, female dress in public space and marriages of the large cohort of third-generation Bangladeshis who were leaving school and university.

This social and cultural process clearly overlapped with the political developments outlined above. The *Satanic Verses* controversy, the 1991 Gulf War, the attack on the World Trade Centre in 2001 by mostly Saudi dissidents, and the recent war in Iraq were dramatic, violent instances of a wider struggle over what Islam means to both Muslims and non-Muslims. These apparently global Islamic events highlighted to Bangladeshi Muslims the variations in the politics and practices of global Islam while at the same time pointing to a nascent idea of the Muslim *ummah*. Migration from rural Sylhet to Britain encouraged people to compare themselves with Muslims from other parts of the world and to give new meanings to the concept of a global *ummah*. In the context of Tower Hamlets this struggle involved the everyday politics of ordinary people's lives, as well as the narrower arena of formal politics and community representation. Furthermore, the ways in which global and local processes worked themselves out in Tower Hamlets differentiated Bangladeshis from their compatriots in Oldham, where riots took place in the summer of 2001. Whatever the causes of the riots, they did not reflect in any straightforward way events occurring in the Middle East, the US or Bangladesh.

The Islamicisation process inevitably involved the expanding numbers of local mosques and prayer halls. At these public meeting points men (primarily) discussed political, social and cultural developments at local and more global levels, as well as performing their religious obligations. Islamist organisations sought to attach themselves to these centres and the East London Mosque provided the most striking example of this process. This was one of the oldest mosques in Tower Hamlets, which reopened in 1986 in an imposing new building on the busy Whitechapel Road. It provided facilities unavailable elsewhere, such as meeting rooms around the spacious prayer hall, a gallery for female worshippers, and a funeral parlour at the back of the mosque. In 2002 a large site to the west of the main building was developed for housing and recreational facilities. Not surprisingly, prominent Islamist organisations tried to link themselves closely to the mosque – the Da'wat ul Islam and the Young Muslim Organisation, for example. Moreover, the mosque's leaders were eager to claim a central position within not just the borough but East London in general (see Eade 1997; Eade, Fremeaux and Garbin 2000; Garbin 2003).

Faith-based community organisations

The assurance and self-reliance of Bangladeshi Muslims is partly reflected in the success of the organisational profiles of faith-based community organisations in Tower Hamlets. These organisations stand at an exciting turning point within the bigger picture of national regeneration priorities. During the past five years the UK government has become increasingly interested in the potential of faith groups to become key agents in improving their local environments. Faith groups are believed to sustain a high degree of solidarity and mutual aid amongst their members. They are seen as vital links between their constituencies and mainstream service delivery and also as vehicles through which people connect with the wider local community (SEU 2000; Smith 1999, 2003; Harris 2003). The growing Islamicisation of Bangladeshi populations in Tower Hamlets corresponds with the more general growth of faith-based community organisations, which carry out a mixture of community and religious functions. This separate but related development has had a cohesive impact on the way in which different members of the local Bangladeshi populations have voiced their criticisms – both of the wars in Afghanistan and Iraq and of the racism directed at their communities by service providers. Increasingly, the two leading mosques are engaged in partnerships with the local authority to carry out social welfare functions. Numerous other community-based partnerships involving faith-led groups have been instrumental in responding to the emerging 'youth at risk' agenda – preventive work on drugs, youth homelessness and teenage pregnancy – and in curbing the anti-social behaviour of young Bangladeshi men, in particular, through community-based projects rooted in Islamic principles and delivering public services to young Bangladeshis. The success of these projects in reaching out to disaffected Bangladeshi young men ensures that these faith-based organisations are engaged in mainstream service delivery channels and remain open and accountable, a requirement for public funding.

The role of faith-based community organisations must also be placed in the context of the wider debate concerning the ability of these communities to create, sustain and deliver social capital and social connections. The creation of social capital in Tower Hamlets has been a powerful catalyst in bringing together different faith communities, particularly Christian and Islamic communities, and has provided some lessons about how to create socially cohesive neighbourhoods between disconnected communities (Begum 2003). Whilst most faith communities regularly deal with isolation, discrimination and exclusion, in many cases this leads to a strong and positive community identity, which can provide a sense of place and self-esteem to individual members. If people feel that they belong and have a sense of who they are, and are comfortable in their environments, they are more likely to become involved, to practise and implement positive neighbourhood messages concerning community safety and local political participation, and to develop collective political opposition. Ironically, while 'faith' has been a battle cry for international terrorists of different religious persuasions, it has equally been a catalyst for community and social cohesion at the local scale in Tower Hamlets and in other parts of East London (Smith 1999). The work of the East London Communities Organisation is an exemplar of faith acting as social glue for organising around social justice initiatives.

Opposition and dissent: multiple voices of protest

Given the history of local politics outlined earlier, Bangladeshi Muslims' response to September 11, unsurprisingly, was neither collective nor harmonious. Instead, a diverse array of voices united in opposition to the US-led invasion of Afghanistan and Iraq – an opposition that resonated with the dissenting voices from non-Bangladeshi populations in East London. Consequently, one of the impacts of September 11 has been a surprising alignment in local politics and grassroots politics in which groups across the political, ethnic and religious spectrums have voiced their opposition to the war. These responses may appear to be low-key in comparison with the usual stylised street confrontations between young people and the police, but there is another way to interpret them – as a healthy and vibrant competition between various empowered publics, with Muslim identities dispersed across these micro-publics through community and political structures. There is no denying that September 11 provided a new-found impetus for religious extremists to recruit from alienated sections of Bangladeshi communities – mainly young, male, British Bangladeshis. However, the potential for recruitment in Tower Hamlets was significantly weaker compared with other parts of the country. There are pockets of religious extremism among Bangladeshi Muslims in the borough, as well as bigotry from white enclaves, but on the whole neither the local far right and its supporters or the Islamic extremists have been powerful local agents in the wake of September 11.

Inter-generational similarities and differences
A plethora of alliances and informal groupings emerged during the lead-up to the war in Afghanistan and Iraq. One alliance involved the old-guard, first-generation Bangladeshis, whose identities are rooted in Bangladesh and shaped by a mainly spiritual, faith-based connection to the practice of religion. The onset of the war in Iraq sparked off a collective concern among the first generation about the future of the loosely perceived Muslim *ummah,* but this was accompanied by a deeper sense of vulnerability associated with the outbreak of hostilities in Iraq and Afghanistan. These elders were very concerned about how the international hostilities would impact on their citizenship rights and were afraid that their 'loyalty' to the British nation would be called into question. They desperately wished to avoid the widespread questioning of their cultural, national and political allegiances.

Elderly British Bangladeshis, therefore, were poised delicately in relation to political authority, with the risk that their claims to citizenship might be called into question. This meant that many in this group articulated opposition to the war in less visible ways – by constant attention to satellite television channels in private spaces and also by participating in the national 'Stop the War' coalition as individuals rather than as organised groupings. In contrast to their response to the Gulf War, which took place before the proliferation of satellite technology and a diffuse choice of alternative channels such as Bangla TV, Ekushi TV and the Arab-based Al Jazeera, dissent could now mushroom in the private domain of the home. This dissent sometimes reached fever pitch in individual households, but always remained mediated and managed in public spaces, such the street or places of worship.

The first generation also transferred core cultural values and experiences of political life in Bangladesh to the second generation, mostly in the 30–50s age band. As a result, both the first and second generations were accustomed to politics as mediated by village councils (*panchayats*) in their country of origin. Typically, this brought to the men an understanding of power dynamics in which religion was both spiritual and political, and could be mobilised for different strategies – survival, coping, winning recognition, celebrating identities, voicing political dissent to events in the Middle East, and so on. The second generation has been successful in building strong community structures to mitigate the impact of social exclusion and racism (Eade 1989). Second-generation British Bangladeshi women also made some inroads into positions of responsibility in the local Council structures.

The third generation is comparatively disadvantaged in this respect, as they do not possess experience of negotiation gained from Bangladeshi village council structures, nor do they have access, as the third generation does, to political power in UK council structures. Potentially these young Bangladeshi Muslims can remain alienated from mainstream social life in Tower Hamlets. However, the overall community structures established in the 1980s have absorbed the alienation felt by many young people by providing a sense of cultural belonging and working through local community, voluntary and political structures to alleviate symptoms of poverty and exclusion. The local white left, represented in the voluntary and community sectors, was also a powerful absorber of Muslim sentiments in the past. These local organisational networks help to explain why national-level politicians, by contrast, were out of touch with their constituencies – leading to a situation, like the resistance to the poll tax in the late 1980s, in which Muslims and non-Muslims could find common cause over issues of democratic accountability.

In contrast to secular organisations, community groups linked to faith-based organisations have helped to manage the frustration of third-generation Bangladeshi Muslims. These organisations are also key spaces in which local Bangladeshi women have been active for years, and many have been instrumental in curbing nascent confrontational tendencies. They have organised around issues, sometimes within a broader range of community development concerns, while capitalising on the newly politicised mood of young people following September 11 and the wars in Afghanistan and Iraq. Finally, and most importantly, key religious institutions – the pillars of local Bangladeshi community life, such as the mosques – are stakeholders in the regeneration process whereby accountability and transparency are demonstrated. This ensured that key religious spaces have remained open community spaces and unlikely targets for extremists. As a result young Bangladeshi Muslims have a wide range of possibilities to choose from when expressing their frustrations at 'the system' or their internal community power structures. This choice explains how Bangladeshi Muslims responded to September 11 in a diffused manner, rather than mobilising their religious identities in isolation from other axes of identity – as British Bangladeshis, as Londoners, as Eastenders, and as mothers, fathers and young people

One of the notable aspects of these alliances and groupings was their diversity in character – from the formal to the informal, from loose connections based on face-to-face relations to distant and virtual groupings with regional and national alliances configured around the principles of social justice. Yet, whatever their alignments, Bangladeshi Muslims in Tower Hamlets responded to September 11 in less visible ways that did not capture headlines and did not lead to the coupling of Bangladeshis with terrorism in the media. On the whole they did not organise behind groups led by Muslim leaders, and instead aligned themselves with organisations and movements that are better described as protests or movements from below – or what some observers have dubbed 'globalisation from below' (Portes 1997). These popular movements also absorbed dissident Muslim voices. Examples of such organisations include local trade union groups, multicultural youth clubs and community groups. They also contributed to national demonstrations and developed strong anti-Islamophobic messages for the wider community, helped by Tony Blair's message on national television urging resistance to a backlash against domestic Muslim populations. This broad-based organising by schools, youth groups, the Citizens Organising Forum, the East London Communities Organisations Forum and the Asian Dub Education Foundation focused the sentiments of the majority of Muslims, providing an outlet for expression and popular dissent.

Mobilisation of local support

The response of Bangladeshi Muslims has been based, therefore, on broad organising principles that emphasised not only opposition to UK anti-poverty and social exclusion measures but also dissatisfaction with US–British foreign policy in the Middle East. This is why the membership and participation activity rates for many community and voluntary sector groups, as well as mosques, have been very high. Many institutions (secular and religious) have recruited new users as a result of this political mobilisation, often with a religious undertone. Many service providers were successful in galvanising younger groups into rediscovering and reactivating debates about social exclusion and citizenship that created a heightened sense of politics and notions of 'home' and 'place'. Religious organisations, such as the local chapters of the Young Muslim Organisation (YMO) and Hizb al-Tahrir, have also widened their recruitment drive, as has the radical group, al-Muhajiroun.

On the whole, the radical groups have enjoyed less success than other organisations because politically active Muslims in Tower Hamlets had already become immersed in faith-based community organisations and well-established religious associations such as the YMO. The protest of Bangladeshi Muslims in Tower Hamlets cannot be interpreted, therefore, in terms of hegemonic discourses around 'extremists' and 'fundamentalists'. Popular opinion, which ranged across ethnic, religious and class divides, united in opposition to the war in Iraq and had a catalytic effect on local politics. The elected politicians lost touch with their local constituency, and interventions by local union structures and outside pressure were necessary to check the growing anti-war vote. This is why Muslims in Tower Hamlets did not find themselves out on a limb on the Iraq issue. They were in sympathy with what was happening in the rest of the borough, as representative politics became divorced from popular support. Citizenship issues came to the fore as the majority populations became alienated from the power structure.

Another way to view the success of the broad-based alliances between Bangladeshi Muslims in Tower Hamlets and other social groups is to look at the slogans of the Hizb al-Tahrir demonstration. These slogans desperately exhorted Muslims not to participate in the national Stop the War Coalition with the absurd slogan 'Don't Say "No" to War'. This ambiguous statement was partly a call to organise separately outside the national coalition, and partly a rallying cry to Muslims to open their eyes to what in this view was an inevitable confrontation between Islam and the West in which Muslims would be required to take sides.

Abuse and public space

So far we have highlighted the intense way in which British Bangladeshis in Tower Hamlets have responded politically to unfolding events since September 11. Amidst these efforts at reclaiming public space for opposition and dissenting political expression, there has been a gradual increase in fear and perceived vulnerability in public spaces, felt mainly by Bangladeshi Muslim women, particularly those wearing the traditional Islamic *hijab*. There were recorded and unrecorded instances of minor abuse against women – usually occurring as drive-by incidents or in queues for public amenities. Younger Bangladeshi Muslims, women and men, were most sensitive to street-level reprisals in public spaces from white residents, particularly in the Poplar, Roman Road and Globe Town sections of Tower Hamlets, regarded by longer-settled East End populations as the 'last bastion of white communities' within the borough. Many community organisations have stepped up their anti-racist work to include workshops on anti-Islamophobia, particularly on the Isle of Dogs, which has significantly high white and African-Caribbean populations. Docklands Outreach, a local organisation dedicated to supporting young Eastenders at risk, has reoriented its annual residential trip away from anti-racist and anti-sexist work to focus on anti-Islamophobia. Tower Hamlets College and Tower Hamlets Summer University – two more key youth stakeholders – have also stepped up their efforts to raise awareness of Islamophobia. The local police stations were also put on notice to deal with Islamophobic behaviour. Such measures and initiatives have had the cumulative impact of reaffirming to British Bangladeshis a sense of belonging, and, on a wider level, given legitimacy to their fears and concerns.

Conclusion

During the last 25 years Bangladeshi Muslims have succeeded in negotiating their citizenship rights on a local scale and gaining recognition of their collective rights. In this sense they have remained in touch with the recommendations of the first Runnymede Trust report on British Muslims (1997) and the second (Parekh Report, 2000) on multiculturalism in Britain, in their timely and insightful analysis calling for a separation between international issues, on the one hand, and domestic concerns relating to civic and political rights in the UK, on the other. There are some limitations to this position, of course, but the style of opposition and resistance, coupled with a demand that local governance institutions should address their economic and social needs over the long term, has meant that their response has been shaped by both short-term and long-term strategies for belonging.

This does not necessarily lead to the criticism that Bangladeshi groups have compromised their political identities. Rather, the development can be seen as the product of broad-based organising, where diverse organisations build a UK constituency first before striking out on bolder campaigns.

Religious extremism in Tower Hamlets is trying to establish itself as a dissident form of politics. There are pockets of radicalism, which have been ignited by recent international political events. However the overall embedded community structure within a mainstream regeneration regime prevents the alienation of young Bangladeshi Muslims from finding a home in Islamic extremism. One explanation of this situation can be sought in the tradition of East End radicalism, with the Bangladeshi Muslims as the latest dissidents in this narrative of popular protest. However, it is our contention that the circumstances encountered by Bangladeshi Muslims mark a disjuncture from radical East End traditions. Bangladeshis struggled bitterly in the 1980s and early 1990s to forge strong political alliances and created political buy-in into community and voluntary structures that absorbed the potential alienation of the contemporary third generation. The disjuncture from the East End radical tradition of the left was powerfully illustrated by a large number of elderly British Bangladeshi Muslims on the day of the national 'Stop the War' demonstrations. They marched through the streets bearing placards with 'No War' slogans, with Socialist Workers' Party slogans ripped off. They wanted to distance themselves as clearly as possible from the Socialist Workers' Party's atheistic leanings. These particular actions demonstrated once again the distinctiveness of Bangladeshi Muslims in the East End from their socialist predecessors, as well as from other Muslims in contemporary Britain. Above all, their diverse responses demonstrate a surprisingly fluid understanding of *resistance* – located in both spiritual and political-sociological terms – alongside conventional narratives of *resistance and jihad* that highlight less defensive modes of religious expression.

Chapter 13

Tower Hamlets:
Insulation in Isolation

NILUFAR AHMED

The Bangladeshi community in the UK was one of many Muslim communities to experience a backlash after September 11. This chapter considers the effects of September 11 on religious practices within the community and, in particular, on women's experiences in the London borough of Tower Hamlets. It will look at the community prior to September 11, the formation and maintenance of a religious identity, and how this has been affected and altered in the post-September 11 climate. The findings rely on a larger study by Keele University exploring the migration and lives of 100 older Bangladeshi women living in the borough; their experiences were contrasted with interviews held with a number of younger, second-generation British Bangladeshi women. This chapter will draw on findings from the pilot phase carried out in 2000 (Ahmed *et al.* 2001) and fieldwork for the main part of the study carried out across the borough during May–October 2001 (Phillipson *et al.* 2003).

All of the older women in the study, aged between 35 and 55 years, were representative of the first wave of migrants. Focus groups were held throughout the borough to establish the main themes for the study and community organisations were used to recruit women for the pilot interviews. For the main study, 100 women were randomly selected using GP lists across the borough. All respondents were individually interviewed for about an hour in their homes.

Bangladeshis in Britain

Making up just 0.5 per cent of the UK population, Bangladeshis tend to live in concentrated enclaves and have been described as 'encapsulated' communities (Eade *et al.* 1996). The 2001 census reports the number of Bangladeshis resident in the UK to be just below three hundred thousand. The region with the largest number of Bangladeshis is Tower Hamlets, where they make up over 33 per cent of the population. In an area with such a high ethnic population and a high proportion of Muslims (over 71,000, representing 36 per cent of the borough), it was to be expected that September 11 would have an effect on the lives of the borough's residents.

The majority of Bangladeshis who migrated to Britain came from the district of Sylhet. A process of chain migration led to Sylhetis virtually monopolising migration to the UK (Gardner 1998). Substantial numbers came from mainly rural settlements within the region (Eade 1997a). The limited geographical area from which they migrated was mirrored in the few urban areas where they chose to settle in the UK (Ballard 2001). Mass migration from Sylhet began in the 1960s. During this period, migrants were predominantly male sojourners who intended to stay for a limited period and return to Bangladesh after amassing a certain amount of capital. However, the unceasing demand for remittances and the inability to save as much capital as they would need to settle down to a comfortable life in Bangladesh meant that the temporary sojourners soon became settlers (Kershen 2000). The original intention to remain only for a short while in the UK prompted many to leave families behind in Bangladesh. With the realisation that the stay would be long-term if not permanent, coinciding with tightening of immigration legislation, efforts were made to bring wives and families to the UK. All of these factors contributed to Bangladeshis being the last of the groups from the Indian subcontinent to complete their family reunification. The process began in the late 1970s and continued with force through the 1980s and, although numbers began to decline during the 1990s, it still continues into this century. The number of Bangladeshi nationals accepted for settlement in the UK rose steadily from just over one thousand in 1974 to peak at over seven thousand in 1982. Following this, the numbers began to decline steadily and the 1990s saw two to three thousand Bangladeshis being granted settlement per year. In 2001 the number of Bangladeshi nationals who settled in the UK rose to 4,050 (Home Office 2004). A possible contributory explanation for the slight upsurge in numbers at the beginning of this century could be that, with the children of original migrants returning to Bangladesh to marry and bring spouses over, a new wave of family reunification is under way.

Migration and the reproduction of religion

For all migrants, voluntary or forced, migration is a turbulent experience (Papastergiadis 2000) – the expectations of a new life rarely match up with the reality they are faced with on arrival. In the case of women, migration can transform their lives and position in the household in numerous ways (Willis and Yeoh 2000). This is especially true for Bangladeshi women who were not the primary agents in the decision to migrate, but rather came as wives or dependants. The absence of a hierarchical family/village system allowed women the opportunity to experiment with their roles, but also placed new demands and responsibilities on them (Ahmed *et al.* 2001). Vertovec (2000) argues that the role women play in the reproduction of religious practices may be enhanced by migration, most notably by their domestic practice of religion.

Most of the women who migrated found their new lives isolating and different beyond their original expectations. One response to this was an increased commitment to religious values, in new as well as more traditional forms.[1] Many sought to retain familiar customs and rituals in an attempt to maintain some kind of equilibrium in their lives. Religion appeared to play an important role in this process, perhaps reflecting Warner's (1998) point that: 'Religious identities ... often [but not always] mean more to individuals away from home, in their diaspora, than they did before'.

In Bangladesh, women could more or less take their faith for granted as they were living within an Islamic setting. However, in the UK they often felt their faith was threatened by an un-Islamic way of life, and even more so in the case of their children – they were worried about how their children would gain an appropriate religious upbringing in a culture where faith could not be taken for granted. Thus, efforts were habitually channelled into religious education and practice at home (this reaction to migration is true for other faiths as well – see, for example, Rayaprol 1997). While living in Bangladesh they had, to a large extent, not consciously thought about their faith, and certainly not considered it under threat, as its practice and visual definers such as dress and prayer cap were never questioned, and children grew up surrounded by lives organised around Islam and its rituals.

For the generation of women interviewed for this study, religion formed a major part of life. Most of them identified their faith as playing a significant role in their daily lives and almost 80 per cent strongly identified themselves with being Muslim. When asked to describe a typical day in their lives, the majority cited religious practices, including prayers, as being central to their day. As well as this, for many women their activities would include taking their children to extracurricular religious classes after school. Nuresa provides a fairly typical example:

> In the morning I get the children ready for school, dress them, feed them breakfast, then drop them off. Then at home I have my youngest and he needs looking after. I do the cooking and cleaning – that needs to be done every day. I pray at prayer times. Then I go and pick up the children from school at 3.30. Then at 4.30 I drop them off to Bangla School and pick them up at 6. At 7 they go to Arabic classes and come home at 9. They go to Arabic classes on Thursday, Friday and Saturday, and Bangla classes Monday to Thursday. (Nuresa, aged 35, living in the UK for 16 years)

More assiduous religious practice was one response to the greater time and isolation that women were faced with in the UK. Most of the women migrated before the advent of satellite television and the widespread availability of an ethnic-language press. Focusing on faith provided a familiar source of comfort and solace in their isolation. The growing availability and accessibility of Islamic literature cultivated their knowledge about Islam, making them no longer reliant on others for their understanding of the faith.

> I would say that it is better here. I have learnt more, and understand more. In Bangladesh, my grandfather told us to pray five times a day so we did. We did whatever our grandparents taught us, whether it was Islamic or Hindu tradition. And Bangladesh has a lot of Hindu tradition. Looking back I can see all the Hindu traditions we followed, that are not Islamic at all. Now I understand more about what is Islamic. (Maya, aged 50, living in the UK for 17 years)

Many of the women reported an intensification in their religious behaviour after migrating to the UK. Echoing the experiences of others, Ruheli, who has been living in Tower Hamlets for 14 years, describes how she became more immersed in these practices following migration to the UK: 'I've always been Islamic-minded ... but it increased after coming to this country.' This was a fairly common response amongst the interviewees; the new environment in which they were living allowed them more time to reflect on issues such as faith. Women reported having more time and fewer distractions in practising their faith:

> There is more time here. You are on your own in your house so you will pray. There is time for it. In Bangladesh there are so many people you are always busy: you just do the basic five prayers, you don't have much time to read. Here there is lots of time. (Henna, aged 38, living in the UK for 17 years)

This experience of reinforcing religious practice was not specific to those who had migrated from Bangladesh: some of the younger women spoke about how they felt inclined to increase their outward religious behaviour when they were removed from the relatively safe Islamic environment of Tower Hamlets.

> It's funny: when I was younger I used to go to a youth club. We used to go on trips and camping. And every time we went on a trip I used to become more Bengali. We'd go to Scotland and Yorkshire, and every time we went I would pray all the time; at home I didn't used to pray, but when I was out of Tower Hamlets I used to pray, everything. There were other people who would rebel when they were out of Tower Hamlets, but I used to be more Bengali and more Muslim when I was out of the house than when I was at home! (Seema, aged 23, community worker)

Seema's experience mirrors the way the first-generation female migrants felt on arriving in a new country. They had left behind the security of an environment within which it was the norm to be a Muslim and to practise openly. Seema, like the older women, felt a need to reassert her Muslim identity when she was removed from her original secure and openly Islamic environment of Tower Hamlets. In doing so, Seema was reproducing what the older women had done on arrival in the UK. She felt a need to assert her own identity, as much to validate her beliefs for herself as to show others that she was a Muslim.

Sinke (1992, 1995) refers to the concept of social reproduction in exploring the gendered connections between the international labour market, marriage and women's migration. She demonstrates how women are involved in the work of social reproduction in ways that extend further than child-bearing and taking care of their families: these include activities that imitate and replicate family, community and cultural models, thus allowing them to create as well as recreate selected cultural norms and religious behaviours. The women in

Tower Hamlets were very much involved in this type of social reproduction through the practice of their faith at home and the importance placed on religious and Bengali language classes.

The large size and close-knit nature of the community in Tower Hamlets offered individuals a safe environment in which to express and practise their faith, and allowed this type of social reproduction to flourish collectively across the community. As well as the impressive East London Mosque, which dominates the landscape at the City end of the borough, there are numerous local places of worship ranging from converted houses to purpose-built mosques to serve the community and allow easy access to worship for all residents. The borough also boasts a number of *madrassas* and other religious establishments, making access to religious teaching available to all. There are, of course, cost implications to the availability of these services, which means that not all people who would want to make use of the services are able to do so without making sacrifices.

> We got a *Measaab* [Imam] to come and teach them at home. In this country you have to pay for religious teaching. The government doesn't pay towards that; we have to pay for it ourselves. I have gone without so that we could teach the children about their faith. (Gulabi, aged 40, living in the UK for 21 years)

> We did want to send them [children] to *madrassa* but it is too expensive to send them. In Bangladesh we wouldn't have to pay for *madrassa* education. (Husna, aged 40, living in the UK for four years)

These experiences demonstrate the necessary modification of religious practice that migration produces. Facilities for learning the faith, which could be taken for granted in Bangladesh, were an added cost in their new homeland, and a luxury that could only be afforded either by those more financially able or by making sacrifices in other domains (usually the home). But few were deterred by the cost. Mariam, who has been widowed for 13 years, explains:

> I have sent one [son] to the *madrassa* here – that costs £1,500. I sent another [son] to Bangladesh and kept him there for a year at the *madrassa* .... That takes money doesn't it.... I am turning my blood into water, but I want to make them good people.... My children can't say that their mother never sent them because of money; I have gone without food to look after them. (Mariam, aged 45, living in the UK for 24 years)

The importance of religion and the desire to instil a religious under-standing in their children have motivated many families to endeavour at all costs to provide religious instruction. Many felt it was an obligation they owed not only to their children but also to Allah.

Religious identity

The majority of women who identified themselves as Muslim stated it was the most important aspect of their identity; but for many it was not the sole aspect of their identity, as two-thirds still identified themselves as Bengali alongside being Muslim. Identities are not fixed, but rather fluid and multi-layered and are always situational. At different times separate identities may come to the fore, such as in a home/family setting. Bangladeshis may feel more 'Bengali' at home than when in a work environment, or conversely, as in the earlier example of Seema, more 'Bengali' and 'Muslim' outside of the home. This process of shifting identities is usually subconscious – few would consciously engage in thinking about which identity is more appropriate in a particular setting.

For the younger women interviewed, however, the Bengali aspect of their identity was not as salient to them as it was for the older women. For younger women their Muslim identity was not only the way they identified themselves, but also the way that they wanted others to identify them.

> When you go to Uni your behaviour is more dictated by your religious beliefs than your cultural beliefs. When I'm at Uni I don't drink ... I don't eat *haram* foods, things like that. More people know me as a Muslim; they don't know that I'm a Bengali or anything like that. (Samina, aged 21, student)

Interestingly, they spoke about their gradual understanding and uptake of religious practices as an aspect of forming identity, as this excerpt from a discussion with sixth-formers demonstrates:

> *Nusrat*: A few years ago I never saw myself wearing a scarf. I don't wear it properly but a few years ago I never saw myself doing that ... and two years ago I never saw myself going to the mosque, and wearing it properly and going to the mosque for prayers. But it's progressing and I do want to see myself wearing it properly.

> *Nadia*: I only recently started wearing a scarf. I never thought I'd be wearing a *hijab* properly and doing all my prayers.

Silma: I don't see myself wearing a hijab, but I do my prayers.

Nusrat: My life goes topsy-turvy if I don't do my prayers.

Silma: I plan my revision around my prayers! I use my prayers as breaks between topics!

The discussion highlights the importance of religion for these young women and the fluid and fluctuating nature of identities. Their statements demonstrate how identities are not established as complete entities, but instead often emerge tentatively and through negotiation with oneself and others as to what is comfortable and right for one at that particular point in life.

Racism

As with all minority groups, the Bangladeshi community has been subject to overt racism in the UK. Many felt that their traditional beliefs were devalued by the indigenous population. Such antagonism towards migrants and their values served to increase efforts to sustain and reinforce cultural and religious practices (Sarup 1994). The literature on migration carries the implicit notion that migration leads to individuals leaving behind the traditional and progressing to the new and alternative, with what is left behind being largely abandoned (Papastergiadis 2000). This approach suggests that tradition is discordant with modern life. However, this is not necessarily the case: although there is an inevitable shift in cultural behaviours, much remains and much is modified alongside the incorporation of ideas and perspectives from the host society (Rait and Burns 1997).

The religious landscape of Tower Hamlets offered its inhabitants relative security. Some problems with racism were reported, but most experiences were of racist incidents in the past, when the number of Bangladeshis in the community was still quite small. But these experiences nevertheless had long-lasting effects on feelings of safety and the establishment of a sense of belonging.

My husband got beaten up by racists. Skinheads beat him up and he needed stitches on both sides of his head. This was many years ago, just after my eldest son [now 20 years old] was born. In those days there weren't many Bengalis in this area. It was in the summer time and he was coming home, it was about 9 o'clock, it was still light, the days were long. He came to get into the lift; as he got in they got in with him and started hitting him. He fainted. After that I was very scared and didn't go out for a long time. (Neefa, aged 42, living in the UK for 22 years)

Racist incidents were seen to be part of the experience of being a migrant to the UK – those who had not directly experienced it themselves knew of someone who had experienced some degree of racism. Many were relatively immune to it, in that they accepted it as part of the price of living in a foreign land.

I should be more scared I suppose because it is quite racist sometimes, and there are lots of robberies, but I have been here so long I am used to it. (Saleha, aged 37, living in the UK for 20 years)

Much of the racial abuse encountered, although severe at times, was not obviously related to religion.

There is a lot of trouble in this area. When we go out the white boys will push us or they spit at you. It happens all the time. I am scared of going out. They have thrown paint on my front door. My son was shot twice with an airgun and we complained to the police after it happened the second time. But nothing has happened. They shot my mother-in-law once too. She is very scared. They shoot from the opposite building. It is difficult to see who does it. (Farida, aged 36, living in the UK for 20 yrs)

Thus, despite some incidents of racial aggravation, the Bangladeshi community of Tower Hamlets prior to September 11 was one comfortably steeped in religious and cultural traditions, where the practice of those traditions was not only shared by a closely connected community but also supported in numerous ways by the local authorities. The area continued to be a magnet for those wanting to live a 'Bengali' way of life, as close as possible to living in Bangladesh. This is not to suggest that racist episodes were felt any less keenly by those subjected to them, but the community structure allowed greater support from within its own networks. Also, while intergenerational differences and modifications to religious and cultural practices transferred from Bangladesh most certainly existed, these changes were occurring at a steady pace and were managed, on the whole, without tension.

Post-September 11

Although the physical environment remained unchanged for the residents of Tower Hamlets following September 11, for some the religious and cultural landscape began to shift. The security and safety they had enjoyed in practising their faith was under threat. Many felt that all Muslims were being persecuted for the terrorist attacks in America, and that they were just as much at risk in Tower Hamlets as anywhere else. Uncertainty arose over their status in the UK. Muslims were coming under siege from the media and people felt enormously conspicuous going about their daily lives.

Racist encounters reported were increasingly linked to religion. In an interview conducted a few weeks after September 11, the respondent reported the verbal abuse her husband had suffered:

> It is very racist here. My husband was abused yesterday. They were calling him 'Osama'. I am too scared to go out. I don't let my children go out either. We would like to move out of this area. (Husna, aged 40, living in the UK for four years)

However, Husna stressed that this type of experience was not specific to the September 11 aftermath:

> It has always been like this in this area. They take my husband's prayer cap off his head. Once they took it off his head and urinated in it. The English boys go around in big groups. It is very frightening.

In the post-September 11 world Muslims across the country were experiencing a heightened awareness of their Islamic identity. Muslims, including those who had never actively thought about their identity, were not only forcibly made conscious of that identity but were fast becoming aware of the disparaging views held towards Muslims by many non-Muslims.

Sarup (1994) argues that when a minority group is faced with hostility, one of its first responses is to 'draw in on itself; it tightens its cultural bonds' in an attempt to reinvigorate itself and display a strong collective identity to those who oppress it. Sarup argues that presenting this collective identity and focusing energy on validating aspects of one's own culture necessarily leads some members of the minority group into deliberate disassociation from the host society.

The level of hatred towards Muslims may well have been exaggerated in media representations of anger towards Muslims. The majority of the women interviewed in this study were not involved in employment and their days were spent mostly in the home. Most of these women relied solely on the media (mainly Bengali language newspapers and specialised channels such as Bangla TV, but also terrestrial news channels) for their information, and so were faced with reports of violence against Muslims on a regular basis. The negative images portrayed of Muslims in the media led to two extreme responses. The first, as Sarup suggests, was a hardening of their Islamic identity, often rationalised by the notion that these were testing times for all Muslims. The second response was one of trying to play down the Islamic identity and 'blend in' with surroundings more. This second response was by far the more reflective of the attitudes of the older generation.

Some of the Bangladeshi women interviewed were afraid of leaving their homes, having heard reports of Muslims being targeted in violent attacks. Reports of young Muslim men being detained and interrogated further led to families cancelling their trips to Bangladesh for fear of similar problems. They were also afraid for their children, whom they felt were easy targets for those looking to attack Muslims. Many felt that their children should not express their faith through visible definers such as dress. In several of the interviews conducted after September 11, women spoke of how they were worried about their daughters going to work wearing the *hijab*. Some had advised their daughters to remove the *hijab* to try to deflect potential abuse.

> I have said to them, 'Your lives will be hard, the way you are going. You have to get on with the world and its ways.' But they don't want to. They think carefully about what they do, and the jobs they will do. One of them worked in a bank and she was allowed to wear what she wanted, and so she took the job.... I tell them to go to Sainsbury's [for work], but they don't want to wear the uniform. (Saleha, aged 37, living in the UK for 20 years)

After September 11, Muslims were forced to reflect on their own identity – and for many this experience sharpened their religious thoughts and ideals. Identities are only really questioned and re-evaluated when they are under threat, or when alternatives are presented. When Bangladeshis migrated to East London, by immersing themselves into the local Bangladeshi community on arrival, and by drawing in on themselves, they were able to preserve much of their identity; there was no need for them to validate themselves to themselves or to others. However, with the heightened focus on Muslims and their activities, these identities started to be examined by individuals.

With the declaration of the 'War on Terror', many felt they were in a no-win situation, and that the antagonism towards Muslims would only grow with such a move. They felt unable to voice their anger and discontent at what they felt was an unfair war, in the fear that such an opinion would expose them as supporting the terror attacks. Again, this attitude was far more prevalent amongst the older generation than the younger women, who were more confident of their views and able to express them more vociferously than their mothers.

Regarding the way British Muslims deal with threats to their identity, Jamil Ali (1998) writes that 'whilst the original migrants approached problems on a cautious, almost apologetic basis, the demands of younger Muslims have been expressed in a more forthright manner'. This was evident in the older women interviewed wanting to maintain a low profile, keeping their children at home more and in some cases encouraging their daughters to change their way of dress. The younger women interviewed felt no fear in continuing to go about their lives as they had always done; indeed, they felt anger at being made scapegoats for the attacks. Their confidence in their primary identification as Muslims, coupled with the certainty they felt about their right to be in the UK, allowed them to carry on to a large degree as normal, without the fears their mothers expressed. To downplay their identity as Muslims was no part of their strategy:

> In Islam, nationalism is prohibited. It is absolutely forbidden you to do that. That's why I only see myself as a Muslim and nothing else. (Jamila, aged 25, health advocate)

> Whether I am living in Britain, whatever culture I have, wherever my Mum was born, wherever my grandfather was born, that doesn't matter. My identity is Muslim. (Parveen, aged 20, community worker)

Baumann (1996) argues that issues surrounding identity come to the fore when doubts arise about belonging. The continuing backlash against Muslims experienced across the UK and being covered in both the mainstream and the ethnic press led many to speak about their fears of repatriation. This was a very real fear for some, and it demonstrated the fragility of the attachment that these women had to their adoptive country. Even though they had been living in the UK for an average of almost 18 years, and many of them had spent a greater proportion of their lives in the UK than they had in Bangladesh, they still did not feel secure about their future here. This was perhaps why none of the women interviewed identified themselves as British.

A safe place?

Although there were a few reports of increased racism and there was undoubtedly a heightened awareness of one's own identity as a Muslim, it can be argued that the very fact of the concentrated numbers of Bangladeshis living in Tower Hamlets helped to create a buffer against any major hostility. Indeed, Tower Hamlets was relatively safe from the more severe country-wide attacks on Muslims, particularly Muslim women, who had to endure their *hijabs* being pulled off and more overt racism.[2]

The sheer size of the community also served to protect it from the 'riots' between Muslims and non-Muslims that have in the past occurred in other areas with concentrated numbers of Asians/ Muslims, and similar deprivation levels to Tower Hamlets. In such areas Muslims make up a far smaller proportion of the local population than the 36 per cent found in Tower Hamlets. According to the 2001 census, Bradford's Muslims make up 16 per cent of the population; the Muslim populations of Burnley and Oldham are 6 and 11 per cent respectively. The lower proportion of Muslims in these and other towns where Muslim communities make up only a small minority of the population may explain the higher incidence of aggravated attacks based on religion that occurred as a response to September 11. The residents of Tower Hamlets were to a large degree able to insulate themselves from such attacks, drawing on the protective force of the large Muslim community. Increased levels of racism were reported only in those parts of the borough, such as Poplar, that house a smaller proportion of Bangladeshis and historically have experienced greater racial tension between the white locals of the area and locals of Bangladeshi origin.

Concluding thoughts

Although outwardly the community remained relatively insulated from tension following September 11, an introspective process was triggered for many. Women living in Tower Hamlets were forced to re-examine their identities and consciously think about their place in the UK. Issues around belonging and identity came to the fore as individuals were forced to consider their identity as Muslims living in a non-Muslim country.

Media reports of attacks on Muslims across the country contributed to this heightened awareness of their identity as Muslims.

People generally felt fortunate to be living in Tower Hamlets where reports of racist attacks were far fewer. Many women had family or friends living in provincial towns where situations were more volatile and tensions more tangible. The comparative safety of the residents of Tower Hamlets was testament to the old adage of 'safety in numbers'.

The world-wide response to Muslims following September 11 exposed the fragility of the ties that women who had raised children and lived a large proportion of their lives in the UK felt to this country. The realisation of the lack of a real sense of belonging to this country came as a surprise to many who had hitherto felt that they were part of the UK (not least because of their children), and could not return home to Bangladesh. This heightened awareness led them not only to consider their place as Muslims living in the UK, but also to be continually cognisant of the way others perceived them. Daily activities were carried out with this new awareness; and their interactions with neighbours and local people changed, lest they in any way provoke abuse.

However, issues around personal identity would most likely have arisen and been dealt with in any case – and for some they had already been consciously raised by other situations, including changes in religious and cultural practices such as marriage. September 11 simply catalysed a widespread re-examination, both individually and collectively, of self and ideals.

Notes

1 Examples of new ways of practising the faith could include *tafseer* (exegesis) sessions, with women gathering in each other's homes where a learned person gives a breakdown of the meaning of the Qur'an, or attending the mosque for prayers and religious sermons – mosques are still male-dominated arenas in Bangladesh.

2 See reports in the *Muslim News* (such as, for example, 'Muslims Face September 11th Backlash'):
http://www.muslimnews.co.uk/news/news.php?article=5080.

Chapter 14
Flying the Flag for England? Citizenship, Religion and Cultural Identity among British Pakistani Muslims

PAUL BAGGULEY AND YASMIN HUSSAIN

Introduction

The year 2001 will be remembered in Britain not only for the events of September 11, but also for the worst outbreak of urban violence since the 1980s. There were 'riots' in Bradford, Burnley and Oldham in May, June and July, largely involving South Asian men of either Bangladeshi (in Oldham) or Pakistani origin, in response to mobilisations by the neo-fascist British National Party (BNP). In Oldham on 26–29 May around 500 people were involved, two police officers and three members of the public were injured, and the damage caused was estimated at £1.4 million. In Burnley about 400 were involved on 24–26 June, with 83 police officers and 28 members of the public injured, and damage estimated at over £0.5 million. Finally, in Bradford up to 500 people were involved in riots over the weekend of 7–9 July. The injured included 326 police officers and 14 members of the public, with estimates of damage to property ranging up to £10 million. There were other less serious disturbances at Easter in Bradford, in Leeds on 5 June and in Stoke-on-Trent on 14–15 July. Around 400 people have been arrested in relation to the disturbances in Bradford, Burnley and Oldham (Denham 2002: 7). In the aftermath of these disturbances, as government-appointed commissions were carrying out their investigations, the World Trade Centre was attacked on 11 September.

Britain has witnessed sequences of riots involving racial factors since the late 1950s, when whites and African-Caribbeans fought in Nottingham and in Notting Hill, London (Fryer 1984: 376–81; Ramdin 1987: 204–10). Subsequent commentators have seen the riots of 1981 and 1985 as community insurrections against the police. The precipitating factors on those occasions involved heavy policing of predominantly African-Caribbean communities, with African-Caribbean men assumed to have been the principal participants. However, in 2001 the predominance of British Muslims of Bangladeshi and Pakistani origin as participants in the riots and as the target of subsequent state and media responses is quite different from the 1980s. Between the disturbances of the 1980s and 2001 was the riot in Manningham, Bradford on 10–12 June 1995, mainly involving young South Asians. This was again popularly blamed on heavy policing, although the official reports simply blamed it on 'anti-social' individuals (Bradford Commission Report 1996: 11). The riots of 2001 are more complex: whilst there are characteristics similar to previous disturbances where policing is involved, other factors have also emerged.

The 2001 riots cannot be divorced from a context in which minority ethnic communities were alarmed by the increasingly high profile of neo-fascist movements such as the BNP and the National Front (NF). Ethnic minority communities in all the areas where violence erupted have had their lives marked by ongoing, mundane and persistent racism. It is important to note that the signs in some places were clear beforehand. The spread of unrest was linked to an increase in racial violence, long-standing mistrust of and disillusionment with the police, the overt and taunting presence of the BNP and other far-right groups, and the entrenched poverty and unemployment that existed within the cities (Ray and Smith 2002).

The official response to the 2001 riots has been divided between a national-level focus on community cohesion, social capital and policy prescriptions based upon them (Cantle 2001; Clarke 2002; Denham 2002; Ritchie 2001), and a local criminal justice response that has been highly repressive. The former has had the potential to garner greater media and political attention than the latter. The local responses have been managed through central government steering and financial incentives. The criminal justice system's response has been extremely repressive, especially in the case of those arrested for the Bradford riots (Bagguley and Hussain 2003).

In the first part of this chapter we pay particular attention to how British Muslim communities of Bangladeshi and Pakistani origin have been constructed within the official reports about the riots. The reports construct these communities as being in a 'state of crisis', segregated by their own choice from the wider white society, which is said to contribute to the undermining of 'social cohesion'. The official reports that we are principally concerned with here are those by Denham (*Building Cohesive Communities*, 2002), which arose from a Ministerial Group on Public Order coordinated by the Home Office, and, closely associated with this, by Cantle (*Community Cohesion*, 2002), produced by an 'independent' Community Cohesion Review Team (CCRT). We also consider the Ritchie (2001) report on the situation in Oldham, also funded by the Home Office, and to a lesser extent the *Report of the Burnley Task Force* (Clarke 2002) – this was commissioned locally, and on several key points it differs markedly from the reports commissioned by the Home Office. In the subsequent sections we move to an analysis of our interview data,[1] focusing particularly on issues of identity in relation to nationhood, ethnicity, religion and some of their symbolic manifestations. Here we attempt to analyse the lived realities of participants, especially young British Pakistani Muslims, in the context of the riots. The official reports are instances of a particular regime of representation of South Asian Muslim communities in Britain that has the effect of essentialising identities, and we wish to contrast that regime of representation with the complex, negotiated lived identities of British Pakistani Muslims in Bradford.

Constructions of British Muslim communities in the official riot reports

The official reports into the riots focus on issues of segregation and social cohesion within a discourse that constructs the segregated communities as 'the problem'. Whenever the reports discuss the British Muslim communities, apart from generalised and stereo-typical discussion of culture and food, they are pathologised, notably in their depiction as communities in a state of 'crisis'. They are repeatedly represented as disintegrating from within, as lacking leadership (Clarke 2002: 49) and being riven by intergenerational conflict:

> Cantle, Clarke, Ouseley and Ritchie all draw attention to the extent to which young people's voices have been largely ignored by decision-makers in the areas where there were disturbances. Some young people complained that the older community and religious leaders who claimed to represent them failed to articulate the experiences of the young. (Denham 2002: 14)

It is worth noting how this issue has become racialised and the significance of Islam rendered problematic through the use of the term 'community and religious leaders'. This immediately marks out the problem of 'intergenerational conflict' as one specific to the South Asian Muslim community, with Islam presented solely in terms of its failure to represent young people. This overlooks the possibility that young people of all communities are largely ignored and not represented by their 'community leaders'. Furthermore, with respect to policing and crime Cantle (2001: 40) argues that: 'Minority communities must also face the fact that over time they have adopted a toleration of certain types of criminality.' In context this can only mean racially motivated crime, or crimes that are seen as specific to the Muslim community in Britain.

The Ritchie report into the events in Oldham also presents aspects of South Asian ethnic identities and cultural practices as 'the causes' of the 'loss of social cohesion'. Language especially, but also transnational kinship relations and long holidays in Pakistan and Bangladesh are cited as factors that single out these communities as 'problematic'. Yet languages such as Bengali, Punjabi and Urdu are central to the formation of the ethnic identities of the second generation. Contacts with Bangladesh and Pakistan are important for maintaining family connections, and families in Britain often own property in those countries or provide economic support to relatives living there. Their 'difference' in these senses is identified as 'the cause' of the 'problems' underlying the riots. This is presented in a way that sees the 'problems' faced by the South Asian community as somehow inherent in its cultural practices, as if in some way its established cultural beliefs and practices are 'dysfunctional' or 'incompatible' with British society. Again, these beliefs and practices are constructed in a manner suggesting that the community itself and its leaders are at fault for its problems, its lack of 'integration' with mainstream white institutions:

> Police links with minority ethnic communities are at present based on a network of community leaders who in our view lack authority and credibility. A new network of facilitators with credibility in the local community is necessary to build bridges. (Ritchie 2001: 13)

The reports do not raise issues concerned with the processes of racism, Islamophobia and the essentialisation of 'non-Western' identities that function to exclude British Muslims from social institutions. On the contrary, Cantle (2001: 19) for example argues that it is necessary for 'the minority, largely non-white community, to develop a greater acceptance of, and engagement with, the principal national institutions'. Furthermore, through suggesting that the South Asian community is 'corrupt', Cantle (2001: 24) recommends that probity for those involved in local politics needs redefining in order to 'specifically tackle the problem of the provision of monocultural community facilities in exchange for political allegiance from specific communities'. As in the other reports anecdotal evidence of gender inequalities is presented in a racialised manner (Cantle 2001: 44). These are largely the impressions of the report writers based upon the views of often unnamed 'service providers':

> one concern expressed by service providers as well as others has been the difficulty of accessing the views of women in the Pakistani and Bangladeshi communities, and the perceived lesser status of women, in terms of access to education, employment and leisure opportunities. (Ritchie 2001: 9)

This is not to deny that there are issues of gender inequality within the South Asian communities, but to argue that the reports construct these questions in a racialised way, glossing over the diversity, change and forms of resistance to gender inequality that are found among British Muslim women.

In an argument that directly paraphrases the BNP's slogan of 'white rights', Cantle like Clarke (2001: 55) takes the view that the 'equalities agenda' has been far too closely associated with ethnic minority groups. They may not be the groups in greatest need, he argues, and the equalities agenda should be addressing wider issues of poverty and social exclusion: 'We must, therefore, redefine the equalities agenda, which clearly and fundamentally relates to need and is not seen to exclude any community, such as the white community' (Cantle 2001: 39). As Beynon and Kushnick (2003: 239) have argued, 'the BNP is the other side of the New Labour coin'. In this way Cantle structures communities in a racialised manner, and in particular writes class out of the picture. Although issues of racism, economic marginalisation and Islamophobia are mentioned in passing (Cantle 2001: 39–40), they are not systematically discussed and there is little in the way of specific proposals that address these issues.

In this section we have attempted to demonstrate the particular features of the regime of representation of British Muslims that can be found in the official reports. The discourses and underlying assumptions of the reports construct a 'crisis' of the South Asian Muslim communities that is structured around themes of inter-generational conflict, tolerance of criminality, a failure to integrate with mainstream white society and the oppression of women. But in doing so this regime of truth essentialises and reifies British Muslim identities in a way that ignores their diversity and lived realities.

Flags, football and cultural citizenship

It may seem strange to shift suddenly from a consideration of official reports into the riots to questions of flags, football and citizenship. However, our interviews in Bradford during the summer of 2002 coincided with England playing in the World Cup, and this context brought to the surface and made explicit precisely the diversity and complexity of British Muslim identities that the official reports missed. In this section we examine these complexities through an analysis of some of our interviews about the riots with British Pakistanis in Bradford.

Public discourse about Britain itself still hangs on to notions of empire and monarchy. However, when we look at contemporary society from a different perspective it can appear multicultural. The sporting mood of the Pakistanis of Bradford in 2002 allowed them to grasp something other than former glories, something that is more tangible, in the form of the flag of St George. Although Bradford had been divided during the riots, it was interesting to see how sport erased those divisions. Along the roads of Bradford St George's flags were flying from bedroom windows, from corner shops and taxis. The feeling of patriotism was almost palpable, in particular among young respondents, both male and female. In these circum-stances, then, as others have noted in relation to the 1998 World Cup (Kumar 2003: 262–3) the St George's flag was felt to represent a multi-ethnic Britain, whereas the Union Jack is associated with colonialism and white racism. The obvious irony, of course, is the St George's flag's older historical symbolism of the crusades, of an earlier conflict between Christian Europe and Islam. Yet British Muslims readily took it up as a symbolic component of their identity, as a symbol of their belonging within and support for England.

If many writers on the subject of citizenship take it to mean participation in the nation-state (Kymlicka 1995), in the context of this research we can see it as cultural participation in a wider and ethnically diverse 'cultural nation'. These Pakistani respondents, just like other British citizens, displayed pride in their nation by flying the 'English' St George's flag. The flag became a prominent symbol of unity, expressive of their desire that England should win the World Cup:

> We live in this country, why shouldn't we support England? At the end of the day whether you support England in a sport or not is no big deal but this is our country and we are going to care about it ... this our home at the end of the day. (Shabnam Ishaq, aged 21)

One of the respondents related the flying of the flag to Norman Tebbitt's 'cricket test' in 1990:[2]

> I was talking to some colleagues about when Lord Tebbitt said 'failing the cricket test'. I hope people know that they have passed the 'football test' – because there are so many taxi drivers, businesses, even young people flying St George's flag. (Khalid Hussain, aged 30)

What this reveals is that the display of the St George's flag was also linked to the ongoing political debates about ethnicity and national identity.

In this way questions around national symbols such as flags generated discussions on allegiance and identification. The Union Jack was not seen as a patriotic symbol of national belonging; instead it has become a symbol of the far right. For instance, according to Khalid Hussain 'there is a difference between St George's flag and the Union Jack, because with the Union Jack you think of the BNP and racists'. It was the view of our younger respondents that the Union Jack has become the property of the far right and a symbol of the political beliefs of the BNP. The Union Jack was not displayed in Bradford because of this political meaning: ordinary people can no longer display the flag without being labelled right-wing racists. Displaying the St George's Flag was more express-ive of an 'authentic' national identity that has not been politically soiled by racism. The Union Jack was no longer representative of the whole nation, only of a minority of extremists.

Those who were born in Britain celebrate a positive image of their Britishness. It is almost as if the younger generation have reclaimed their citizenship as a positive identity in the wake of racism. They have created a concept of England, no longer something vacuous but a developed and inclusive identity that encapsulates diversity:

there were young Pakistani lads with St George's flag and middle-aged Pakistani taxi drivers ... it showed that the Pakistani community are saying that they are not just Pakistani. They are trying to show that England means something to them and that England is our team. We are from England. But if you say they are only English if they sit down and have roast beef and roast potatoes then it is not going to happen. (Khalid Hussain, aged 30).

Englishness, on the one hand, is a 'common sense' feeling of belonging based on the space we all occupy together; a space that happens to be called England. Multiculturalism and Englishness are not opposites, you cannot have one without the other. On the other hand, however, Englishness is rendered problematic as a source of identity for those we interviewed, as the BNP's notion of Englishness and racial purity is contested by the participants because it is narrowly defined culturally as 'roast beef and roast potatoes'. The notion of Englishness in some respects has become the property of the extreme right, but with this transfer the symbols associated with the BNP, the bulldogs and the Union Jack, become symbols of defiant racism. The paradox here, of course, is that the Union Jack is officially the British flag. Yet our second-generation interviewees see themselves as British citizens, as really belonging to Britain in contrast to their parents:

our parents in their days might have had a bit of trouble and they might have thought, oh they'll (meaning British authorities) – we will get rid of them ... at our age we are thinking we are not here to go, we are here to stay cos' we have been born here and this is our home town, home country. (Kamran and Omar, aged 19 and 20)

Finally, the irony of the St George's flag's older symbolism of the crusades against Islam should not be overlooked – an irony that emerged in its fullness in Khalid Hussain's observation that 'there were so many taxi drivers, businesses, even places like the Book Centre [an Islamic bookshop] in Bradford with St George's flag in the window'.

In this section we have attempted to analyse the contradictory, contested and contextual identifications that especially younger British Pakistanis have with England and Britain. Whilst the English football team is strongly supported and the St George's flag widely displayed as a symbol of national sporting pride, Britishness is regarded more ambivalently. The Union Jack, the flag that 'represents'

Britain, is seen as a racist flag, the symbol of colonialism and the BNP. However, as we shall see, Britishness as an identity of citizenship is central to their understanding of themselves and their actions in response to the riots.

Ethnic, cultural and religious identities

Young South Asian people in the UK understand their ethnic and religious culture within the broader British culture, in that they wish to celebrate their ethnic, cultural and religious differences in relationship with those of the wider society (Modood *et al.*, 1994). For example, according to Shabnam Ishaq (aged 21),

> White people, they like going out, they like clubbing and all that is for forbidden and they think by showing their flesh that is how they attract other people and if they ask if you are going to get married they automatically ask if you are going to have an arranged marriage because that is what they think Asians do.

Defining ethnicity carries with it notions of language, culture, religion, nationality and a shared heritage (Fenton 1999; Modood *et al.* 1994; Song 2003). Ethnicity is increasingly recognised as a political symbol that does not merely exclude groups and individuals from mainstream society but also serves as a mode of identity – a symbol of belonging and political mobilisation (Werbner 1990; Song 2003). Ethnic identities remain ambivalent; people do not have unitary or singular identifications, and many second-generation individuals identify with being 'British' as well as being 'Pakistani' or 'Muslim':

> I would never say I am English because I am not and I am sure my daughter will grow up with her Pakistani identity because that is what life is. You have to look at what makes up that identity. Being Muslim, how many times do you hear about Britain accepting Muslims as part of their community ... but if you start talking to young people they will say they are British Muslim, even more so now I think. (Khalid Hussain, aged 30)

Here we can see how the adoption of 'English' or 'British' identities by individuals from an ethnic minority remains complex; because of the racialised nature of British identity, with its connotations of European heritage, being 'white' and the colonial legacy (Ahmad and Husband 1993). However, the second and subsequent generations also challenged such racialised constructions of Britishness, in contrast to their parents' generation, whose sense of Britishness was often a pragmatic reflection of being born and living in Britain. For young people, however, identification with Britishness held a much more distinct meaning. For our young respondents, going beyond reservations and negative experiences enhanced their sense of Britishness as *citizens*. And to this extent, external factors can influence and modify the young person's sense of ethnicity.

Socialisation into cultural and religious values, against the backdrop of a potentially hostile majority culture, is a major concern of minority ethnic groups (Ahmad 1996; Anthias 1992; Modood *et al.* 1997). The potential for greater freedom afforded to the second generation compared to their parents introduces them to influences against which many parents would wish to guard their children (see Ahmad 1996). The older generations have many concerns about new freedoms that may threaten prized cultural values – such as parental authority, sanctions on marriage choice and sexual restraint – that are held strongly by the older generations of South Asian people. Lived religion is often difficult to differentiate from culturally specific norms and expectations; nevertheless, Islam can offer an important mode of being for young Pakistani people living in Britain. No young person that we interviewed was totally detached from parental ethnic, religious and cultural traditions. Most young people manage to acquire a working knowledge of religious and cultural traditions and identify with their families' religion and ethnicity. The younger generation, especially the women, demonstrate sophisticated understandings of how religious and ethnic traditions intersect and use these arguments to challenge parental perspectives or expectations:

> Young people will turn their parents' arguments back to them. On one hand they will say we are Muslims or we are all Pakistanis or whatever, and they will say well so and so they are Muslim or they are Pakistani, but then their parents will say, 'Oh no, you can't marry them.' In the same way they might say, well, that is your uncle or your aunt. And people say, hang on a minute, why does it matter what they say, why does it matter what they think, how about what *I* think? What about what *I* want? (Khalid Hussain, aged 30)

Most young people know enough about their religious and cultural values to feel both that they belong to their religious community and that they need to behave 'appropriately' – examples include knowledge of culturally appropriate gender roles

(Atkin and Hussain 2003). Second and subsequent generations of Muslims are reclaiming their religious identity and rediscovering Islam. Their ability to read English fluently allows them to research in the dominant tongue, the language of the web and text books. This diasporic awareness is reconfirming yet also redefining their roots, and some made subtle distinctions between the religious and cultural strands, bringing to the surface their own reflexivity in this process:

> They are bringing religion into a thing where children are not looking at it specifically. I mean if you look at the whites, the whites have Christianity but when you are talking about them we don't say the Christian community, we say the white community. And they say the Muslim community have done this, not the Asian community. Like I said, we are British Pakistanis now and we are in a culture not in a religion no more. (Serena Khan, aged 19)

Thus the separation of an idealised notion of Islam from lived religion, perceived by some of our younger respondents to be corrupted through conflation with ethnic customs and traditions, is important (Ahmed 1988; Mumtaz and Shaheed 1987). This reflects a wider process where religion has risen in importance as a distinct identity and an aspect of mobilisation in recent years (Ahmed and Donnon 1994; Samad 1992; Werbner 2000). The decline of class- and colour-based analysis of ethnic and race relations in recent years is paralleled by an increasing recognition of the significance of religious identity (Samad 1992). For our discussion, one development is significant in this regard: the reimagining of Islam as a global religion, without its ethnic connotations (Ahmed and Donnon 1994). Consequently, for British Pakistanis of the first and second generations there have always been conflicts of identity, most particularly between religion and citizenship in the context of Islamophobia. This is illustrated by our younger respondents especially, who emphasised responses to the attack on the World Trade Centre on September 11. According to Shabnam Ishaq (aged 21),

> it is especially after September 11 it has got worse. Everywhere you go people are disrespecting us ... I was scared ... I have heard that people have pulled girls' scarves off. So it was a bit difficult and I didn't tend to go out alone and I remember I went to town a few weeks after it had happened people were just giving me mucky looks and I think that is sad because you can't just judge by what people are wearing.

Others also remarked upon this noticeable change due to events elsewhere in the world. They related experiences of public harassment, and the consequent feelings of exclusion from Britain. Although they feel themselves to be British, Islamophobia has excluded them from the 'British nation':

> I think there is this phobia, isn't there, that if you are Muslim that people don't want to know you and with all the propaganda to do with Islam at the moment? Islamophobia and all that. People actually fear Muslims, don't they? (Alisah Khaleeq, aged 38).

> Oh yeah. September 11 didn't help. That didn't help at all. I think American values and beliefs are being forced onto British society ... apart from the division within the community. We feel like outsiders in our own country.... Because before I was part of a community, whether there was integration or not, that is completely irrelevant. I was part of a community, a British community in England. Now I am part of a criminal element in Bradford.... I am not respected as a Muslim. I am just respected for the fact that I could actually help a political party get into power or that I generate so much income for the British government. I am not respected as a Muslim. (Imran Ishmail, aged 28).

A sense of difference, enforced by Islamophobia, racism and discrimination, thus remains an important influence on how British Muslims understand their lives. Substantive citizenship rights are often denied to minority ethnic groups. Whilst they may hold British passports or have British citizenship by virtue of being born here, they often experience difficulty accessing the wider benefits of social citizenship in education and health care, for instance (Castles and Davidson 2000). However, despite these all-too-common experiences of institutionalised racism, second-generation Pakistanis in Britain firmly assert their identities as British citizens by virtue of being born in the country.

Conclusions

In the US, 2001 will be remembered for the events of September 11, but for many in Britain 2001 will also be well remembered for the spring and summer of rioting. In this chapter we have attempted to link these two events together because they are both integral to British Muslims' recent experiences of Islamophobia and racism at the hands of the state and neo-fascist mobilisations. We have tried to examine the responses of the state to the riots through an analysis of the reports arising from Home Office investigations. These give us an insight into the dominant ways of thinking about British Muslims and South Asians in Britain as leading politicians sanction them at the heart of the British state. We have contrasted these official views of British Muslim communities with the lived realities and identity claims of British Pakistanis in Bradford, the city most seriously affected by the riots.

Official reports can be seen to have used the ideas of segregation and social cohesion to construct a racialised and, in parts, Islamophobic narrative of British Muslim communities in crisis. By highlighting issues of intergenerational conflict, and presenting British Bangladeshis' and British Pakistanis' cultural and religious practices as incompatible with 'British society', the reports present an essentialised and static view of British Muslim and South Asian identities. Questions of class inequality, racism and Islamophobia are considered in passing, but are ultimately swept aside in the rush to 'redefine the equalities agenda' (Cantle 2001: 39).

These reified constructions in the official reports contrast with the complex and heterogeneous identity claims of British Muslims. In the aftermath of the riots and September 11 we have found British Pakistanis in Bradford to be proud of their cultural heritage and religious beliefs, whilst quite happily flying the St George's flag in support of their English football team. However, they have rejected the Union Jack as a symbol appropriated by the racist BNP. These findings indicate the complex and multifaceted identity claims of the second generation in particular. Their ethnic identifications are heterogeneous, drawing upon a Pakistani identity, being Muslim and also part of a wider South Asian diaspora, yet simultaneously asserting their identities as British citizens. These are identity claims that express resistance to the backlash in the wake of September 11 as well as the racist mobilisations of the BNP that led to the riots of 2001. Racism, therefore, can be an important influence on young people's sense of identity. As well as offering a form of self-identification, a symbol of belonging and mobilisation, cultural identities also have a wider political significance, resisting exclusion.

Acknowledgement
The research reported in this paper was supported by the British Academy. Grant Number SG-35152.

Notes

1   Fieldwork was conducted in Bradford, where existing community and professional networks facilitated sample recruitment. Organisations included community groups and community centres, religious institutions, council organisations, disability groups and the Fair Justice for All Campaign. Further contacts were also made informally by the use of snowballing techniques. The semi-structured interviews were framed around the following headings: reasons for riots; generation and gender; integration; media; authorities; knowledge of rioters; differences between riots; race and community; the far right; and future expectations. All the interviews were tape recorded and transcribed later. Informants were offered a choice of languages; all the young and middle-aged interviewees chose to be interviewed in English. The older participants spoke either Urdu or Punjabi. Interviews conducted in languages other than English were translated and transcribed simultaneously. In total 34 interviews and one focus group were conducted with 19 male and 21 female participants. Informants' ages ranged from 16 to over 60, with slightly more young women and older men. All of those interviewed have been given pseudonyms.

2   In 1990 a minister in the then Conservative government, Norman Tebbitt, questioned the loyalty of ethnic minority groups to Britain on the basis of whom they supported when the English cricket team played against India, Pakistan or the West Indies.

Chapter 15
Pakistanis in Northern Ireland
in the Aftermath of September 11

GABRIELE MARRANCI

Introduction

This chapter discusses the effects that September 11 and the resulting 'War on Terror' have produced on the lives of the Northern Irish
Pakistanis. In Northern Ireland people might have the occasion to
enjoy their cultural differences and might create a peaceful multicultural society; notwithstanding these potentialities, Northern
Ireland today is still affected by religious discrimination. Catholics
and Protestants have shared the same history, but not its understanding: the Catholic population felt discriminated against by the
Protestants; the Protestant population felt threatened by the
Catholics. In 1921 Britain and the new-born Irish state signed a
treaty that divided Ireland into two parts, the Irish Free State and
Northern Ireland; in the latter Protestants were the majority.

This historical event has produced a fracture within the Northern
Irish society, which the 1998 Good Friday Agreement has tried to
resolve. Today, Unionist Protestants are worried that Northern
Ireland could become one of the Irish counties, challenging their
British Protestant identity, while Nationalist Catholics are worried
that the discrimination suffered during the last century could still
affect them, disrupting their Christian Irish identity, although the
'troubles', which started during the 1960s, have found in the Good
Friday Agreement the first hopeful sign of a resolution. Today Northern Irish society is still not a stable European society; religious
hostility among Christians persists, as shown by the so-called 'Holy
Cross affair' (which has seen the schoolgirls of the Holy Cross
Catholic Primary School prevented from reaching their school).[1]

Thirty years of 'troubles' in this region had concealed the presence of Muslim immigrants; during the last twenty years, the Northern Irish people failed to notice an increase in the Pakistani population. Today, the 2001 census has revealed that in Northern Ireland there are 1,973 Muslims, of whom 678 are Pakistanis (378 males and 300 females).[2] Most of them run successful businesses, have university degrees (or equivalent qualifications) and are home owners. However, September 11 and the 'War on Terror' have drastically changed their lives as well as shifted their religious and political opinions. On the one hand, the Pakistanis, from being unnoticed members of Northern Irish society, have become mistrusted; on the other, the 'War on Terror' has transformed their previously introverted approach to Islam, and they have become more passionate and radical.

Interviews were conducted from the spring of 2000 to the summer of 2003 among thirty Pakistanis, who were members of different families living in Belfast, Craigavon, Coleraine and Derry. The majority of the interviews were informal, although, to clarify relevant points, some semi-structured interviews were recorded. On each occasion, an event or an interview was either tape-recorded or noted in shorthand, the respondent's permission was sought and the right to withdraw, when required, was granted. After September 11, the respondents showed some concern about the author's research; they feared potential violent and mindless reactions because of the terrorist attacks. It was therefore decided not only to use pseudonyms, but also to restrict the disclosure of personal details concerning the respondents.

The first section of this chapter provides a brief but necessary history of Pakistanis in Northern Ireland. The second section discusses how, after September 11 and the 'War on Terror', Northern Irish people challenged Pakistani political neutrality. The last section observes Pakistani reactions to these events, which, it is argued, have modified their relationship with Islam.

A brief history of South Asians in Northern Ireland

In Northern Ireland South Asians are not recent immigrants, as many might think.[3] The first South Asian, a member of the East India Company, had reached Ireland around 1780 and lived in Cork, while the region of Ulster received its first South Asian Muslim settler during the 1920s (see also Corrigan 2001; Donnan 1983;

Donnan and O'Brien 1998). These first immigrants were self-employed in the rag trade, and sold their products door-to-door. Their businesses became successful and other South Asians joined them, mainly through family networks. So, before the end of the 1930s, several South Asian families lived in what, after 1921, had become Northern Ireland.

Today, the Pakistanis emphasise that these first immigrants were so committed to their businesses that they had forgotten their religion; this in contrast to the current generation, who are zealous in their Islamic faith. Karim, a Pakistani man who arrived in Northern Ireland when Pakistan was still India, said:

> They [the first immigrants] did not know even how to perform basic Islamic rituals. Somebody told me that when one of these first Muslims died they discovered that, to relatives' distress, nobody had an idea of the ritual and worship in Islamic practice. What they were interested in were their businesses and money. Some of them even anglicised their names, giving up their Islamic ones.

Of course, this does not mean that the immigration experience had disrupted their Islamic faith, but that they had temporarily lost their Islamic practices. This explains the subsequent efforts that the Pakistani immigrants made to establish an Islamic space within Northern Ireland.

From the 1940s to the 1950s, the majority of South Asians arrived from west Punjab, Azad Kashmir, and other frontier provinces. Then an increasing number of South Asians arrived in Northern Ireland from England, particularly from Birmingham, Manchester, Yorkshire, Cardiff and Glasgow. These Pakistanis had very few contacts with the other Muslim immigrants, such as the doctoral and post-doctoral Arabs, because nobody was interested in organising a mosque. In the following years, however, the South Asians increased in number and many of them lived in the city of Craigavon.[4] This led the Pakistani businessmen in Craigavon to buy a semi-detached house, located in Legahory, a Protestant neighbourhood. Even though religious affiliations and sectarian divisions mark Northern Ireland, the decision to build the mosque in a Protestant British estate was not politically motivated. Some Pakistanis living in Craigavon originally came from British cities and could be expected to be more familiar with British Protestants than Irish Catholics.

This mosque provided the Pakistanis with the Islamic facilities they needed in the area. This organisation of their religious life acquired a symbolic meaning; for instance, in one interview an Indian man emphasised that the regular Friday prayers had transformed their community from a group of immigrants into a real *ummah* (community of believers). Although in Craigavon there was a mosque, the Muslims still needed a central mosque in the capital city of Belfast. In 1972, again with the support of the Pakistani businessmen, the Muslims in Belfast started the Islamic Society of Northern Ireland (ISNI), which, among other activities, was to collect funds to build the first 'real' Northern Irish mosque. Although they worked towards the project of establishing a mosque with a minaret, the unsettled political situation in the region as well as lack of money forced the Belfast Muslims to buy a small property and, as in Craigavon, transform it into a mosque.

During the late 1970s, terrorist activities increased in the region, also affecting Belfast. Because of this dangerous situation, South Asians felt that they should involve the Arabs in organising a strong Muslim community, as Mohammed, a 54-year-old Pakistani man, recalled:

> During the end of 1970s, the political situation was very dangerous here in Northern Ireland. Terrorist actions were so common. We needed to stay together, in particular because we did not have any Pakistani or Arab neighbourhoods.

The mosque in Belfast became the point of reference for the Northern Irish Muslims, whose ethnic and religious diversity was increasing. Shi'a Muslims from Lebanon, Iran, Iraq and some parts of Yemen, as well as Pakistan, Bangladesh and India, joined the Sunnis in worship. However, this meant that in Belfast the recently purchased premises were no longer able to contain an enlarged community.

Diversity within the community facilitated rivalry among the groups as well as between the Belfast and Craigavon mosques. Nevertheless, the reasons for these divisions were largely to be found in economic competition among Pakistani businessmen rather than religious antagonism, as the fieldwork of Corrigan (2001) has demonstrated. In 1985 Belfast Muslims bought a new semi-detached house in order to accommodate the community. It became the Belfast Islamic Centre (BIC), with a committee usually controlled by influential Pakistani businessmen although there is Arab participation throughout the organisation, up to and including the position of president.

Until September 11, nobody in Northern Ireland worried about which religion Pakistanis might profess. In fact, during the previous sixty years, most of the Northern Irish population had seen the Pakistanis and Bangladeshis manly as 'blacks' rather than Muslims. This is not surprising in a region that, until recently, lacked African and Caribbean people (Lentin and McVeigh 2002). In 1998, the Good Friday Agreement established the Northern Irish peace process. Many in Northern Ireland hoped that something might change; so did the BIC committee, which 'opened' the community to the wider society, making the Muslim presence noticeable.

Pakistanis were enjoying the new peaceful atmosphere when September 11 happened. This event shocked the Muslims and changed their lives. The Pakistani population feared an increase in the number of attacks; some even thought they might become the next target of either the IRA or other Northern Irish paramilitary groups. Indeed, the BIC had two windows smashed; four South Asians were attacked; and other Muslims, in particular Pakistani women wearing the *hijab* (headscarf), were verbally abused by young people in the streets.

From 'Paki' to 'bin Laden', from Muslims to IRA terrorists

On 12 September 2001 the BIC door was shut, two plywood panels replaced the ground-floor windows, and the green-and-white sign reading 'Belfast Islamic Centre' in English and Arabic was withdrawn. The BIC committee had suspended all the activities of the mosque, apart from prayers, and only a few Muslims attended those. In addition, parents prevented their children from attending the weekend religious classes held at the centre in the weeks following the attacks, worried that the mosque could be targeted.

Although September 11 had distressed the entire community, Pakistanis suffered more consequences. Attacks against them increased and their businesses suffered economic damage. Yet Pakistanis also had a new concern. During the life of their community in Northern Ireland, they had always tried to maintain a low profile. For instance, Donnan and O'Brien (1998) observed that, when questioned, Pakistanis played down racism in the region, even though the problem strongly affected them. During the interviews for this chapter, indeed, sentences such as 'well, there is no racism in Northern Ireland – you know, they are too busy killing each other' were common.

Nevertheless, Jarman (2002) showed that racism exists in Northern Ireland, and that South Asians are often victims of it. But Pakistanis wished to avoid any attention being drawn to them. Even an event such as the Rushdie affair, which enflamed other British Pakistanis (Malise 1990; Werbner 2002), produced hardly any visible reaction among Northern Irish Pakistanis. Abu-Karim, a forty-year-old man, observed:

> We were very upset and offended by the book [*The Satanic Verses*]. However, Belfast was not the right place to show our anger. Northern Ireland is a place where we have to live a local life, if we don't want troubles. I mean, we have to survive in this difficult political situation and we did not want that some international events could create more problem than we had because of the skin.

However, September 11 has changed Pakistani lives unexpectedly. For a long time they had organised their lives locally, but now they were projected into an unsettling trans-local dimension. Before September 11, the Northern Irish people saw Pakistani colleagues, fellow students, or general practitioners as immigrants; and at worst as 'blacks' or 'Pakis'. After September 11, Pakistanis no longer represented a politically neutral presence; they became a new local–global threat. If Northern Irish children, in the Shankill Road[5] for instance, used to shout 'Paki!' at the South Asian passer-by, they now shout 'Bin Laden!' The idea that the Pakistanis were Muslims, and hence in the imaginary of some Northern Irish people potential terrorists, spread from the offensive, but harmless, 'Bin Laden!' to something more sinister: Northern Irish politics.

For instance, the *Ballymena Guardian* on Wednesday 27 March 2002 carried the headline 'DUP Muslim Snub Row'. The article explained how a Democratic Unionist Party (DUP) councillor had refused a gift from the Muslim community: a brass replica of the Islamic designs and Arabic texts on the Ka'bah's door. The gift, according to the councillor, had showed 'incomprehensible symbols' (by these he meant Arabic). Then he had asked rhetorically: 'If a paramilitary group came to us with a gift or request for an exhibition, would we accept it?' The following day, the same councillor asked a *Belfast Telegraph* journalist another of his rhetorical questions: 'If I walked into Ballymena council with a barrel load of sashes or other articles associated with the Orange culture, would I be accepted?' The councillor was comparing the sectarian symbols of Northern Ireland, such as sashes, to the Ka'bah door and its Arabic inscriptions.

Thus, the Protestant community, after September 11 and the 'War on Terrorism', has increasingly seen Pakistani Muslims as allies of the Catholic Nationalist movement, if not quite honorary members of the IRA. In any case they were becoming the 'Catholic Muslim'.[6] Although the Pakistani members of BIC committee received several threatening letters, it was the Palestinian president who suffered the most significant attack. On 12 July 2002, a day made highly volatile in Northern Ireland by the Orange parades, a mob of young Loyalists forced the president of the BIC to leave his home. He had lived in this area with his family for many years without any problems, but now for the first time a member of the Islamic community, like many in Northern Ireland in the past, had suffered from the effects of religious discrimination.

During the 'War on Terror', the Protestant Loyalist community seemed to find more evidence to support their allegations that Pakistani Muslims were supporting the Nationalist Catholic cause. The associations who campaigned against the war, as well as the marches they organised in support of Palestinian and Iraqi people (in which many Pakistanis took an active part) also included members of Sinn Fein and other Catholic Nationalist organisations. This produced new attacks against the Pakistanis, in which family members were victims. For instance, a group of youths belonging to a Loyalist paramilitary group recently attacked Pakistani families in Craigavon. During a BBC radio interview the mother of one family described how

> My son walked in and said: 'Mum, are we Prod [Protestant] or are we Catholic?' I said, 'you are Muslim'. And he said 'I know I'm a Muslim, but am I a Prod or am I Catholic?' (BBC Radio Ulster, 10 July 2003)

The neutrality of the Pakistani population was no longer trusted; Pakistanis had to decide which Northern Irish faction they officially wanted to support. The reasons for this development may be found in the Northern Irish 'war symbols' that, since September 11, have affected Pakistani Muslims, particularly those living in Craigavon. Northern Ireland has a long tradition of war symbols: in other words, Northern Irish society tends to transform any event, object, or cultural item into a symbol suitable for the conflict between Catholics and Protestants. Symbols are important, emotionally provocative, multi-meaningful, and (sometimes) dangerous. In Northern Ireland, symbols surely *are* dangerous. As Buckley explains (1997: 3), 'the symbolic picture, the symbolic wall, the symbolic ship, the symbolic ring gain their meanings through having been set aside. Symbolic objects have been bracketed off from ordinary objects'.

Hence, the global events of the 'Islamic terrorist' attack against America are entangled with the Northern Irish socio-political discourse. For a long time, Pakistanis in Northern Ireland had tried to distance themselves from international events involving the Islamic world, in contrast to other Pakistani communities in Britain (Archer 2002; Hopkins and Hopkins 2002; Werbner 2002). Indeed, Northern Irish Pakistanis had created what they saw as a local *ummah*. Yet after September 11 they lost the control of the global–local dimensions and Northern Irish politics trapped them in an unexpected trans-local position.

Many Northern Irish people had previously seen the Pakistani businessmen as an exotic element in Northern Ireland and, after the Good Friday Agreement, even the symbol of the 'new' multi-ethnic and multi-faith Northern Irish society. But now Protestant Loyalists see Pakistanis as a new threat. This development is described as a cataclysm in the lives of the latter, affecting not only the social-political position of Pakistanis, as discussed above, but also their relationship with Islam.

Distancing from Pakistan, becoming Islamic

Before September 11, Islam was *one* of the important aspects of a South Asian's identity; yet it was not the *only* aspect. After September 11 and the 'War on Terror', Islam became 'their identity'. One Pakistani man, who has lived for 35 years in the region, tried to explain such a shift:

> Don't be wrong. We have always been religious people and we have always respected Islam. However, our business and our traditions were similarly important. Our children had some Islamic education, but the main interest for the parents was that their children got good result at the mainstream schools. After September 11 many things have changed. We focus on Islam because we must defend Islam. Islam is under attack, doesn't matter what Bush and Blair said. Do you remember the satanic book [*The Satanic Verses*]? This was an attack against the Prophet; it was a very bad thing. But Bush's war on terrorism is an attack against Islam and all Muslims. We must defend Islam by our words, our actions, our behaviour and our intelligence. Bin Laden's actions are not clever; they are only blind violence.

Indeed, before September 11 Pakistani Muslims were not very active in supporting what they now call 'Islamic causes', such as the Palestinian Intifada. For instance, during the 1990s Arab students tried to involve Pakistanis in awakening Northern Irish public opinion to the issue of Palestine, but pressure on the Pakistani population had disappointing results. Most of the South Asians justified their disengagement by emphasising their duty towards their families as well as towards their businesses; some of them, when rebuked, pointed out that money coming from their businesses was vital in meeting the needs of the Muslim community. Young Pakistanis, though showing some interest in the problem, recalled that other Muslims were suffering around the world and have less chance to make their voices heard. They mentioned, of course, the cases of Muslims in Kashmir and India to support their point.

However, when Pakistanis realised after September 11 that their local, apolitical *ummah* could no longer protect them from sectarianism, they drastically changed their previously private commitment to Islam into something more open and public. 'Islam is my identity,' young Pakistanis often said, whilst their parents, on the other hand, willingly admitted they would need to reach a 'real' Islamic identity.

When Pakistan supported the Bush administration, not only in principle but also in practice, Northern Irish Pakistanis saw this as treason towards Pakistan's Islamic mission. Some of the Pakistanis in Northern Ireland are of Pashtun[7] origin and have relatives on Afghanistan's border. During the Afghanistan War the news that the Pakistan authorities had agreed with the Bush administration to prevent humanitarian convoys crossing the Pakistani border and reaching the Afghan refugees shocked the Pakistani community, which was pervaded by a feeling of indignation. Iqbal, a 64-year-old Pakistani, expressed his response in these words:

> Pakistan was created as an Islamic republic; its capital is called Islamabad, the city of Islam. Look now; we are Americans, practically we have Bush as leader. Do you think I am a Pakistani now? No! I am Muslim, I am Islamic. For too long we have forgotten our religion. Now that they call us bin Laden, what can we lose? We must show, and our children must show, that we are Muslims rather than 'Paki', as they call us. We have to protect our religion; I mean there are many ways to do *jihad*. Bin Laden is a man of the CIA. The 11 September was *jihad* only for the Western people; they don't know Islam, they don't know the

concept. You know, they don't know Christianity and want to teach us Islam. The eleventh of September was a terrorist attack against Islam!

Nevertheless, on this point young Pakistanis often have divergent opinions from those of their parents. Although they did not see bin Laden as a hero, with many pointing out that he seemed a Western caricature of a *mujahid* (a person who makes *jihad*), they emphasised that he was the only person challenging the 'new American imperialism'.

This terminology was not coincidental. Most young Pakistanis, after September 11, have supported Northern Irish anti- globalisation movements such as Youth against the War, which have also influenced their political discourse. Before September 11, these young people had a modest interest in international events – usually either when the Islamic world was involved or when their parents' country, Pakistan, developed new tensions with India. After Bush started his 'War on Terror', and particularly after Camp X in Guantanamo Bay was organised, these young Pakistanis shifted towards a new political and religious radicalism. Some of them even said that violence and retaliation might be justified because Bush's actions were a direct attack on Islam and Muslims. Salim, a 23-year-old, showed the author two websites discussing Camp X[9] and commented:

> Look, do you think that this is right? I don't think so. This is inhuman terrorism. They threat them [the captives] like beast because they are Muslims. They [the Americans] are hypocritical; they don't put American terrorists in the same camp; and what about here [Northern Ireland] ... at least half of the population support the paramilitary organisations. Yet nobody criminalised them for this. You know? There are many Pakistanis and some British Pakistanis in that camp .... I cannot imagine the agony of their parents. The CIA kidnapped one of them when he was working for a humanitarian organisation. Some people here [Northern Ireland] know what torture and injustice are. We have to learn from them and work together to defend our ideas and our Islamic identities. If somebody forces Muslims out their homes we have the right to fight back for our brothers.

Other young Pakistanis used the example of the IRA and the 1981 internment of Catholic Nationalists (see Arthur and Jeffery 1996) to make their points. For instance, 25-year-old Rajab argued:

> Sometimes violence may be useful; I know people do not like this, but they accept when their states say that they use war to help people. The

IRA and the Catholic community would not have achieved the Good Friday Agreement without struggling for freedom. Nobody would have paid attention to them. Bush and his friends are very violent, they like violence, and they stop many countries to reach freedom. Their idea of democracy is that they rule the world and impose their faith. You could, as Bush said, only be with him or against him. It was the same for the Protestant and Catholic here. The Protestant saw the Catholic as monkeys that were unable to take their decisions. The American and British governments think the same about us. We must act; we need to act in the correct way. If somebody attacks your family, you defend your wife and children, don't you? Islam is more important than your family and so is your duty towards millions of Muslims.

This new political and religious activism was not limited to male Pakistanis. Young women started to show an aggressive interest in the political situation. They expressed an Islamic commitment that had not been expressed before. Abida actively joined the Northern Irish movement against the war after watching some reportage about Iraqi children broadcast by Al Jazeera. She explained:

Today in Northern Ireland many [Pakistani] women feel that as Muslim mothers, Muslim sisters and Muslim daughters, we have a strong duty towards our Muslim brothers and sisters that are losing their lives for freedom. I used not to wear the *hijab*; now, as you see, I wear it. I want to show that I am a Muslim. Before September 11, I was very worried that if I had worn the *hijab* in public, I could have been attacked. Now, here [in Northern Ireland] we are often called 'bin Laden's wives' and we are seen as terrorists in any case. Protestants see us as supporters of the Catholics. We are no longer safe here [Northern Ireland] whether or not you wear a *hijab*. But I certainly send a message to this society when I wear it.

The quiet, docile attitude that Pakistanis had towards Islam before the 'War on Terror' has now turned into its opposite. Their behaviour and feelings about Islam are now similar to those that Werbner (2002) reported for Pakistanis in Manchester. In one of her anecdotes a Pakistani mother, whose son was called 'dirty Paki' by some 'English louts', asked the little boy not to retaliate. Werbner (2002: 132) observes that

unknown to the English louts, there is an invisible shield protecting the little boy and mother. The shield is Islam ... which is worse? The attack on the little boy or the attack against the Prophet?... For an ordinary Pakistani the answer to my question is equally obvious – attack me, attack my son, attack my wife, but do not attack my Prophet.

Before September 11, the Pakistanis in Northern Ireland have a priority in their lives: to protect their family and wealth. September 11 destabilised their local lives and socio-political position within Northern Ireland by projecting them into unknown global dimensions.

Conclusions

For a long time, South Asians in Northern Ireland adapted to the social-political context of the region. They focused on maintaining the Muslim community as well as steering clear of the conflict between the Catholic Nationalists and the Protestant Loyalists, their main interests were their businesses and families. Religion was part of their cultural heritage: in most cases, worshipping, fasting, and *zakat* (charity) were considered part of their everyday life, yet bore no emphatic meaning.

Very soon after September 11, however, South Asian Muslims understood the implications that the 'War on Terror' might have for their lives. Now they had to cope with two apparently distinct but actually strongly correlated issues. On the one hand, they had to face the same stereotypes and mistrust that South Asian Muslims often suffer from in Britain; on the other hand, coming up against the peculiar power that symbols exercise in Northern Ireland, they had to face the new political values that the words Muslim and Islam have acquired in that society. Paradoxically, these two circumstances have driven Pakistanis in Northern Ireland towards a political and religious activism that was unusual before this date and before the rise in consciousness of Muslims in Northern Ireland. In this way, September 11 and the 'War on Terror' have also influenced intergenerational relationships. As we have seen, parents started to consider the identity processes of their children as a valuable experience. The generational gap that before September 11 distinguished the Muslim families was transformed into a 'dialogue of identities' between the generations. The aftermath of September 11 has changed the role of Islam in Northern Ireland: once a shield against the political turmoil of the region, it has become an affirmation of identity and a powerful social force.

Notes

1   In November 2001 some Protestant families protested against the Catholic schoolgirls who used to cross the Protestant neighbourhood to reach their school, the Holy Cross Primary. The Protestant families declared that it was an action against the schoolgirls' parents, whom they accused of attacking Protestant homes.

2   During his research the author had the impression that the 2001 census may have underestimated the number of Muslims and Pakistanis living in Northern Ireland because many of them refused to answer questions related to ethnicity and religion.

3   I use the term 'South Asian' here because Pakistan was only established with the Indian Independence Act (1947). Yet the majority of the first immigrants to reach Northern Ireland before 1947 came from areas that would be assigned to Pakistan at Independence. In the other parts of the paper 'South Asians' refers to Indian and Pakistani Muslims.

4   Craigavon is a town in County Armagh, bordered on the north by Lough Neagh. It is about 50 kilometres from Belfast.

5   The Shankill Road is one of the most notorious Protestant areas and is still affected by paramilitary activities.

6   There is an old joke, most famously addressed to Jewish people, but during the 1980s applied to Muslims and commonly relayed. Someone asks a Muslim man, 'Are you Catholic or Protestant?' When he answers 'Muslim', the other man is impatient with this reply. 'Yes, but Catholic Muslim or Protestant Muslim?'

7   Most of the Taliban in Afghanistan were Pashtun. This may explain the strong link that Pakistan had with the Taliban regime (see Marsden 2002).

8   One from the BBC and the other from the controversial organisation Hizb al-Tahrir.
    (http://www.alkhilafah.info/massacres/afghanistan/campxray3.htm; http://news.bbc.co.uk/hi/english/static/in_depth/americas/2002/inside_camp_xray/default.stm)

An Afterword on the Situation of British Muslims in a World Context

JOHN REX

The dialectics of the war against terror

We live today in what might be called the Fourth World War. The First World War was that fought in the trenches in France. The second was the war against Nazism and Fascism. The third was the Cold War between capitalism and communism. This Fourth World War is generally seen as the war against terror.

The most oversimplified account of this latest war is that, since September 11, America and its allies have had to fight against terrorism in many parts of the world orchestrated by an organisation called al-Qa'ida. This is, however, a very oversimplified account. To understand this we have to look at both the way in which America has attempted to create a Coalition of the Willing and the way in which dozens of terrorist groups are mobilised and act together.

The Coalition of the Willing was organised first of all in relation to the war against Iraq. The first ally of the Americans in this war was Britain. The war against Iraq was then explained as a war against terrorism as such. It had many sites in Afghanistan, Pakistan, Sudan, Morocco, Saudi Arabia, Indonesia, Singapore, Malaysia and the Philippines, but the most significant of these was the bombing of a nightclub in a tourist centre in Bali. In these extensions of the war the Coalition of the Willing recruited some surprising allies. On the one hand Australia, the country from which most of the victims of Bali came, moved into the centre. On the other hand Russia and its President Putin were now defined as allies.

The terrorist groups had various origins. Some were nationalist or ethnic. Some were Muslim. They were sometimes quite independent of one another but also had a loose relationship with al-Qa'ida which, if it became involved, could provide finance and training in terrorism. All of them saw terrorism as the best available weapon of the weak against the strong. While this terrorism was directed against specific oppressors, it could involve collateral injury to non-combatants, to women and children, or, in the case of suicide bombing, to the perpetrators themselves.

It was essential to al-Qa'ida (which literally means 'The Base') that it should have potential allies both in situations of active terror and in other countries where sleepers could stand ready for action if called upon. Such sleepers were looked for in Britain, Europe and America itself. They could receive financial support and might be summoned to terrorist training camps. Al-Qa'ida was not of itself a purely Islamic organisation, although it was concerned during the Kuwait war with keeping the Muslim holy cities out of non-Muslim control. Much more specifically Muslim was the Taliban (this term means 'Student') who were concerned with establishing a funda-mentalist Islamic state. Both al-Qa'ida and the Taliban had partici-pated during the last stages of the Cold War in fighting against the Russians. Having gained their initial strength there, they were available in a struggle, which was no longer bi-polar, to fight against the Coalition of the Willing. In the Russian case the original issue had been that of the political independence of Chechnya, but undoubtedly Muslim fundamentalists drawing their strength from other countries such as Afghanistan penetrated the nationalists of Chechnya.

The founder and leader of al-Qa'ida was the immensely rich Osama bin Laden, who originally had support from the Saudi govern-ment. When, however, he began to draw upon radical Saudi support, he was forced to leave Saudi Arabia and worked in the Sudan before moving his secret headquarters to Afghanistan and Pakistan. He remains in charge of the organisation. Afghanistan has been the crucible of al-Qa'ida activity. Militant Afghan Muslims fought the Russians in Chechnya and their allies in Central Asia; and in the Bali bombing Australians were targeted because of their government's policies toward Afghan refugees.

It is a strange fact that it was in the war against Iraq that the idea of a Coalition of the Willing came into currency, because Iraq did not form part of an international network of terrorists, and it was not seriously claimed that the dictatorship of Saddam Hussein was part of such a network. The Iraqi government did not see itself as part of the Coalition of the Willing against al-Qa'ida organised terror. Rather, it faced its own ethnic, religious and regional resistance movements, which it succeeded in repressing. So far as the actual Coalition of the Willing was concerned, it had to deal with the resistance of the Iraqi people after the fall of Saddam Hussein, as well as an international anti-war movement that was hardly recognisable as a terrorist network.

The position of British Muslims

It is against this background that the situation of British Muslims has to be understood. They are identified by many governmental organisations as a threat, and, as earlier chapters in this volume make clear, there is now a strong growth of Islamophobia in Britain (Runnymede Trust 1997). This is a wider phenomenon than the fear of terror as such. The image of Muslims is that they are irrational fundamentalists, the book burning of the Rushdie affair (Samad 1992) being taken as an illustration of this. But they are also associated with terrorism, and the imprisonment of British Muslims in Guantanamo Bay is seen as proof of this.

A further factor defining the situation of British Asian Muslims has come into play since the riots involving Asians in Northern cities. Until these occurred the general view – with 1981 and 1985 in mind – was that African-Caribbeans were the principle rioters. The Asians of Southall rioted not against the police but as vigilantes whose behaviour was made necessary through the failure of police protection. In the new disturbances in the Northern cities, however, Asians were in open conflict with the police as well as with the far-right BNP. In the various diagnoses of these events the danger most commonly referred to was that of segregation. Asians living in segregated areas and going to overwhelmingly Asian schools were seen as uncommitted to an overall local British citizenship.

In the Northern cities the Asians involved were seen as poor working-class people whose needs had not been met by the city councils. This is also an issue in the cases discussed here in an earlier chapter. In the West Midlands, however, the Asian community has made some progress in terms of political empowerment. They share in the government of cities like Birmingham. The discussion following the Northern riots made little mention of Islam as an exacerbating factor. Nor did the young white rioters often mention Islam as the basis of their hostility. They simply saw Asians as taking resources away from themselves and leaving then to live in poverty. Muslim leaders on the whole played a moderating role. They were associated with the councils, whose policies the whites felt had let them down, and with the Labour Party locally and nationally.

More generally and at a national level the period after 2001 produced a number of policy responses. The first of these was concerned with security. In this area the government seemed to have little detailed knowledge of the nature of any terrorist threat. What it did was to cast its net as widely as possible. Individuals could be held without charge under the Prevention of Terrorism Act and Britain had its own centres equivalent to the American Guantanamo Bay. Anyone associated with one of the more radical Muslim sects who had visited Afghanistan, Saudi Arabia or the Gulf States could be detained in this way. Moreover, any radical imam in a British mosque became an object of suspicion.

This was an important aspect of the general climate of Islamophobia. As to understanding Islam in Britain, there was little recognition of the actual diversity of Muslim groups in Britain. Much of this diversity preceded September 11 and had nothing to do with it. There was a central division amongst the Sunnis between Deobandis, who were concerned to purge Islam of all Hindu and pagan elements, and the Barelvis who added to their beliefs the practices of Sufism. More radical than the Deobandis were organisations like Jamiat al-Hadith, which refused to accept any teaching except that which was in the Qur'an and the Hadith. These were essentially theological differences. There was also a broad distinction to be drawn between those who believed in the ideal of an Islamic state and those who adjusted themselves to secular government. These organisations jostled each other for internal control of the Muslim community.

Most of these organisations financed themselves in part by subsidies from the oil-rich Middle Eastern states and could in part be influenced by the political struggles between these benefactors. All of this could happen without the intervention of al-Qa'ida. There were missionary organisations like the Jamaat-Tabligh, which operated from centres in Yorkshire and Lancashire and sought to intensify the religious practice of those who were already Muslims. There were also Shi'a groups ranging from the business-oriented Ismailis to some more working-class groups who recognized the Ayatollah in Iran, though very rarely accepting the *fatwa* against Rushdie. We could go into much more detail about these groups.[1]

What has to be noted here, however, is that any one of the distinct elements among them could be seized upon after 2001 and presented as the agent of an international network like al-Qa'ida, or simply feared as being 'fundamentalist'. A distinction was then made between acceptable and extreme Islam. On another level public political discourse might turn against multiculturalism of any sort and insist upon rapid assimilation through learning English and adopting a British identity, along the lines of French assimilationism. Alternatively there was discussion in a series of reports of the need to promote social and community cohesion and avoid segregation. Finally, emphasis might be placed upon social inclusion and exclusion so that all potential problems were brought under the rubric of traditional sociological explanations in terms of equality.

The most important of these reports were those commissioned by the Home Office and led by Cantle (2001), and that undertaken in Bradford two years earlier by Ouseley though only published in 2002 (Ouseley 2002). Cantle distinguished between social cohesion, which referred to the internal solidarity of ethnic groups, and community cohesion, which united individuals across ethnic lines. Ouseley saw dangers in multiculturalism, which he thought of as producing segregation in housing and education.

Many other diagnoses were offered, such as that produced by the Runnymede Trust on the future of a multi-ethnic Britain (Runnymede Trust 2000), which outlined the programmes in each of a number of institutional spheres to produce a multi-ethnic society. In another book produced in the same year, Parekh (2000) celebrated cultural diversity, arguing that a multicultural society necessarily changed in accommodating diverse cultures. This was in many ways an opposite argument to that of Cantle and Ouseley. What was striking, however, was that the whole of this discussion was seen as related to the findings of the Macpherson enquiry into the death of Stephen Lawrence, which argued that British society was characterised by institutional racism (Macpherson 1999). Even the separate question of refugees and asylum seekers was seen in a similar light.

The whole question of racism in British society was now placed at the centre of all discussion. The far-right BNP had won a number of local council seats in Lancashire in what had been working-class Labour wards, and in national elections; although the party did not win seats in Parliament, it had a significant minority following. Moreover, in an attempt to recover its support, the major political parties adjusted their policies to compete with the BNP. Another factor in the situation was the role of the police, which was important in several ways. The Ouseley Report was sympathetic to the police, arguing that they were placed in an impossible situation in a segregated society of having to control racial conflict. The Macpherson Report, while admitting that there was individual racism amongst the police, drew attention to institutional racism. This institutional racism, however, was seen, not simply as a matter of the racist culture of police stations, but rather as something to be found in all institutional areas. When this was said, it was possible for the police to claim that it could not be expected that they alone should be found guilty of institutional racism if this pattern of behaviour was endemic in British society.

For my part I have argued that a different view, and one which is more sympathetic to multiculturalism, can be derived by combining T. H. Marshall's notion of citizenship with a definition of integration as it applies to immigrants offered in 1966 by Roy Jenkins. Marshall (1950) did not address himself to the question of the position of immigrant minorities. Rather, he was concerned with the question of the replacement of class identity with one based on citizenship. This had to be achieved, first, in terms of equality before the law; second, in political terms through the establishment of a universal franchise; and, finally, in social terms through the establishment of the welfare state. In outlining this third phase, Marshall drew on the work of Beveridge on full employment (Beveridge 1944) and on his Report, *Social Insurance and Allied Services* (1942). Jenkins made his statement to a conference of non-governmental organisations called by the National Committee for Commonwealth Immigrants (Joppke 1999). Jenkins *did* deal with the question of immigrant integration and implicitly offered a distinctive definition of a multicultural society. 'Integration', he wrote, had to be conceived 'not as a flattening process of uniformity but as cultural diversity coupled with equal opportunity in an atmosphere of mutual tolerance'.

In my own work (Rex 1998) I have made two central points about this definition. First, it distinguishes Jenkins's concept of multiculturalism from any other idea about it through its insertion of the notion of equality of opportunity, thus relating it to Marshall's concept of citizenship. Second, it implies the existence of two separate domains, one being the public sphere while the other is that of culturally diverse communities. In the public domain all individuals are treated equally. In the domain of the separate communities each of these may speak its own language, practise its own religion and adhere to its own customs and family practices. So far as Muslims are concerned this recognises their right to practise their own religion but does not recognise their right to have their religion made part of the public domain.

This theory of multiculturalism could draw upon the sociology of Emile Durkheim (1933), who had argued for the necessity under conditions of organic solidarity for there to be some group standing between the family and the state within which individuals could feel at home. While Durkheim had the rather romantic idea that such a group could take the form of an occupational guild, it does seem that the concept of separate communal cultures and immigrant group organisation that is envisaged here would fulfil this function.

A further question which arises relates to the teaching of citizenship in schools. The Qualifications and Curriculum Authority appointed Bernard Crick to consider this question. In his final report in 1998 he suggested that there should be teaching of citizenship as part of the school curriculum. All children should be required to attend these lessons. A different nuance was introduced into this debate, however, by the Home Secretary David Blunkett who, after the Northern riots, saw citizenship education as part of a package of measures including identity cards and a requirement that immigrants should learn English. In this conception of citizenship the problem was seen as lying with the immigrant communities. Other people were regarded as already citizens. The immigrants were seen as having outside loyalties, such that special efforts had to be made to educate them into their citizenship duties.

Conclusion

What this book is concerned with is the position of Muslims in Britain after September 11. The answer has to be a very complex one.

First, the problems of the relation between Muslims and any society in which they exist as a minority have to be rethought in the light of the so-called 'War on Terror' and resistance to American world domination. There is no doubt that in this new situation Islam should be seen by Americans and their Coalition of the Willing partners as one of the possible bases for terrorist organisation. Equally the resistance might well define itself in Islamic terms with the Americans seen, to use the Iranian term, as the Great Satan. Here there is the possibility that financial assistance and training in terrorism will be given to those who decide to use it. Clearly there are some young British Muslims who have gone to the Gulf States, to Afghanistan and to Pakistan under these plans. On the other hand, the existence of such individuals means that all Muslims who visit these territories are likely to be viewed with suspicion.

Other problems may arise in connection with the way in which British Muslims react to the concept of multiculturalism that has been advocated here. Some of them may reject the notion of public and private domains, arguing that Islam is a whole way of life. They may wish to remain separate and some may even consider seceding from British society. This possibility was explored by the Muslim Institute in London, which published a Muslim Manifesto (Siddiqui 1990) and urged the setting up of a Muslim Parliament; it should be pointed out that this movement does not appear to have given any support to the idea of violence or terror.

Given this range of possibilities in the attitudes of Muslims to the societies in which they live as immigrants, there is also a range of possibilities in the way in which they are discussed in the discourse of their host societies. The most complete intellectual rejection of the possibility of their acceptance is that of Samuel Huntington, who argues that Western and Muslim civilisations exist on very different levels (1993). For him the transition to secular rationalism which has existed in the West simply cannot happen for Islam. This surely provides the most complete intellectual basis for Islamophobia. Muslims are the most unassimilable minority. A similar notion of the unacceptability of Muslim immigration is shared by the British demographer David Coleman (*Guardian*, 7 August 2002) and the organisation Migrationwatch UK, of which he is one of the leading figures. For him, while some limited immigration is acceptable, it is right that it should be selective and that Muslims should be excluded on the grounds of their unassimilability.

A more common view is that while some Muslims may be accommodated there clearly are a minority at least who are unassimilable and possibly dangerous to public order. Thus many British politicians go out of their way to say that they see a place for Muslims in British society, but that these acceptable Muslims have to be distinguished from a fringe of followers who are fundamentalist and extremist. How wide that fringe is varies in the definition offered by different policy makers.

These, then, are some of the problems faced by a Muslim minority in Britain after September 11. They are the problems of living in the world of the 'War on Terror'.

Note

1   I have done this in my chapter on Islam in the UK in the book *Islam Europe's Second Religion* edited by Shireen Hunter and published by Praeger in 2001.

Bibliography

Abbas, T. (2000) 'Images of Islam', *Index on Censorship*, Vol. XXIX, No. V.

Abdou, N. (2003) 'Veiled is beautiful, say Egypt's feminists and fashionistas', *Independent*, 13 December 2003, p. 16.

Ahmad, W. and C. Husband (1993) 'Religious identity, citizenship and welfare: the case of Muslims in Britain', *American Journal of Islamic Social Sciences*, Vol. CII, No. II.

Ahmad, W. (1996) 'Family obligations and social change in Asian Families', in W. I. U. Ahmad, and K. Atkin (eds.), *'Race' and Community Care*, Buckingham: Open University Press.

Ahmed, A. S. and H. Donnan (eds.) (1994) *Islam, Globalisation and Identity*, London: Routledge.

—— (2004) *Islam, Globalisation and Modernity*, London: Routledge.

Ahmed, N. M., F. Bodi, K. Kazim and M. Shadjereh (2001) *The Oldham Riots: Discrimination, Deprivation and Communal Tensions in the United Kingdom*, London: Islamic Human Rights Commission.

Ahmed, N., C. Phillipson and J. Latimer (2001) *Transformations of Womanhood through Migration,* Centre for Social Gerontology, Working Paper No. 8, Keele University.

Ahmed, S. T. (2003) 'Young British Muslims: social space and active identity', unpublished PhD thesis, University of Leicester.

Ahsan, M. M. (2003) 'Introduction', in M Seddon, D. Hussain and N. Malik (eds.), *British Muslims: Loyalty and Belonging*, Leicester: The Islamic Foundation and the Citizen Organising Foundation.

Ahsan, M. M. and A. R. Kidwai (1991) *Sacrilege versus Civility: Muslim Perspectives on the Satanic Verses Affair*, Leicester: Islamic Foundation.

Akbar, A. S. (1988) *Discovering Islam: Making Sense of Muslim History and Society*, London: Routledge and Kegan Paul.

Al-Hujwari, Ali B. Uthman al-Jullabi (1976) *The Kashf al-Mahjub*, translated by R. A. Nicholson, London: Luzac.

Ali, J. (1998) 'Changing identity constructions among Bangladeshi Muslims in Britain', unpublished MA thesis, Centre for the Study of Islamic and Christian–Muslim Relations, University of Birmingham.

Ali, M. (1989) *The Emergence of Pakistan*, Lahore: University of Punjab Press.

Al-Jabri, M. A. (1999) '"Clash of civilisations": the relations of the future?', in G. M. Munoz (ed.), *Islam, Modernism and the West*, London: I. B. Tauris.

Allen, C. (2001) 'Islamophobia in the media since September 11', paper given at the conference on 'Exploring Islamophobia', University of Westminster, London, 29 September 2001.

—— (2002) *The Select Committee on Religious Offences: a Response*, London: Forum Against Islamophobia and Racism.

—— (2003) *Fair Justice: the Bradford Disturbances, the Sentencing and the Impact*, London: Forum Against Islamophobia and Racism.

—— (2004) 'Endemically European or a European epidemic? Islamophobia in a post-September 11 EU', in T. Gabriel, R. Geaves and Y. Haddad (eds.), *Islam and the West after September 11 (tbc)*, London: Ashgate.

Allen, C. and J. Nielsen (2002) *Summary Report on Islamophobia in the EU after 11 September 2001*, Vienna: European Monitoring Centre on Racism and Xenophobia.

Al-Shingiety, A. Y. (1991) 'The Muslim as the "other": representation and self-image of the Muslims in North America', in Y. Yazbeck (ed.), *The Muslims of America*, Oxford: Oxford University Press.

Alsumaih, A. M. (1998) 'The Sunni concept of Jihad in classical Fiqh and modern Islamic thought', unpublished PhD thesis, University of Newcastle-upon-Tyne.

Amnesty International (2001) *September 11 Crisis Response Guide: Human Rights Education Program for Junior and High Schools*, New York: Amnesty International.

Anderson, B. (1983) *Imagined Communities*, London: Verso.

Anderson, L. (1997) 'State policy and Islamist radicalism', in J. Esposito (ed.), *Political Islam: Revolution, Radicalism, or Reform?* London: Lynne Rienner.

Ansari, Humayun (2002) *Muslims in Britain*, London: Minority Rights Group International.

Ansell, A. E. (1997) *New Right, New Racism: Race and Reaction in the United States and Britain*, London: Macmillan.

Anthias, F. (1992) *Ethnicity, Class, Gender and Migration*, Aldershot: Gower.

Anwar, M. (1979) *The Myth of Return: Pakistanis in Britain*, London: Heinemann.

—— (1994) *Race and Elections*, Coventry: Centre for Research in Ethnic Relations.

—— (1998) *Between Cultures*, London: Routledge.

—— (2000) 'The impact of legislation on British race relations', in M. Anwar *et al.* (eds.), *From Legislation to Integration?*, London: Macmillan.

Anwar, M. and F. Shah (2000) 'Muslim women and experiences of discrimination', in J. Blaschke (ed.), *Multi-Level Discrimination of Muslim Women in Europe*, Berlin: Edition Parabolis.

Anwar, M. and Q. Bakhsh (2003) *British Muslims and State Policies*, Centre for Research in Ethnic Relations, University of Warwick.

Archer, L. (2002) 'Change, culture and tradition: British Muslim pupils talk about Muslim girls' post-16 "choice"', *Race, Ethnicity, and Education*, Vol. V, No. IV.

Arthur, P. and K. Jeffery (1996) *Northern Ireland since 1968*, Oxford: Blackwell.

Asad, T. (1990) 'Multiculturalism and British identity in the wake of the Rushdie affair', *Politics and Society*, Vol. XVIII, No. IV.

Ashraf, S. A. (1985) *Education and the Muslim Community in Britain Today: Areas of Agreement*, Cambridge: Islamic Academy and Department of Education, University of Cambridge.

—— (1993) 'Recommendations of the five World Conferences on Muslim education – a plan for implementation II', editorial, *Muslim Education Quarterly*, Vol. X, No. II.

Atkin, K. and Y. Hussain (2003) 'Disability and ethnicity: how young Asian disabled people make sense of their lives', in S. Riddell and N. Watson (eds.), *Disability, Culture and Identity*, Harlow: Pearson Education Ltd.

Back, L., M. Keith, A. Khan, K. Shukra and J. Solomos (2002) 'The return to assimilation: race, multiculturalism and New Labour', *Sociological Research Online*, Vol. VII, No. II, <http://www.socresonline.org.uk/7/2/back.html>.

Bagguley, P. and Y. Hussain (2003) 'The Bradford "riot" of 2001: a preliminary analysis', in C. Barker and M. Tyldesley (eds.), *Ninth International Conference on Alternative Futures and Popular Protest*, Manchester: Manchester Metropolitan University.

Bakhsh, Q. and D. Sullivan (1985) *Multi-Faith Britain: a Way Forward*, London: Cheeta Books.

Baktiari, B. (2000) 'Cybermuslim and the Internet: searching for spiritual harmony in a digital world', in M. S. Bahmanpour and H. Bashir (eds.), *Muslim Identity in the 21st Century*, London: Institute of Islamic Studies and BookExtra.

Ballard, R. (1990) 'Migration and kinship: the differential effect of marriage rules in the processes of Punjabi migration to Britain', in C. Clarke, C. Peach and S. Vertovec (eds.), *South Asians Overseas*, Cambridge: Cambridge University Press.

Ballard, R. (2001) 'The impact of kinship on the economic dynamics of transnational networks: reflections on some South Asian developments', Centre for Migration and Development Working Paper Series, Princeton, NJ: Princeton University Press.

Banton, M. (1955) *The Coloured Quarter*, London: Jonathan Cape.

Barber, B. (1996) *Jihad vs. McWorld: How Globalisation and Tribalism are Reshaping the World*, London: Ballantine.

Barker, M. (1981) *The New Racism*, London: Junction Books.

Basit, T. N. (1997) *Eastern Values, Western Milieu: Identities and Aspirations of Adolescent British Muslim Girls*, Aldershot: Ashgate.

Baumann, Z. (1996) 'From pilgrim to tourist', in S. Hall and P. du Gay (eds.), *Questions of Cultural Identity*, London, Sage.

Begum, H. (2003) *Social Capital in Action: Adding up Local Connections and Networks*, London: London School of Economics/National Council for Voluntary Sector Organisations.

Bennett, C. (1992) *Victorian Images of Islam*, London: Grey Seal.

Beveridge, W. (1942) *Social Insurance and Allied Services*, London: HMSO, Cmnd 6404.

—— (1944) *Full Employment in a Free Society*, London: Allen and Unwin.

Beynon, H. and L. Kushnick (2003) 'Cool Britannia or Cruel Britannia? Racism and New Labour', in L. Panitch and C. Leys (eds.), *Socialist Register 2003. Fighting Identities: Race, Religion and Ethnonationalism*, London: The Merlin Press.

Bhachu, P. (1985) *Twice Migrants: East African Sikh Settlers in Britain*, London: Tavistock.

Blair, Tony (2002) 'The Power of World Community', in M. Leonard (ed.), *Reordering the World*, London: The Foreign Policy Centre, pp. 119–24.

—— (2003) 'History will be our judge': Friday 18 July 2003. Speech by the Prime Minister, Tony Blair, to the US Congress, Washington DC.

Bradford Commission (1996) *The Bradford Commission Report*, London: The Stationery Office.

Brah, A. (1988) 'Black struggles, equality and education', *Critical Social Policy*, Vol. XXIV.

British Muslims Monthly Survey (2001), Vol. XI, No. XII.

Brierley, P. (ed.) (1990) *UK Christian Handbook*, Eltham: MarcEurope Britain.

Brierley, P. and Longley, D. (eds.) (1992) UK *Christian Handbook*, 1992/3 edition, Eltham: Marc Europe Britain.

British National Party (2002) *The Truth about ISLAM: Intolerance, Slaughter, Looting, Arson and Molestation of Women*, pamphlet.

Brown, M. (2000) 'Religion and economic activity in the South Asian population', *Ethnic and Racial Studies*, Vol. XXIII, No. VI.

Brown, M., J. E. Malcolm and C. Tew (2004) 'Learning through linking: teachers without borders', *Race Equality Teaching*, Vol. XXII, No. II.

Buckley, A. (ed.) (1998) 'Introduction: daring us to laugh: creativity and power in Northern Irish symbols', in A. Buckley (ed.), *Symbols in Northern Ireland*, Belfast: Institute of Irish Studies.

Bunglawala, I. (2002) 'British Muslims and the media', in *The Quest for Sanity: Reflections on September 11 and the Aftermath*, London: Muslim Council of

Britain.

Bunt, G. (2000) *Virtually Islamic: Computer-Mediated Communication and Cyber Islamic Environments*, Cardiff: University of Wales Press.

Cantle Report (2001) *Community Cohesion: a Report of the Independent Review Team*, London: Home Office.

Castles, S. and G. Kosack (1973) *Immigrant Workers and the Class Structure in Western Europe*, London: Institute of Race Relations and Oxford University Press.

Castles, S. and A. Davidson (2000) *Citizenship and Migration: Globalization and the Politics of Belonging*, London: Routledge.

Centre for Bangladeshi Studies (1994) *Routes and Beyond: Voices from Educationally Successful Bangladeshis*, London: Centre for Bangladeshi Studies.

Cesari, J. (1998) 'Islam in France: social challenge or challenge of secularism?', in S. Vertovec and A. Rogers (eds.), *Muslim European Youth: Reproducing Ethnicity, Religion, Culture*, Aldershot: Ashgate.

Choudhury, G. W. (1968) *Pakistan's Relations with India: 1947–1956*, London: Pall Mall.

Clarke, T. (2002) *Report of the Burnley Task Force*, <http://www.burnleytaskforce.org.uk/>

Coles, M. I. (2004) *Education and Islam: a New Strategic Approach*, Leicester: School Development Support Agency.

Corrigan, M. (2001) 'A sociological study of Pakistani Muslims in Northern Ireland', unpublished PhD thesis, Queen's University of Belfast.

Coward, H., J. Hinnells and R. Williams (eds.) (2000) *The South Asian Religious Diaspora in Britain, Canada and the United States*, Albany: State University of New York Press.

Crick, B. (1998) *Final Report of the Advisory Group on Citizenship Qualifications and Curriculum Authority*, London: HMSO.

Davis, M. (2001) 'The flames of New York', *New Left Review*, Second Series, No. XII.

Dayan, D. (1998) 'Particularistic media and diasporic communications', in T. Liebes and J. Curran (eds.), *Media, Ritual and Identity*, London: Routledge.

Deakin, N. (1970) *Colour, Citizenship and British Society*, London: Panther.

Denham, J. (2002) *Building Cohesive Communities: a Report of the Ministerial Group on Public Order and Community Cohesion*, London: Home Office.

Department for Education and Skills (2003) *Aiming High: Raising the Achievement of Minority Ethnic Pupils*, London: Department for Education and Skills.

Department of the Environment, Transport and the Regions (1997) *Involving Communities in Urban and Rural Regeneration: a Guide for Practitioners*, London: DETR.

Department of Transport, Local Government and the Regions (2001) *Housing in England: Survey of English Housing 2000/1*, London: DTLR.

—— (2002) *Survey of English Housing*, London: DTLR.

DES (1989) *The Education Reform Act 1988: Religious Education and Collective Worship*, Circular 3/89, Department of Education and Science, London: HMSO.

Donnan, H. (1983) 'New minorities, South Asian in the North', in T. Eriksen (ed.) *Ethnicity and nationalism: anthropological perspectives*, London: Pluto Press.

Donnan, H. and M. O'Brien (1998) ' "Because you stick out, you stand out": perception of prejudice among Northern Ireland's Pakistanis', in P. Hainsworth (ed.), *Divided Society, Ethnic Minorities and Racism in Northern Ireland*, London: Pluto Press.

Durkheim, E. (1933) *The Division of Labour in Society*, Glencoe: Free Press.

Eade, J. (1989) *The Politics of Community: the Bangladeshi Community in East London*, Aldershot: Avebury.

—— (1992) 'Quests for belonging: Bangladeshis in Tower Hamlets', in A. Cambridge
    et al. (eds.), *Where You Belong: Government and Black Culture*, Aldershot:
    Avebury.
—— (1996) 'Nationalism, community and the Islamicisation of urban space', in B.
    Metcalf (ed.), *Making Muslim Spaces in North America and Europe*, Berkeley:
    University of California Press.
—— (1997a) 'Keeping the options open: Bangladeshis in a global city', in A. Kershen
    (ed.), *London: the Promised Land? The Migrant Experience in a Global City*,
    Aldershot: Avebury.
Eade, J., C. Peach and T. Vamplew (1996) 'The Bangladeshis: the encapsulated
    community', in C. Peach (ed.), *Ethnicity in the 1991 Census. Volume 2, The Ethnic
    Minority Populations of Britain*, London: Office for National Statistics.
Eade, J., I. Fremeaux and D. Garbin (2002) 'The political construction of diasporic
    communities in the global city', in P. Gilbert (ed.), *Imagined Londons*, Albany:
    State University of New York Press.
Esposito, J. (1997) 'Introduction', in J. L. Esposito (ed.), *Political Islam: Revolution,
    Radicalism, or Reform*, London: Boulder.
—— (1997) 'Political Islam and Gulf Security', in J. L. Esposito (ed.), *Political Islam:
    Revolution, Radicalism, or Reform*, London: Boulder.
—— (1999) 'Clash of Civilisations'? Contemporary images of Islam in the West', in G.
    M. Munoz (ed.), *Islam, Modernism and the West*, London: I. B. Tauris.
—— (2002) *Unholy War: Terror in the Name of Islam*, Oxford University Press.
Euben, R. L. (2002) 'Killing (for) politics: *jihad*, martyrdom, and political action',
    Political Theory, Vol. XXX, No. I.
EUMC (2001) *Anti-Islamic Reactions in the EU after the Terrorist Acts against the
    USA*, Vienna: European Monitoring Centre on Racism and Xenophobia.
Fenton, S. (1999) *Ethnicity: Racism, Class and Culture*, Basingstoke: Macmillan.
Firestone, R. (1999) *Jihad: the Origin of the Holy War in Islam*, Oxford: Oxford
    University Press.
Fremeaux, I. (2002) 'The strategic use of the notion of community in cultural projects
    within urban regeneration schemes', unpublished PhD thesis, London Guildhall
    (now Metropolitan) University.
Fremeaux, I. and D. Garbin (2002) 'The political construction of diasporic
    communities in the global city', in P. Gilbert (ed.), *Imagined Londons*, Albany:
    State University of New York Press.
Fryer, P. (1984) *Staying Power: the History of Black People in Britain*, London:
    Pluto Press.
Gabriel, T., R. Geaves and Y. Haddad, (2004) *Islam and the West after September 11
    (tbc)*, London: Ashgate.
Gale R. (1999) *Pride of Place and Places: South Asian Religious Buildings and the
    City Planning Authority in Leicester*, Working Paper 124, University of Wales,
    Department of City and Regional Planning, Cardiff.
Garbin, D. (2004) 'Migration, territories de diasporiques et politiques identitaires:
    Bengalis musulmans entre "Banglatown" (Londres) et Sylhet', unpublished PhD
    thesis, University of Tours (France).
Gardner, H. (1995) *Leading Minds: An Anatomy of Leadership*, New York: Basic
    Books.
Gardner, K. (1998) 'Women and Islamic revivalism in a Bangladeshi community', in
    P. Jeffrey and A. Basu (eds.), *Appropriating Gender: Women's Activism and
    Political Religion in South Asia*, London: Routledge.
Geaves, R. (1999) 'Britain', in D. Westerlund and I. Svanberg (eds.), *Islam Outside the
    Arab World*, Surrey: Curzon Press.
Gellner, E. (1994) 'Forward', in A. S. Ahmed and H. Donnan (eds.), *op. cit.*

Gluckman, M. (1958) *An Analysis of a Social Situation in Modern Zululand*, Rhodes-Livingstone Paper 28, Manchester: Manchester University Press.

Goddard, H. (1990) 'Stronger than fiction: the affair of *The Satanic Verses*', *Scottish Journal of Religious Studies*, Vol. XII.

Griffith, P. and M. Leonard (2002) *Reclaiming Britishness*, London: Foreign Policy Centre.

Guardian (2001) Diary, 13 March and Faisal Bodi, 'Opportunistic Cronies', 13 November.

—— (2001), Letters, 'Questions of Loyalty for Muslims', 16 November.

—— (2002), Review of Migrantwatch demographic estimates by Heather Stewart and Richard Adams, 7 August.

Habermas, J. (1994) 'Struggles for recognition in the democratic constitutional state', in A. Gutmann (ed.), *Multi-culturalism: Examining the Politics of Recognition*, New Jersey: Princeton University Press.

Halliday, F. (1992) Arabs in Exile: Yemeni Migrants in Urban Britain, London: I. B. Tauris.

Hardt, M. and A. Negri (2000) *Empire*. Harvard: Harvard University Press.

Hargreaves, A. and T. Stenhouse (1995), *Immigration, Race and Ethnicity in Contemporary France*, London: Routledge.

Hassan, Nasra (2001) `An Arsenal of Believers', The New Yorker 19 November.

Harris, M. (2003) 'Faith and Regeneration', paper presented at the conference on 'An Independent Sector?' 7 March 2003, LSE Centre for Civil Society.

Haw, K. (1994) 'Muslim girls' schools – a conflict of interests?' *Gender and Education*, Vol. VI, No. I: 73–5.

Hepple, B. and T. Choudhry (2001) *Tackling Religious Discrimination: Practical Implications for Policy Makers and Legislators*, London: Home Office.

Hodgins H. (1981) *Planning Permission for Mosques: the Birmingham Experience*, Research Papers – Muslims in Europe, 9, Selly Oak Colleges, Birmingham.

Home Office (2004) figures received through personal communication.

Hopkins, V. K and N. Hopkins (2002) '"Representing" British Muslims: the strategic dimension of identity construction', *Ethnic and Racial Studies*, Vol. XXV, No. II.

Hoveyda, F. (2002) *The Broken Crescent,* London: Praeger.

Hunter, S. (ed.) (2002) *Islam, Europe's Second Religion*, Connecticut and London: Praeger, Westport.

Huntington, S. P. (1993) 'The clash of civilizations', *Foreign Affairs*, Vol. LXXII.

—— (1996) *The Clash of Civilizations and the Remaking of World Order*, London: Simon and Schuster.

Husband, C. (2002) 'Diasporic identities and diasporic economies: the case of minority ethnic media', in: M. Martiniello and B. Piquard (eds.), *Diversity in the City*, Bilbao: Universidad de Deusto.

Iqbal, N. (2003) 'Pakistan Workshop 2003', *Anthropology Today*, Vol. XIX.

Islamic Human Rights Commission (2000) *Anti-Muslim Discrimination and Hostility in the United Kingdom*, London: Islamic Human Rights Commission.

Jackson, S. A. (2001) 'Domestic terrorism in the Islamic legal tradition', *The Muslim World*, Vol. CIX, No. II.

Jacobson, J. (1998) *Islam in Transition. Religion and Identity among British Pakistani Youth*, London: Routledge.

Jarman, N. (2002) *Overview Analysis of Racist Incidents Recorded in Northern Ireland by RUC 1996–1999*, Belfast: OFM and DFM.

Jewett, R. and J. S. Lawrence (2003) *Captain America and the Crusade against Evil: the Dilemma of Zealous Nationalism*, Cambridge: William B. Eermans Publishing Company.

Joppke, C. (1999) *Immigration and the Nation State: the United States, Germany and Britain*, Oxford: Oxford University Press.

Kapil, A (1991) 'Les Parties Islamistes en Algerie: Elements de presentation', *Maghreb-Machrek*, Vol. 133: 103–11.

Kawale, R. (2003) 'A kiss is just a kiss … or is it? South Asian lesbian and bisexual woman and the construction of space', in N. Puwar and P. Raghuram (eds.), *South Asian Women in the Diaspora*, Oxford: Berg.

Kepel, G. (1997) *Allah in the West: Islamic Movements in America and Europe*, Cambridge: Polity.

—— (2000) *Allah in the West: Islamic Movements in America and Europe*, Cambridge: Polity Press.

Kershen, A. J. (2000) 'Mother tongue as a bridge to assimilation? Yiddish and Sylheti in East London', in A. J. Kershen (ed.), *Language, Labour and Migration*, Aldershot: Ashgate.

Kettani, M. A. (1986) *Muslim Minorities in the World Today*, London: Mansell Publishing.

Khan, V. (ed.) (1979) *Minority Families in Britain: Support and Stress*, London: Macmillan.

Klug, F. (2002) 'Human rights: a common standard for all peoples?', in P. Griffith and M. Leonard (eds.), *Reclaiming Britishness*, London: Foreign Policy Centre.

Knott, K. (1991) 'Bound to change ? The religions of South Asians in Britain', in S. Vertovec (ed.), *Aspects of the South Asian Diaspora*, New Delhi: Oxford University Press.

Knowles, C. (1992) *Race, Discourse and Labourism*, London and New York: Routledge.

Kumar, K. (2003) *The Making of English National Identity*, Cambridge: Cambridge University Press.

Kundnani, A. (2000) '"Stumbling on": race, class and England', *Race and Class*, Vol. XXXXI, No. IV.

Kymlicka, W. (1995) *Multicultural Citizenship*, Oxford: Oxford University Press.

Lawrence, B. B. (1998) *Shattering the Myth: Islam beyond Violence*, Princeton: Princeton University Press.

Leicester City Council (1988) *Survey of Leicester: Ward Tables*, Leicester: Leicester City Council.

Lentin, R. and R. McVeigh (eds.) (2002) *Racism and Anti-racism in Ireland*, Belfast: Beyond the Pale.

Leveau, R. (1992) 'Les associations musulmanes', *Projet*, 231: 78–80.

Lewis, B. (1988) *The Political Language of Islam*, Chicago: Chicago University Press.

Lewis, P. (1994) *Islamic Britain: Religion, Politics and Identity among British Muslims*, London: I.B. Tauris.

LFS (2000) unpublished data, Spring–Winter, Labour Force Survey.

Mac an Ghaill, M. (1999) *Contemporary Racisms and New Ethnicities: Social and Cultural Transformations*, Buckingham: Open University Press.

MacArthur, J. (2001) *Terrorism, Jihad and the Bible: a Response to the Terrorist Attacks*, London: W Publishing Group.

Macpherson. W. (1999) *The Stephen Lawrence Inquiry: Report of an Inquiry by Sir William Macpherson of Cluny*, HMSO Cmnd 4262-I.

Malise, R. (1990) *A Satanic Affair: Salman Rushdie and the Rage of Islam*, London: Chatto and Windus.

Mandaville, P. (2001) *Transnational Muslim Politics: Reimagining the Umma*, London: Routledge.

Mani, B. (2002) ' Undressing the diaspora', in N. Puwar and P. Raghuram (eds.), *South Asian Women in the Diaspora*, Oxford: Berg.

Marsden, P. (2002) *The Taliban: War and Religion in Afghanistan*, New York: Zed

Books.

Marshall, T. H. (1950) *Citizenship and Social Class*, Cambridge: Cambridge University Press.

Mastnak, T. (1994) *Islam and the Creation of a European Identity*, CSD Research Papers 4, London: University of Westminster Press.

McRoy, G. A. (2001) *Rushdie's Legacy: the Emergence of a Radical British Muslim Identity*, unpublished PhD thesis, London Bible College.

Medway D. and D. Phillips (2000) 'Punjabi Hindus in diaspora: socio-religious transformations amongst British Indians in Bradford', paper delivered to the Social and Cultural Research Group, Institute of British Geographers Annual Conference, University of Sussex, 7 January.

Moaddel, M. and K. Talatoff (eds.) (2000) *Contemporary Debates in Islam: an Anthology of Modernist and Fundamentalist Thought*, Basingstoke: Macmillan.

Modood, T. (1990) 'British Muslims and the Rushdie affair', *Political Quarterly*, Vol. LXI, No. II.

—— (1992) 'British Asian Muslims and the Rushdie affair', in: J. Donald and A. Rattansi (eds.), *'Race', Culture and Difference*, London: Sage.

Modood, T., R. Berthoud, J. Lakey, J. Nazroo, P. Smith, S. Virdee and S. Beishon (1997) *Ethnic Minorities in Britain: Diversity and Disadvantage*, London: Policy Studies Institute.

Modood, T., Beishon, S. and S. Virdee (1994) *Changing Ethnic Identities*, London: Policy Studies Institute.

Mumtaz, K. and F. Shaheed (1987) *Women of Pakistan*, London: Zed Books.

Munoz, G. M. (1999) *Islam, Modernism and the West*, London: I. B. Tauris.

Naylor, S. and J. Ryan (2002) 'The mosque in the suburbs: negotiating religion and ethnicity in South London', *Social and Cultural Geography*, Vol. III.

Nielsen, J. (1981) *Muslims in Europe: An Overview*, Birmingham: Centre for the Study of Islam and Christian-Muslim Relations.

—— (1992) *Muslims in Western Europe*, Edinburgh: Edinburgh University Press.

Office of Population Censuses and Surveys (1993) *1991 Census: Ethnic Group and Country of Birth (Great Britain)*, London: HMSO.

ONS (2004) *2001 Census*, Office for National Statistics . http://www.statistics.gov.uk/census2001.

Osler, A. (1997) *The Education and Careers of Black Teachers: Changing Identities, Changing Lives*, Buckingham: Open University Press.

—— (2003) 'Muslim women teachers: life histories, identities and citizenship', in: H. Jawad and T. Benn (eds.) *Muslim Women in the United Kingdom and Beyond: Experiences and Images*, Leiden: Brill.

Osler, A. and K. Vincent (2002) *Citizenship and the Challenge of Global Education*, Stoke: Trentham.

—— (2003) *Girls and Exclusion: Rethinking the Agenda*, London: RoutledgeFalmer.

Osler, A. and Z. Hussain (1995) 'Parental choice and schooling: some factors influencing Muslim mothers' decisions about the education of their daughters', *Cambridge Journal of Education*, Vol. XXV, No. III.

Ouseley, H. (2002) *Community Pride, not Prejudice – the Ouseley Report on Bradford*, Bradford: Bradford Vision.

Papastergiadis, N. (2000) *The Turbulence of Migration*, Cambridge: Polity Press.

Parekh Report (2000) *The Future of Multi-Ethnic Britain*, London: Profile Books. (See also Runnymede Trust)

Parekh, B. (1990) 'The Rushdie affair: research agenda for political philosophy', *Political Studies*, Vol. XXXVIII.

Parekh, B. (2000) *Rethinking Multiculturalism: Cultural Diversity and Political Theory*, Cambridge, Massachusetts: Harvard University Press.

Parker-Jenkins, M. (1994) 'Islam shows its diverse tendencies', *Times Educational Supplement*, 21 October.

Peach, C. (1990a) 'Estimating the growth of the Bangladeshi population of Great Britain', *New Community*, Vol. XXXI.

—— (1990b) 'The Muslim population of Great Britain', *Ethnic and Racial Studies*, Vol. XIII.

—— (1996a) Editor and contributor to *The Ethnic Minority Populations of Britain, Volume 2, Ethnicity in the 1991 Census*, London: ONS and HMSO.

—— (1996b) 'Does Britain have ghettos ?', *Transactions IBG*, Vol. XXII.

—— (1997) 'Estimates of the 1991 Muslim population of Great Britain', Oxford Plural Societies and Multicultural Cities Research Group, Working Paper I, Oxford School of Geography, Oxford.

—— (1999) 'London and New York: contrasts in British and American models of segregation', *International Journal of Population Geography*, Volume V.

Peach, G. C. K. and S. W. C. Winchester (1974) 'Birthplace, ethnicity and the under-enumeration of West Indians, Indians and Pakistanis in the censuses of 1966 and 1971', *New Community*, Vol. III, No. IV: 386–93.

Petch, A. (1986) 'Parental choice at entry to primary school', *Research Papers in Education*, Vol. I.

Phillips D. and M. Brown (2000) 'Religion and identity in the suburbanising South Asian population of Leeds', paper given at the Symposium on New Landscapes of Religion in the West, University of Oxford, 27–29 September.

Phillipson, C., N. Ahmed and J. Latimer (2003) *Women in Transition: a Study of the Experiences of Bangladeshi Women Living in Tower Hamlets*, Bristol: Policy Press.

Pipes, D. (2002) 'Jihad and the Professors', commentary, November 2002, www.danielpipes.org/article/498.

—— (2002) 'What is *Jihad?*', New York Post, 31 December 2002, www.danielpipes.org/article/990

Piscatori, J. (2001) 'Managing God's guests: the pilgrimage and the politics of Saudi legitimacy', conference presentation, University of Oxford.

Poole, E. (2002) *Reporting Islam: Media Representations of British Muslims*, London: I. B. Tauris.

Portes, A. (1997) 'Globalisation from below: the rise of transnational communities', Working Paper 98–99, Centre for Migration and Development, Princeton, NJ.

Poston, L. A. (1991) 'Da 'wa in the West', in Y. Yazbeck (ed.), *The Muslims of America*, Oxford: Oxford University Press.

Q-News (2001a) Readers poll, November 2001/Ramadhan 1422, No. 337, p. 9.

—— (2001b) 'Ready for *Jihad*: young, Muslim and angry', November 2001/Ramadhan 1422, No 337, p. 15.

Radcliffe, L. (2003) 'A Muslim lobby at Whitehall? Examining the role of the Muslim minority in British foreign policymaking', unpublished M.Phil. thesis, Department of Politics and International Relations, University of Oxford.

Rait, G. and A. Burns (1997) 'Appreciating background and culture: the South Asian elderly and mental health', *International Journal of Geriatric Psychiatry*, Vol. XII, No. X.

Ramadan, T. (2004) *Western Muslims and the Future of Islam*. Oxford: Oxford University Press.

Ramdin, R. (1987) *The Making of The Black Working Class in Britain*, Aldershot: Wildwood House Ltd.

Rampton, S. and J. Stauber (2003) *Weapons of Mass Deception: the Uses of Propaganda in Bush's War on Iraq*, London: Robinson.

Ray, L. and D. Smith (2002) 'Racist offending, policing and community conflict', paper presented to the British Sociological Association Conference.

Rayaprol, A. (1997) *Negotiating Identities: Women in the Indian Diaspora*, Delhi: Oxford University Press.

Reber, A. S. *(1985) Dictionary of Psychology*, London: Penguin.

Rex, J. (1998) *Ethnic Minorities in the Modern Nation State*, Basingstoke: Macmillan.

—— (2002) 'Islam in the United Kingdom', in S. Hunter (ed.), *Islam: Europe's Second Religion*, Washington: Center for Strategic and International Studies and Praeger.

Rex, J. and R. Moore (1967) *Race, Community and Conflict: a Study of Sparkbrook*, London: Institute of Race Relations and Oxford University Press.

Rex, J. and Y. Samad (1996) 'Multiculturalism in Birmingham and Bradford', in *Innovation: the European Journal of Social Sciences*, Vol. IX, No. I.

Ritchie, D. (2001) *Oldham Independent Review*, Oldham: Oldham Independent Review Panel and Government Office North West.

Roberts, A. (2004), 'The Changing Faces of Terrorism', http://www.bbc.co.uk/history/war/sept_11/changing_faces_01.shtml

Roberts, H. (1991) 'A trial of strength: Algerian Islamism', in J. Piscatori (ed.), *Islamic Fundamentalism and the Gulf Crisis*, Chicago: American Academy of Arts and Sciences.

Robinson, F. (ed.) (1996) *The Cambridge Illustrated History of the Islamic World*, Cambridge: Cambridge University Press.

Robinson, V. (1986) *Transients, Settlers and Refugees: Asians in Britain*, London: Clarendon Press.

Rose, E., N. Deakin, M. Abrams, V. Jackson, M. Peston, A. Vanags, B. Cohen, J. Gaitskell and P. Ward (1969) *Colour and Citizenship: a Report on British Race Relations*, London: Institute of Race Relations and Oxford University Press.

Runnymede Trust (1997) *Islamophobia: a Challenge for Us All*, London: Runnymede Trust.

—— (2000), *The Future of Multi-ethnic Britain. The Parekh Report*, London: Profile and Runnymede Trust.

—— (2001) *Addressing Prejudice and Islamophobia. Resources, References and Guidance on the Internet*. Runnymede Trust, Commission on British Muslims and Islamophobia.

Ruthven, M. (2000) *Islam in the World*, new edition, London: Penguin.

Sahgal, G. (2002) 'Blair's *jihad*, Blunkett's crusade: the battle for the hearts and minds of Britain's Muslims', *Radical Philosophy*, Vol. CXII.

Said, E. (1979, 1985) *Orientalism*, Harmondsworth: Penguin.

Saikal, A. (2003) *Islam and the West: Conflict or Cooperation,* Basingstoke: Palgrave–MacMillan.

Samad, Y. (1992) 'Book-burning and race relations: political mobilisation of Asians in Bradford', *New Community*, Vol. XVIII, No. IV.

Sardar, Z. (2002) 'The excluded minority: British Muslim identity after 11 September', in P. Griffith and M. Leonard (eds.), *Reclaiming Britishness*, London: Foreign Policy Centre.

Sardar, Z. and Z. A. Malik (1996) *Introducing Muhammad*, Cambridge: Icon Books.

Sarup, M. (1994) 'Home and identity', in G. Robertson, M. Mash, L. Tickner, J. Bird, B. Curtis and T. Putnam (eds.), *Travellers' Tales: Narratives of Home and Displacement*, London: Routledge.

Sarwar, G. (1991) *British Muslims and Schools: Proposals for Progress*, London: Muslim Educational Trust.

Sayyid, B. (1997) *A Fundamental Fear: Eurocentrism and the Emergence of Islamism*, London: Zed Books.

Seldon, A. and Marquand, D. (1996) *The Ideas That Shaped Post-war Britain*, London: Fontana.

Shaw, A. (1998) *A Pakistani Community in Britain*, Oxford: Blackwell.

—— (2002) 'Why might young British Muslims support the Taliban?', *Anthropology Today*, Vol. XXVIII, No. I.

Sheriff, S. (2001a) 'Mosques firebombed, Muslims assaulted – British Muslims under siege', *Muslim News*, No. 149, 28 September 2001/10 Rajab 1422, p. 1.

—— (2001b) 'Comfortable with being British but not British foreign policy', *Muslim News*, No. 152, 21 December 2001/6 Shawwal 1422, p. 12.

Siddiqui, K. (1990) *The Muslim Manifesto*, London: Muslim Institute.

—— (1992) 'The Muslim Parliament of Great Britain: political innovation and adaption', inaugural address (xerox), London: Muslim Parliament of Great Britain.

Sikand, Y. (2001) 'Changing course of Kashmiri struggle: from national liberation to Islamist *jihad*?', *Economic and Political Weekly*, Vol. XXXVI, No. III.

Silverman, A. L. (2002) 'Just war, *jihad*, and terrorism: a comparison of western and Islamic norms for the use of political violence', *Journal of Church and State*, Vol. XLIV, No. I.

Sinke, S. (1992) 'The international marriage market and the sphere of social reproduction', in D. Gabbaccia (ed.), *Seeking Common Ground*, Westport, CT: Greenwood Press.

—— (1995) 'The international marriage market: theoretical and historical perspectives', in D. Hoerder and J. Nagler (eds.), *People in Transit*, Cambridge: Cambridge University Press.

Smith, G. (1998) 'More than a little quiet care: the extents of the churches' contribution to community work in East London in the 1990s', London: Aston Charities Communities Involvement Unit.

—— (1999) 'East London is no longer secular: religion as a source of social capital in the regeneration of East London', *Rising East: The Journal of East London*, Vol. IV, No. III.

Smith, S. J. (1989) *The Politics of 'Race' and Residence*, Cambridge: Polity Press.

SEU (2000) *National Strategy for Neighbourhood Renewal*, London: Social Exclusion Unit.

Song, M. (2003) *Choosing Ethnic Identity*, Cambridge: Polity Press.

Strategy Unit (2003) *Ethnic Minorities and the Labour Market*, London: Cabinet Office.

Streusand, D. E. (1997) 'What does *jihad* mean?', *Middle East Quarterly*, 1997, www.meforum.org/article/357.

Taji-Farouki, S. (2000) 'Islamists and the Threat of Jihad: Hizb al-Tahrir and al-Muhajiroun on Israel and the Jews', *Middle Eastern Studies*, Vol. XXXVI, No. IV.

Taylor, C. (1994) 'The politics of recognition', in A. Gutmann (ed.), *Multiculturalism*, Princeton: Princeton University Press.

Thomas, D. (2003) *Le Londonistan: La voix du djihad*, Paris: Éditions Michalon.

Tikly, L., A. Osler, J. Hill and K. Vincent (2002) *Ethnic Minority Achievement Grant: Analysis of LEA Action Plans*, Research Report 371, London: Department for Education and Skills.

Troyna, B. and B. Carrington (1987) 'Anti-sexist anti-racist education – a false dilemma: a reply to Walkling and Brannigan', *Journal of Moral Education*, Vol. XXXI.

Vallely, P. (2000) 'It's time to say what's good about being a Muslim', *Independent*, 31 October.

Vandewalle, D. (1997) 'Islam in Algeria: religion, culture, and opposition in a rentier state', in J. Esposito (ed.), *Political Islam: Revolution, Radicalism, or Reform*,

London: Boulder.

Vertovec, S. (1995) 'Introduction' (with Alisdair Rogers), in A. Rogers and S. Vertovec (eds.), *The Urban Context: Ethnicity, Social Networks and Situational Analysis*, Oxford: Berg, pp. 1–33

—— (1998) 'Young Muslims in Keighley, West Yorkshire: cultural identity, context and "community"', in S. Vertovec and A. Rogers (eds.), *Muslim European Youth: Reproducing Ethnicity, Religion, Culture*, Aldershot: Ashgate.

—— (2000) 'Religion and diaspora', paper presented at the conference on 'New Landscapes of Religion in the West', University of Oxford, September.

Vertovec, S. and A. Rogers (eds.) (1995) *The Urban Context: Ethnicity, Social Networks and Situational Analysis*, Oxford: Berg.

Wahhab, I. (1989) *Muslims in Britain: Profile of a Community*, London: Runnymede Trust.

Warner, R. S. (1998) 'Approaching religious diversity. Barriers, byways, and beginnings', *Sociology of Religion*, Vol. LIX.

Watson, C. W. (2000) *Multiculturalism*, Buckingham: Open University Press.

Weller, P. (ed.) (1993) *Religions in the UK: a Multi-Faith Directory*, Derby: University of Derby.

—— (1997) *Religions in the UK: A Multi-Faith Directory*, Derby: University of Derby and the Inter-Faith Network for the United Kingdom.

Weller, P., A. Feldman and K. Purdam (2001) *Religious Discrimination in England and Wales*, London: Home Office.

Werbner, Pnina (1990) *The Migration Process: Capital, Gifts and Offerings among British Pakistanis*, Oxford: Berg.

—— (1994) 'Diaspora and millennium: British Pakistani global– local fabulations of the Gulf War', in A. S. Ahmed and H. Donnan (eds.), *op. cit.*

—— (1997) 'Essentialising essentialism, essentialising silence: ambivalence and multiplicity in the constructions of racism and ethnicity', in P. Werbner and T. Modood (eds.), *op. cit.*

—— (2000) 'Divided loyalties, empowered citizenship? Muslims in Britain', *Citizenship Studies*, Vol. IV, No. III.

—— (2002) *Imagined Diasporas among Manchester Muslims*. World Anthropology Series, Oxford: James Currey.

Werbner, P. and T. Modood (1997) *Debating Cultural Hybridity: Multi-cultural Identities and the Politics of Anti-racism*, London: Zed Books.

Whitaker, B. (2002) 'Worst impressions', *Guardian*, 24 June.

Willis, K. and B. Yeoh (2000) *Gender and Migration*, Cheltenham: Edward Elgar.

Wills, M. (2002) 'What defines British values?', in P. Griffith and M. Leonard (ed.), *Reclaiming Britishness*, London: Foreign Policy Centre.

Yalcin-Heckmann, L. (1998) 'Growing up as a Muslim in Germany: religious socialisation amongst Turkish families', in S. Vertovec and A. Rogers (eds.), *Muslim European Youth: Reproducing Ethnicity, Religion, Culture*, Aldershot: Ashgate.

Yuval-Davis, N. (1992) 'Fundamentalism, multiculturalism and women in Britain', in: J. Donald and A. Rattansi (eds.), *'Race', Culture and Difference*, London: Sage.

Websites

http://www.hvk.org/articles/0503/146.html

http://www.minorityrights.org/admin/Download/pdf/muslimsinbritain.pdf

http://www.telegraph.co.uk/news/main.jhtml?xml=/news/campaigns/war/recruit. xml 'Britain a perfect haven for Islamic radicals looking for recruits' (11.09.2002)

Notes on the Contributors

Tahir Abbas is Lecturer in Sociology and Director of the Centre for the Study of Ethnicity and Culture at the University of Birmingham. Previously he was Senior Research Officer at the Home Office and the Department for Constitutional Affairs, and ESRC Research Fellow at the UCE Business School, where he explored issues of 'ethnic enterprise in an inner city context', in particular the independent restaurant sector in Birmingham. He has published over twenty journal articles and book chapters and in 2004 his monograph, *The Education of British South Asians: Ethnicity, Capital and Class Structure*, is published by Palgrave Macmillan.

Nilufer Ahmed currently holds the post of Research Fellow at St George's Hospital Medical School, where she is researching the effects of psychosocial adversity on asthma. She has worked extensively with the Bangladeshi community and her academic interests include transnational migration, ethnicity and mental health. Recent publications include *Women in Transition*, examining the lives of Bangladeshi women living in Tower Hamlets. She was previously active in the voluntary sector, where she deployed her skills in various community organisations and acquired expertise in working with Asian women before returning to academia. These links remain and she is involved in the management committees of a number of Asian women's organisations in East London.

Sameera T. Ahmed's research experience at Warwick (Centre for Research in Ethnic Relations – CRER), Manchester and Nottingham universities has examined issues relating to Muslims in Europe, minority ethnic media consumption, housing needs, social disturbances in the north-west and youth crime in Birmingham. Her research interests are centred on Muslims and the media, British Muslim identity and globalisation, and her publications include *'Muslim Voices' in the European Union*; *The Stranger Within: Community, Identity and Employment*; and *Tradition, Change and Diversity: Understanding the Housing Needs of Minority Ethnic Groups in Manchester*. Currently, she is President of the Association of Muslim Researchers and a writer for the *Muslim News*.

Parveen Akhtar is a PhD research student in the Department of Politics and International Relations, University of Birmingham, who is currently working on an ESRC-funded project looking into the representation of women in higher education, with a particular focus on the discipline of Political Science. Her specialist area is 'Political participation and British Muslims', the topic of her ESRC-funded PhD. Her wider research interests include the nature of democracy and the nation-state, new forms of political participation and radical Islam. She teaches in the areas of political theory, sociological theory and multiculturalism.

Chris Allen is currently completing doctoral research at the University of Birmingham that explores the discourse and manifestation of Islamophobia in the

UK. He has written widely on the topic, co-authoring the European Union Monitoring Centre on Racism and Xenophobia's, *Summary Report on Islamophobia in the EU after 11 September 2001* (2002). He is joint-editor of a collection of essays, *Challenging Islamophobia: New Perspectives and Contemporary Agendas* (forthcoming 2004) and is preparing a solo publication, *Islamophobia* (forthcoming 2005). In addition to regular contributions to the press and work with the media, he is the Director of the Religions in Britain Research Organisation.

Humayun Ansari is Senior Lecturer in History and Director of the Centre for Ethnic Minority Studies, Royal Holloway, University of London. Dr Ansari has written extensively on the subject of equal opportunities, the employment and career opportunities of ethnic minorities, racial equality, cross-cultural communications and managing cultural diversity. He has conducted extensive research into Muslims in Britain and is co-author, with June Jackson, of *Managing Cultural Diversity at Work*, (Kogan Page). His recent publications include *Muslims in Britain* (Minority Rights Group International, 2002) and *The 'Infidel' Within* (Hurst, 2004).

Muhammad Anwar is Research Professor at the Centre for Research in Ethnic Relations, University of Warwick. Formerly Director of CRER (1989–94) and Head of Research at the Commission for Racial Equality (1981–9), he has written extensively on ethnic and race relations in publications such as *Between Two Cultures* (1976), *The Myth of Return: Pakistanis in Britain* (1979), *Race and Politics: Ethnic Minorities and the British Political System* (1986) and *Between Cultures* (1998). He is joint editor of *Black and Ethnic Leaderships: the Cultural Dimensions of Political Action* (1991) and *From Legislation to Integration* (1999). His research interests include Muslims in Britain and Europe, the political participation of ethnic minorities and race relations legislation.

Paul Bagguley, Senior Lecturer in Sociology, School of Sociology and Social Policy, University of Leeds, carried out extensive research (with Dr Yasmin Hussain) on the urban 'riots' in 2001 funded by the British Academy ('The Bradford "riot" of 2001: a preliminary analysis'; 'Citizenship, ethnicity and identity: British Pakistanis after the 2001 "riots"'; and 'Conflict and cohesion: constructions of "community" around the 2001 "riots"'). With Dr Yasmin Hussain, he is now working on a project funded by the Joseph Rowntree Foundation on 'The role of higher education in providing opportunities for Young South Asian Women'.

Halima Begum is Research Associate at the Centre for Civil Society, London School of Economics, where she is developing a paper on social capital and civil society interventions in London's East End. Halima is currently employed as a policy adviser at the UK Department for International Development. She completed her undergraduate and postgraduate studies at the LSE. Her PhD (Queen Mary University of London) examined the role that culture and creativity can play in fostering civic engagement in Tower Hamlets. Her research interests are in the area of social capital, British Bangladeshis, community development, and arts-led civic renewal. She has also written for the *Guardian* and *Time Out* magazine.

Jonathon Birt is completing a DPhil in Social Anthropology at the University of Oxford on the development of Islamic youth movements in the UK. He is part-time

Research Fellow at the Islam in Europe Unit, Islamic Foundation. He has written, 'Wahhabism in the United Kingdom: reactions and manifestations' in Madawi al-Rasheed (ed.), *Transnational Connections: the Arab Gulf and Beyond* (Routledge Curzon, forthcoming) and co-written (with Phillip Lewis) 'The pattern of Islamic reform in Britain: the Deobandis between intra-Muslim sectarianism and engagement with wider society' in Martin van Bruinessen and Stefano Allievi (eds.), *Producing Islamic Knowledge in Western Europe* (Routledge Curzon, forthcoming). He is also joint editor with Chris Allen of a forthcoming volume, *Challenging Islamophobia: New Perspectives and Contemporary Agendas*.

John Eade is Professor of Sociology and Anthropology at the University of Surrey Roehampton, and is currently seconded to the University of Surrey where he is Executive Director of the multidisciplinary Centre for Research on Nationalism, Ethnicity and Multiculturalism. His main research interests are urban ethnicity, globalisation, travel and pilgrimage. His publications include two monographs: *The Politics of Community: the Bangladeshi Community in East London* (1989) and *Placing London: From Imperial Capital to Global City* (2000). He edited *Living the Global City* (1996) and co-edited *Understanding the City: Contemporary and Future Perspectives* (2002), *Reforming Pilgrimage* (2004) and *Contesting the Sacred* (1991/2000).

Ron Geaves is Senior Lecturer in the Department of Theology and Religious Studies at the University College, Chester. His PhD on *Sectarian Influences within Islam in Britain* was published as a monograph by the Community Religions Project at the University of Leeds and in 2002 *The Sufis of Britain* came out from Cardiff Academic Press. He is also interested in Hindu and Sikh diaspora communities and is currently working on a monograph looking at South and North Indian Saivite traditions that have transmigrated to the UK. He has recently edited *Islam and the West post-9/11*, along with Theodore Gabriel, Yvonne Haddad and Jane Smith (forthcoming 2004 from Ashgate).

Yasmin Hussain is Research Fellow in the School of Sociology and Social Policy at the University of Leeds. Her main interests are in the areas of ethnicity and gender. She has published several articles in these fields and is the author of *Diasporic Womanhood*, (forthcoming 2004, Ashgate), which critically assesses the literature and films produced by British South Asian women. Her current project – 'The role of higher education in providing opportunities for South Asian women' – draws on the experiences of young South Asian women in Leeds and Birmingham prior to, during and immediately after their higher education. It is funded by the Joseph Rowntree Foundation.

Stephen Lyon returned to Britain after several years teaching English as a foreign language in France to do a PhD in Social Anthropology at the University of Kent. His doctoral research was on local politics, patron–client networks and cultural models in Punjab, Pakistan. While carrying out his field research in northern Punjab, he worked as research assistant on an ESRC-funded project examining ethnicity in the ethnically diverse area of Attock District, Punjab, Pakistan. In addition he worked closely with the Pakistan Agricultural Research Council on an agricultural development project. His current research interests include Pakistani and Turkish migration, conflict resolution and the politics of Islamist parties in Pakistan and Turkey. He is the author of *An Anthropological Analysis of Power and Patronage in Pakistan* (Edwin Mellen Press, 2004).

Gabriele Marranci is Lecturer in Divinity and Religious Studies at the School of Divinity and Religious Studies, History and Philosophy, University of Aberdeen. His main area of interest is the cultural and identity aspects of the Muslim diaspora in Europe. He has recently conducted fieldwork in Northern Ireland on the local Islamic community. As well as participating in international meetings and conferences, he has published several book chapters and articles in journals such as *Ethnologies, Building Environment*, and *Culture and Religion*. Currently, he is writing a book concerning concepts of *jihad* among ordinary Muslims for Berg Books (forthcoming, 2005).

Tariq Modood is Professor of Sociology and Director of the Centre for Ethnicity and Citizenship at the University of Bristol. He is the founding editor of the new international journal, *Ethnicities* (Sage). A leading authority in the field of ethnicity, he was the principal researcher on the Fourth National Survey of Ethnic Minorities in Britain, published as *Ethnic Minorities in Britain: Diversity and Disadvantage* (PSI, 1997). His other publications include *Not Easy Being British* (Trentham, 1992), *Changing Ethnic Identities* (with S. Beishon and S. Virdee, PSI, 1994) and *Employment in Higher Education* (with S. Fenton and J. Carter, PSI, 1999).

Audrey Osler is Professor of Education at the University of Leeds and Director of the Centre for Citizenship and Human Rights Education. Her research focuses on issues of identity, equality and diversity in education. She has published widely and her books include *The Education and Careers of Black Teachers: Changing Identities, Changing Lives* (Open University Press, 1997); *Citizenship and Democracy in Schools: Diversity, Identity, Equality* (Trentham, 2000); and the winner of the Times Educational Supplement/National Association of Special Educational Needs prize, *Girls and Exclusion: Rethinking the Agenda* (Routledge Falmer, 2003, with Kerry Vincent).

Ceri Peach is Professor of Social Geography, Fellow and Tutor at St. Catherine's College, University of Oxford. He has held Visiting Fellowships at the Australian National University, Berkeley, Yale, the University of British Columbia and Harvard. He is currently working on an ESRC-funded project on Muslim, Sikh and Hindu ethnic concentrations in Britain. His research interests are in patterns of migration, segregation and intermarriage. He recently completed the Leverhulme Trust Domesday Survey of the Impact of Muslim Mosques, Sikh Gurdwaras and Hindu Mandirs on the Cultural Landscapes of English Cities. With funding from the Canadian government he and Dr Ali Rogers (School of Geography and the Environment) have worked on comparative levels of segregation of ethnic groups in the USA, Canada and the UK.

John Rex is Professor Emeritus at the Centre for Research in Ethnic Relations, University of Warwick. He has taught and carried out research in sociological theory and ethnic relations since his arrival from South Africa in 1949. He founded the departments of Sociology at Durham in 1964 and Warwick in 1970. His best known books are *Key Problems of Sociological Theory* (1964), *Race Relations in Sociological Theory* (1970) and *Race and Ethnicity* (1986). His most recent book is *Ethnic Minorities in the Modern Nation State: Working Paper in the Theory of Multi-Culturalism and Political Integration* (1996). He was a member of the UNESCO Committee of experts on the nature of race and race prejudice in 1967 and was president of the International Sociological Association's Research Committee on racial and ethnic minorities.

Index